THE MYTH OF THE LOST CAUSE
AND CIVIL WAR HISTORY

The Myth of the Lost Cause and Civil War History

Gary W. Gallagher and Alan T. Nolan, Editors

INDIANA UNIVERSITY PRESS

Bloomington and Indianapolis

This book is a publication of
Indiana University Press
601 North Morton Street
Bloomington, IN 47404-3797 USA

http://www.indiana.edu/~iupress

Telephone orders   800-842-6796
Fax orders   812-855-7931
Orders by e-mail   iuporder@indiana.edu

The paper used in this publication meets the minimum requirements of
American National Standard for Information Sciences—Permanence of Paper
for Printed Library Materials, ANSI Z39.48-1984.

Manufactured in the United States of America

Library of Congress Cataloging-in-Publication Data

The myth of the lost cause and Civil War history /
Gary W. Gallagher and Alan T. Nolan, editors.
p.   cm.
Includes bibliographical references and index.
ISBN 0-253-33822-0 (cl : alk. paper)
1. Confederate States of America—Historiography. 2. United States—History—Civil
War, 1861-1865—Historiography. 3. Confederate States of America—History. 4. United
States—History—Civil War, 1861-1865.   I. Gallagher, Gary W.   II. Nolan, Alan T.
E487 .M97 2000
973.7'13'072—dc21   00-036978

2 3 4 5   05 04 03 02 01

Contents

THE MYTH OF THE LOST CAUSE
AND CIVIL WAR HISTORY

Introduction

Gary W. Gallagher

White Southerners emerged from the Civil War thoroughly beaten but largely unrepentant. Four years of brutal struggle had ravaged their military-age male population, vastly altered their physical landscape and economic infrastructure, and destroyed their slave-based social system. They grimly acknowledged the superior might of United States military forces and understood the futility of further armed resistance. Yet the majority of ex-Confederates, who had remained hopeful of establishing a new slaveholding republic until late in the conflict, did not believe they had fought for an unworthy cause. During the decades following the surrender at Appomattox, they nurtured a public memory of the Confederacy that placed their wartime sacrifice and shattering defeat in the best possible light. This interpretation addressed the nature of antebellum Southern society and the institution of slavery, the constitutionality of secession, the causes of the Civil War, the characteristics of their wartime society, and the reasons for their defeat. Widely known then and now as the Lost Cause explanation of the Confederate experience, it drew strength from the pages of participants' memoirs, from speeches at veterans' reunions, from ceremonies at the graves of soldiers killed while serving in Southern armies and other commemorative events, and from artwork with Confederate themes.

The architects of the Lost Cause acted from various motives. They collectively sought to justify their own actions and allow themselves and other former Confederates to find something positive in all-encompassing failure. They also wanted to provide their children and future generations of white Southerners with a "correct" narrative of the war.

1

Some tried to create a written record that would influence later historians. In terms of shaping how Americans have assessed and understood the Civil War, Lost Cause warriors succeeded to a remarkable degree. Robert E. Lee serves as an obvious example of that success. The commander of the Army of Northern Virginia was the preeminent Lost Cause hero (by focusing on him rather than on Jefferson Davis, ex-Confederates could highlight the military rather than the far messier political and social dimensions of the war), and by the second decade of the twentieth century Lee had joined Abraham Lincoln as one of the two most popular Civil War figures. Ulysses S. Grant, second only to Lincoln among those who had forged the Union triumph, inspired far less enthusiastic admiration than did the principal rebel chieftain. A speaker at the dedication of an equestrian statue of Lee in Charlottesville, Virginia, in 1924 illustrated this phenomenon, observing that Lee's defeat "was but apparent." "Long since has the impartial verdict of the slow-moving years crowned as the real victor of Appomattox not Ulysses S. Grant and his swarming armies, but the undefeated spirit of Robert E. Lee," stated this man. "Long since have his enemies and detractors surrendered in their turn to this hero of defeat."[1]

Many Northerners who watched the developing Lost Cause school of interpretation worried that it might gain wide acceptance. For example, Frederick Douglass labored throughout the postwar decades to combat what he perceived as Northern complicity in spreading Lost Cause arguments. Aware that most former Confederates had not forsworn their belief in the rightness of their experiment in nation building, he complained in 1871 that "the spirit of secession is stronger today than ever." Douglass described that spirit as "a deeply rooted, devoutly cherished sentiment, inseparably identified with the 'lost cause,' which the half measures of the Government towards the traitors has helped to cultivate and strengthen." Nearly a quarter-century later, a publication sponsored by the Grand Army of the Republic in Massachusetts mounted an attack on what one of its subheadlines termed the "Lost Cause of Historical Truth." Concerned that school textbooks had fallen under the sway of those who sought to mask the true causes and meaning of the Civil War, this article staked its position clearly in referring to the conflict as the "Great Pro-Slavery Rebellion." In 1925, a Pittsburgh newspaper cheered news that a shortage of funds had stopped work on a massive Confederate memorial at Stone Mountain, Georgia: "Just enough work has been done to remind the traveler that 'there is the lost cause, conceived in hatred, and interrupted in its course for want of support.' Nothing could constitute a more appropriate insignia to a lost cause than an unfinished monument halted in its rise for want of sympathy."[2]

The sculptures at Stone Mountain eventually were completed, and Lost Cause symbols and interpretations remained visible and sometimes hotly debated throughout the twentieth century. Controversies erupted in the 1990s over the public display of Confederate flags in South Carolina and Georgia, the inclusion of Robert E. Lee's picture on a flood wall along the James River in Richmond, and the presence of early-twentieth-century statues of Confederate heroes on the campus of the University of Texas.[3] The National Park Service's handling of Civil War themes also has come under scrutiny. Should it administer the "'Stonewall' Jackson Shrine" (the plantation office where Jackson died in May 1863) as part of the Fredericksburg and Spotsylvania National Military Park? Should Gettysburg be interpreted as the "high-water mark" of the Confederacy, a frame of reference well attuned to Lost Cause writings of the late nineteenth century? Should the Park Service try to bring slavery, which Lost Cause writers scrupulously sought to remove from their version of Confederate history, and other nonmilitary dimensions of the conflict into their interpretive schemes at battlefield sites?[4] Public discussion of such questions suggests the degree to which the Lost Cause remains part of the modern Civil War landscape.

The Lost Cause also has attracted significant attention from historians interested in its nineteenth-century manifestations as well as its long-term impact on American understanding of the Civil War. In a pioneering effort, Rollin G. Osterweis depicted the Lost Cause as an extension of antebellum Southern romanticism and found it much in evidence during the mid and late twentieth century. Gaines M. Foster's landmark study, in contrast, argued that the Confederate tradition played an increasingly marginal role in the South after the turn of the century. Charles Reagan Wilson explored connections between the Lost Cause and postwar Southern religion, while Thomas L. Connelly and Alan T. Nolan focused on Robert E. Lee as a pivotal figure whose Lost Cause image gained national favor. The Southern Historical Society's *Papers* and the *Confederate Veteran*, major outlets for Lost Cause authors during a span of several decades, received recent attention from Richard D. Starnes and John A. Simpson respectively. On the artistic side, Mark E. Neely Jr., Harold Holzer, and Gabor S. Boritt analyzed popular nineteenth-century prints and lithographs that formed a Confederate iconography, and Kirk Savage's study of nineteenth-century monuments allotted considerable attention to the heroic statue of Lee on Monument Avenue in Richmond, Virginia. Jim Cullen's investigation of

the war in recent popular culture found many Lost Cause echoes—none
more memorable, or odd, than some Tony Horwitz described in his en-
gaging treatment of Civil War reenactors.[5]

The essays that follow seek to build on previous literature by engag-
ing various aspects of the white South's response to defeat, efforts to
create a suitable memory of the war, and uses of the Confederate past.
Readers should be aware that the collection does not pretend to compete
with the monographic literature on the Lost Cause. Nor does it present
a unified interpretation of the many dimensions of the subject. Instead,
the essays focus on both specific and general topics, revisit some long-
standing debates and well-known actors, illuminate continuities between antebellum and postwar attitudes, and underscore how political
and ideological antagonisms divided white Southerners who generally
accepted basic elements of the Lost Cause interpretation of slavery, secession, and the war. Several of the essays discuss the degree to which
Lost Cause arguments continue to influence modern writers and, by
extension, the large lay audience interested in the Civil War.

The idea for this collection originated with Alan T. Nolan, who has a
long-standing interest in the historiographical impact of Lost Cause
writings. Nolan's opening essay summarizes the arguments with which
Lost Cause advocates consciously sought to establish a retrospectively
favorable account of the Confederate people and their short-lived nation. Among other points, these ex-Confederates denied the importance
of slavery in triggering secession, blamed sectional tensions on abolitionists, celebrated antebellum Southern slaveholding society, portrayed
Confederates as united in waging their war for independence, extolled
the gallantry of Confederate soldiers, and attributed Northern victory
to sheer weight of numbers and resources. Much of this view, which
Nolan labels "a caricature" of the true history of the war, transcended
region to make its way into popular American understanding. Vehicles
that abetted this process included Margaret Mitchell's *Gone with the
Wind*, Shelby Foote's widely admired works, and the National Park Service. After refuting each element of the Lost Cause argument, Nolan
sounds a call to sweep away counterfactual myth and confront the true
history of the Civil War era.

No former Confederate did more to shape Lost Cause writings in the
late nineteenth century than did Jubal A. Early. The second essay, a revised version of a previously published piece, examines Early's goals,
arguments, and influence. Early served for most of the war as a general
officer in the Army of Northern Virginia, an experience that left him
with a reverential admiration for Robert E. Lee. Deeply antagonistic
toward the North and embittered by Confederate defeat, Early under-

stood that accounts by participants would help define later historical writing about the war. He hoped to create a literary legacy emphasizing Lee's greatness and Confederate gallantry in the face of overwhelming Northern manpower and materiel resources. For Early and those who shared his outlook, Grant invited scorn as a marginally able general who nevertheless knew enough to use his unlimited pool of soldiers relentlessly. Many of Early's ideas achieved wide acceptance, and he would find much to applaud in modern works of history and fiction, art created to meet the demand of Civil War enthusiasts, and treatments of the war on television and in film.

Charles J. Holden's essay narrows the interpretive lens to one state, using ex-Confederate general Wade Hampton as his focus in exploring the Lost Cause in South Carolina. Few Confederate generals compiled a more exemplary military record than Hampton, who as governor also played a major role in restoring conservative rule to South Carolina in the late 1870s. But Holden shows that even these accomplishments failed to sustain broad support for Hampton as white South Carolinians moved toward the end of the century. Once Northern influence waned in their state, many of Hampton's fellow Carolinians—including thousands of former Confederate soldiers—expressed unhappiness with his profoundly aristocratic ideas. Martin W. Gary and later "Pitchfork Ben" Tillman led anti-aristocratic forces that ended Hampton's political dominance in 1890. Over the next thirteen years, Hampton steadily regained popularity as a Confederate hero whose aristocratic outlook became less important to South Carolinians. By the time of his death in 1903 he stood second only to Lee as a Lost Cause idol in the Palmetto State. Holden's essay reminds readers that the South of the Lost Cause era, like the Confederacy, was beset by fissures along political and class lines. As Wade Hampton's story demonstrates, politics and economics could trump Confederate credentials among postwar white Southerners.

The fourth essay also maintains a state focus but moves to Georgia and its Confederate veteran reunions between 1885 and 1895. Keith S. Bohannon selected a decade that witnessed the rapid growth of veterans' groups and Lost Cause public ceremonies. Reunions combined social, political, and memorial dimensions, providing an excellent forum for communities to fabricate a collective memory of the past and teach younger people about the sacrifices and accomplishments of the Confederate generation. Speakers at reunions honored the Lost Cause and its heroes but also addressed political issues, including soldier homes, pensions, and other veteran-related subjects (a few speakers even trumpeted the goals of the Farmers' Alliance and Populist Party). Popular figures such as John B. Gordon, whose career in the Army of Northern Virginia had been filled with dashing success, often combined praise for a glorious Confederate past with New South boosterism. Whatever their differences about specific political questions, Bohannon finds that most soldiers held to their earlier views about the war, Reconstruction, and Southern race relations.

Peter S. Carmichael's essay examines attitudes among the generation of slaveholders' sons who attended Virginia universities during the 1850s. These men made up a large proportion of the field officers in the Army of Northern Virginia, stood among the staunchest supporters of the Confederacy, and used wartime examples to prod postwar Virginians toward a New South of economic development, mass education, and social progress. Their goal was to restore Virginia to a position of glory within the United States. Carmichael's subjects had grown disenchanted before the war with their state's political and economic leadership, touting what they called a "progressive" agenda that would bring material prosperity, scientific improvements, and intellectual distinction. After Appomattox, they renewed their antebellum call for change. They pointed out that the Confederate citizenry had built war industries, sacrificed for the national good, and exhibited steadfastness on the battlefield and behind the lines—behaviors postwar white Virginians should emulate. Although fully attuned to Lost Cause thinking regarding slavery, Lee's brilliance, and the pluck of Confederate soldiers, these Virginians reconciled easily with the North and looked more to the future than to the past.

Few former Confederates suffered more at the hands of Lost Cause writers than James Longstreet, who had served as Lee's senior subordinate for most of the war. Like Carmichael's young Virginians, Longstreet urged rapid accommodation with the North. He also called for cooperation with the Republican Party to control newly enfranchised black voters and, most notably, dared to criticize Lee's generalship in public. Jubal Early and many others turned on Longstreet savagely, blaming him for the defeat at Gettysburg and labeling him a traitor to the white South. Jeffry D. Wert examines Longstreet's estrangement from old comrades, reviewing the charges leveled against him, his clumsy attempts to defend himself in print, and the seemingly endless ensuing historical debate over Longstreet's conduct and proper place in Confederate military history. As recently as the 1990s, notes Wert, critics rehearsed familiar Lost Cause criticisms of Longstreet while defenders insisted that "Old Pete" continued to suffer from the slanders of Jubal Early and his minions.

Ulysses S. Grant shared Longstreet's status as a prime target for Lost

Cause controversialists. Brooks D. Simpson's essay discusses the effective campaign ex-Confederates mounted against the Union's general-in-chief. Grant's Southern detractors explained away or ignored his striking successes in the western theater, and concentrated instead on the 1864 Overland campaign that pitted him against their champion Lee. In Virginia, they claimed, only Northern numbers had allowed Grant to emerge victorious over the more talented and admirable Confederate commander. Using material from the Union's official records, including Grant's own report of operations in 1864–65, as well as statements from Northern writers and criticisms from officers who had served in the West with Grant, Lost Cause writers built a devastatingly effective critique that continues to resonate in modern Civil War literature. Grant did his best to defend his reputation and understandably refused to acknowledge Lee's martial gifts—but in the end failed to carry the day. He remains a clumsy butcher to many Americans, who look to a warped historical record that draws heavily on the efforts of Lost Cause writers.

Women joined men in the Lost Cause movement, few more prominently than LaSalle Corbell Pickett. The widow of Confederate general George E. Pickett of Gettysburg fame, LaSalle Pickett published prolifically and appeared at innumerable Lost Cause ceremonies in the late nineteenth and early twentieth centuries. Her books and articles, which included history, reminiscences, and fiction, created a romantic past of graceful plantations, contented slaves, righteous secessionists, and valorous Confederates. They also placed her in a loving marriage to a chivalrous Southern general. In fact, explains Lesley J. Gordon, Pickett's writings departed radically from the truth regarding both Southern history and her own life. Pickett not only glossed over nearly all the South's warts in her recounting of historical events, but also ignored the poverty, illness, long separations, and other troubling aspects of her marriage to the often irresponsible General Pickett. In her writings, LaSalle Pickett appears as a representative member of a completely admirable slaveholding South that persevered despite the cruel tests of a great war. Her message proved attractive to white Northerners as well as old Confederates, and she received plaudits from veterans of both sides at reunions at Gettysburg.

Lloyd A. Hunter closes the volume with an essay on religion and the Lost Cause. He suggests that in the 1870s and 1880s many ex-Confederates and their children embraced a faith centered on the Confederacy and the Old South. At veterans' reunions, memorial day programs, dedications of monuments, and other public events, they invested Confederate symbols and relics with a sacred status. This cultural faith combined

Protestant evangelicalism and Southern romanticism and found expression in the many activities of the United Confederate Veterans, the United Daughters of the Confederacy, and other organizations. Hunter points to the Confederate flag, the gray jacket of Southern soldiers, and the song "Dixie" as especially evocative symbols. Lee and Jefferson Davis served as Christ figures, Stonewall Jackson as a stern Moses, and common soldiers as saints. Steadfast Southern women watched over the tomb of the Confederacy in stark counterpoint to James Longstreet, who functioned for many (though usually not for soldiers who had fought under him) as Judas to Lee's Christ. Hunter alerts readers not to fall into the trap of equating "myth" with "falsehood." Myths arise when people draw on images and symbols to construct a usable truth, which in turn permits them to deal with traumatic events such as the Confederacy's defeat.

These nine essays follow some of the investigative paths that beckon anyone interested in the origins, development, and influence of the Lost Cause movement. Their authors hope that they contribute to a better understanding of a complex and compelling subject. The contributors also expect to see far more work in this field. Increasing scholarly interest in the creation and applications of historical memory makes it a prime area for further work. Moreover, few episodes in American history match the Civil War in its power to make the people who lived through it think seriously about a suitable public memory. And, because the Confederacy lost so unequivocally, its citizens probably devoted more energy to the task than their Northern counterparts. These elements should combine to inspire considerable attention to the many dimensions of the Lost Cause.

Notes

1. John S. Patton, ed., *Proceedings of the 37th Annual Reunion of the Virginia Division of the Grand Camp U.C.V. and of the 29th Reunion of the Sons of Confederate Veterans at Charlottesville, Va., May 20, 21, 22, 1924* (Charlottesville, Va.: The Michie Company, [1924]), 67.

2. David Blight, *Frederick Douglass' Civil War: Keeping Faith in Jubilee* (Baton Rouge: Louisiana State University Press, 1989), 229; *The Grand Army Record* 10 (November 1895): 84; "Let Stone Mountain Alone," *Opportunity* 3 (April 1925): 125 (the National Urban League's *Opportunity* reprinted the piece from the Pittsburgh newspaper). On the history of the Stone Mountain memorial, see David Freeman, *Carved in Stone: The History of Stone Mountain* (Macon, Ga.: Mercer University Press, 1997).

3. For representative coverage of these issues, which constitute just three of many possible examples, see *Newsweek*, January 13, 1997, 16; *Atlanta Journal/Constitution*, May 22, 28, 1994 (flag controversy); *Richmond Times-Dispatch*, June 4, 1999, A1, A14–A15, *Washington Post*, June 17, 1999, Metro B1, B4 (Lee picture); *The Daily Texan* (student newspaper at the University of Texas), September 23, 1999, 4. See also John M. Coski, "The Confederate Battle Flag in American History and Culture," and Kevin Thornton, "The Confederate Flag and the Meaning of Southern History," in *Southern Cultures* 2 (Winter 1996): 195–245.

4. The National Park Service and the Organization of American Historians have undertaken a joint evaluation of interpretation at Antietam, Gettysburg, Richmond, and other Civil War sites. For a discussion of the report on Antietam, see Barbara Franco, "Antietam National Battlefield Visit," *OAH Newsletter* 24 (May 1996): 3.

5. See Rollin G. Osterweis, *The Myth of the Lost Cause, 1865–1900* (Hamden, Conn.: Archon, 1973); Gaines M. Foster, *Ghosts of the Confederacy: Defeat, the Lost Cause, and the Emergence of the New South, 1865–1913* (New York: Oxford, 1987); Charles Reagan Wilson, *Baptized in Blood: The Religion of the Lost Cause, 1865–1920* (Athens: University of Georgia Press, 1980); Thomas L. Connelly, *The Marble Man: Robert E. Lee and His Image in American Society* (New York: Knopf, 1977); Alan T. Nolan, *Lee Considered: General Robert E. Lee and Civil War History* (Chapel Hill: University of North Carolina Press, 1991); Richard D. Starnes, "Forever Faithful: The Southern Historical Society and Confederate Historical Memory," *Southern Cultures* 2 (Winter 1996): 177–94; John A. Simpson, *S. A. Cunningham and the Confederate Heritage* (Athens: University of Georgia Press, 1994); Mark E. Neely Jr., Harold Holzer, and Gabor S. Boritt, *The Confederate Image: Prints of the Lost Cause* (Chapel Hill: University of North Carolina Press, 1987); Kirk Savage, *Standing Soldiers, Kneeling Slaves: Race, War, and Monument in Nineteenth-Century America* (Princeton, N.J.: Princeton University Press, 1997); Jim Cullen, *The Civil War in Popular Culture: A Reusable Past* (Washington, D.C.: Smithsonian, 1995); Tony Horwitz, *Confederates in the Attic: Dispatches from the Unfinished Civil War* (New York: Pantheon, 1998). For photographs of several hundred Confederate monuments, see Ralph W. Widener Jr., *Confederate Monuments: Enduring Symbols of the South and the War between the States* (Washington, D.C.: Andromeda Associates, 1982).

One

The Anatomy of the Myth

Alan T. Nolan

In the period 1861–65, there was a major war in the United States of America (USA). The antagonists were the "North," that is, the United States except for eleven states, and the "South," which claimed to have seceded, that is, withdrawn from the United States to form a new nation, the Confederate States of America (CSA). The citizens of both sides were of the same Caucasian race and national and ethnic origins. They were committed to democratic political principles and were blessed with an unusually rich geography. The Confederate states had an African-American slave labor system. Although it was racist, the North's labor system was free, except in the border states of Kentucky, Missouri, Maryland, and Delaware and in the District of Columbia. Northern people in the main were antagonistic to slavery. The two sides had been unable politically to resolve sectional disagreements.

The United States refused to recognize the existence of the Confederate States of America as a nation. The Confederate states promptly recruited armies and claimed as their own all property within their borders that had been the property of the United States of America; in many cases, the Confederate states seized that property by force. Ultimately, the United States refused to surrender Fort Sumter in Charleston, South Carolina. Thereupon Confederate and South Carolina forces attacked the fort and forced its surrender. Then, in President Abraham Lincoln's words, the war came.

The war ended in 1865 within a period of several weeks after the surrender at Appomattox, Virginia, of Gen. Robert E. Lee's Army of Northern Virginia, the CSA's most prominent army. The United States successfully reclaimed the eleven seceded states and the United States of America survived. During the course of the war and as a consequence, slavery was abolished and African Americans were emancipated. The people of the Confederate States of America were left free by the United States government. There were no large-scale arrests or punishments. As stated by Samuel Eliot Morison, "By 1877, all of the former Confederate states were back in the Union and in charge of their own domestic affairs, subject only to the requirements of two constitutional amendments (Articles XIV and XV) to protect the freedmen's civil rights." Within a few years of the surrender at Appomattox, former Confederate leaders were serving in high offices in the United States government. According to Morison, white supremacy continued in a different form, "as numerous lynchings in rural districts indicated; and presently 'Jim Crow' would emerge" to intimidate and control the Southern Negro.[1]

The war had been enormously destructive. More than six hundred thousand American men, soldiers from both the USA and CSA, died in the war. Thousands more were wounded, many of whom were disabled for life. The destruction of property was also vast.[2]

* * *

The foregoing carefully phrased, simple declarative statements are believed to be undisputed as accurately describing the central aspects of the event generally called today the American Civil War. Despite the undisputed essentials, the war is surrounded by vast mythology. Indeed, it is fair to say that there are two independent versions of the war. On one hand there is the *history* of the war, the account of what in fact happened. On the other there is what Gaines Foster calls the "Southern interpretation" of the event. This account, "codified" according to Foster, is generally referred to by historians today as "the Lost Cause."[3] This version, touching almost all aspects of the struggle, originated in Southern rationalizations of the war. Then it spread to the North and became a national phenomenon. In the popular mind, the Lost Cause represents the national memory of the Civil War; it has been substituted for the *history* of the war.

The Lost Cause is therefore an American legend, an American version of great sagas like *Beowulf* and the *Song of Roland*. Generally described, the legend tells us that the war was a mawkish and essentially heroic and romantic melodrama, an honorable sectional duel, a time of martial glory on both sides, and triumphant nationalism.

Cambridge political scientist D. W. Brogan, a keen and detached observer of the United States, has written that "the country that has a 'history,' dramatic, moving and tragic, has to live with it—with the problems it raised but did not solve, with the emotions that it leaves as a damaging legacy, with the defective vision that preoccupation with the heroic, with the disastrous, with the expensive past fosters."[4]

In the case of the Confederacy, the past was indeed expensive. James M. McPherson has briefly summarized the ultimate consequences of the war in terms of its impact on the South: "The South was not only invaded and conquered, it was utterly destroyed. By 1865, the Union forces had . . . destroyed two-thirds of the assessed value of Southern wealth, two-fifths of the South's livestock, and one-quarter of her white men between the ages of 20 and 40. More than half the farm machinery was ruined, and the damages to railroads and industries were incalculable . . . Southern wealth decreased by 60 percent."[5]

Leaders of such a catastrophe must account for themselves. Justification is necessary. Those who followed their leaders into the catastrophe required similar rationalization. Clement A. Evans, a Georgia veteran who at one time commanded the United Confederate Veterans organization, said this: "If we cannot justify the South in the act of Secession, we will go down in History solely as a brave, impulsive but rash people who attempted in an illegal manner to overthrow the Union of our Country."[6]

Today's historians did not, of course, coin the term "Lost Cause." It goes back almost to the events it characterizes. An early use of the term occurred in 1867 when Edward A. Pollard, the influential wartime editor of the *Richmond Examiner,* published *The Lost Cause: The Standard Southern History of the War of the Confederates.* It is a full-blown, argumentative statement of the Confederate point of view with respect to all aspects of the Civil War. The character of Pollard's insights may be judged from a quotation from another of his books, *Southern History of the War,* published in 1866, in which he wrote of the sectional disagreement in this way: "The occasion of that conflict was what the Yankees called—by one of their convenient libels in political nomenclature— slavery; but what was in fact nothing more than a system of Negro servitude in the South . . . one of the mildest and most beneficent systems of servitude in the world."[7]

The origins and development of the Lost Cause legend have been the concern of several excellent modern books, including Thomas L. Connelly's *The Marble Man: Robert E. Lee and His Image in American Society;* Gaines M. Foster's *Ghosts of the Confederacy: Defeat, the Lost Cause, and the Emergence of the New South, 1865 to 1913;* and *Lee's Tarnished Lieutenant: James Longstreet and His Place in Southern History* by William Garrett Piston. These studies establish that the purpose of the legend was to foster a heroic image of secession and the war so that the Confederates would have salvaged at least their honor from the all-encompassing defeat. Thus the purpose of the legend was to hide the Southerners' tragic and self-destructive mistake. The creators of the myth, certain Confederate leaders, prominent among them Jubal A. Early, William N. Pendleton, and Rev. J. William Jones, and the Virginia Cult, intentionally created the principles and misinformation of the Lost Cause.

The victim of the Lost Cause legend has been *history*, for which the legend has been substituted in the national memory.

My purpose here is not to retell the story of the origin and development of the legend. I am more concerned with its historicity. Thus I will catalogue the assertions of the Lost Cause and compare them to the *history* of the Civil War experience. The goal is to correct the national memory by refuting the Lost Cause legend and reestablishing the war as *history*.

The Lost Cause

The Lost Cause as Advocacy

As has been suggested, the Lost Cause was expressly a rationalization, a cover-up. It is, therefore, distinctly marked by Southern advocacy. As pointed out by Michael C. C. Adams in *Our Masters the Rebels*, long before the secession crisis, Southerners "came to see themselves as representing a minority within the nation."[8] One reason for this was "the need to justify the existence of slavery . . . even before the abolitionist attack from the North, Southerners began the defense of slavery as a social system that provided unique benefits, both for the slaves whom it placed under the fatherly care of a superior race and for the master who was given the freedom from toil necessary to the creation of a superior culture."[9] In short, Southerners were placed in a defensive posture before the war, and this has never changed.

The advocacy aspect of the Southern legend has been express on the part of Southern spokesmen. On the back page of the April 1880 issue of the *Southern Historical Society Papers*, as well as in other issues, the following advertisement for subscriptions appears above the name of Rev. J. William Jones, D.D., secretary of the Southern Historical Society of Richmond, Virginia: "[The contents] will make our Papers interesting to all lovers of historic truth and simply INVALUABLE to those who desire to see vindicated the name and fame of those who made our great struggle for constitutional freedom."[10] Writing whose purpose is to "vindicate" the "name and fame" of the South's "great struggle" plainly proceeds from an advocacy premise.

Douglas Southall Freeman, one of the twentieth century's most prominent historians of the war, was also quite candid regarding his concerns. In *The South to Posterity*, Freeman published a critical bibliography of works about the war. He acknowledged that he was "interested to ascertain which were the books that seemed to have made new protagonists for the South." He states that his effort is to identify the books "that have brought a new generation of Americans to understanding of the Southern point of view."[11] Freeman clearly identified himself as an advocate, and his advocacy marked his view of the war, General Lee, and other Confederate leaders. His books have been highly influential with other historians and the American public.

The Claims of the Legend

Slavery Was Not the Sectional Issue. According to the legend, slavery was not the critical issue between the sections. Slavery was trivialized as the cause of the war in favor of such things as tariff disputes, control of investment banking and the means of wealth, cultural differences, and conflict between industrial and agricultural societies. In all events, the South had *not* seceded to protect slavery!

Kenneth M. Stampp observes that Southern spokesmen "denied that slavery had anything to do with the Confederate cause," thus decontaminating it and turning it into something that they could cherish. "After Appomattox, Jefferson Davis claimed that 'slavery was in no wise the cause of the conflict' and Vice President Alexander H. Stephens argued that the war 'was not a contest between the advocates or opponents of that Peculiar Institution.'"[12] The denial that slavery protection had been the genesis of the Confederacy and the purpose of secession became "a cardinal element of the Southern apologia," according to Robert F. Durden. He finds that "liberty, independence and especially states rights were advanced by countless Southern spokesmen as the hallowed principles of the Lost Cause."[13] And James L. Roark notes that postwar Southerners manifested "a nearly universal desire to escape the ignominy attached to slavery."[14]

The Abolitionists as Provocateurs. The status of the abolitionists in the legend is a corollary to the principle that slavery was not the cause of secession. In the context of the legend, the abolitionists' image is nega-

tive. They are seen as troublemakers and provocateurs—virtually manufacturing a disagreement between the sections that was of little or no
interest to the people and had little substance.[15]

The South Would Have Given Up Slavery. Another of the assertions
of the Lost Cause is that the South would have abandoned slavery of its
own accord. It was simply a question of time. If the war was about slavery, it was unnecessary to the elimination of slavery because it would
have died a natural death. From this premise, it is claimed that the war
was foolish, a vain thing on the part of the North.

The Nature of the Slaves. Given the central role of African Americans
in the sectional conflict, it is surely not surprising that Southern rationalizations have extended to characterizations of the persons of these
people. In the legend there exist two prominent images of the black
slaves. One is of the "faithful slave"; the other is of what William Garrett Piston calls "the happy darky stereotype."[16] It is interesting that the
faithful slave had a more or less official status in the Confederate myth.
In a message to the Confederate Congress in 1863 in which he attacked
the Emancipation Proclamation, President Davis called the slaves "peace-
ful and contented laborers."[17] It was the uniform contention of Southern spokesmen—the press, the clergy, and the politicians—that the
slaves liked their status. Fiction writers from Thomas Nelson Page,
James Dixon, and Joel Chandler Harris to Walt Disney and Margaret
Mitchell in our own time carried this view well into this century.[18] In
the 1930s, Hollywood's slaves were invariably happy in their slavery and
affectionate toward their uniformly kind and indulgent masters. Indeed,
as evidenced by the 1940 film *Santa Fe Trail*, Hollywood embraced the
full range of Lost Cause stereotypes: the abolitionists, the slaves, and
the valiant Southern men.

The Nationalistic/Cultural Difference. Having eliminated slavery as
the source of sectional contention, the South created a nationalistic/
cultural basis for the disagreement. This theory was instituted on the
eve of the war and became a staple of the Lost Cause during and after
it. An extensive statement of the argument appeared in June 1860 in the
Southern Literary Messenger. Northerners were said to be descended
from the Anglo-Saxon tribes that had been conquered by the Norman
cavaliers. The cavaliers were, of course, the ancestors of the Southerners according to this theory. It was written that the cavaliers were "descended from the Norman Barons of William the Conqueror, a race distinguished in earliest history for its warlike and fearless character,
a race in all times since renowned for its gallantry, chivalry, honor,
gentleness, and intellect."[19] As described in *Why the South Lost the
Civil War*, "Without its own distinctive past upon which to base its na-

tionality, the Confederacy appropriated history and created a mythic past of exiled cavaliers and chivalrous knights."[20]

The Military Loss

Like the apologists who created the "stabbed-in-the-back" myth to explain Germany's defeat in World War I, Lost Cause spokesmen sought to rationalize the Southern military loss. This presented a confusing and sometimes contradictory set of assertions, the first of which simply manipulated semantics: the Confederates had not really been defeated, they had instead been overwhelmed by massive Northern manpower and materiel. This was presented with a suggestion that the North's superior resources constituted Yankee trickery and unfairness. Furthermore, the South's loss was said to be inevitable from the beginning; the fact of loss was somehow mitigated in the myth because it was said that winning had been impossible. If the Confederacy could not have won, it somehow did not lose. On the other hand, the myth asserted that had the South won at Gettysburg, it would have won the war. The loss at Gettysburg was attributed to Lt. Gen. James Longstreet. The "Longstreet-lost-it-at-Gettysburg"[21] thesis was presented in this way by Rev. J. William Jones, secretary of the Southern Historical Society. He wrote that "the South would have won at Gettysburg, and Independence, but for the failure of *one man*" (emphasis in original).[22]

Another Lost Cause rationale for the loss at Gettysburg was Stonewall Jackson's death earlier in 1863.

The Idealized Home Front. In the context of the Lost Cause, Southern culture is portrayed as superior. William Garrett Piston finds the prewar South "blessed" in the myth, peopled by cavalier aristocrats and martyrs along with the fortunate happy darkies.[23] Gaines Foster sees "grace and gentility" attributed to the South in the myth. The planter aristocracy, the other whites, and blacks are pictured as united in defense of the South's humane, superior culture. The "moonlight and magnolias" culture as described by Foster[24] is fully displayed in *Gone with the Wind,* America's favorite Civil War story. That story idealized the men and women of the plantation class, suggested the superior valor of Southern manhood, and is strongly peopled with happy slaves and gentle and indulgent masters.

The Idealized Confederate Soldier. Piston writes that the Lost Cause legend "developed a romanticized stereotype of the Confederate soldier."[25] He was invariably heroic, indefatigable, gallant, and law-abiding. It is not my intent in any way to disparage the common soldier of the Confederacy. In many ways he was the principal victim of the Lost

Cause myth. Nor do I contend that the majority of Confederate soldiers believed they were fighting to preserve slavery. In fact, they were, but many of them thought in terms of defending their homeland and families and resisting what their leaders had told them was Northern aggression.

The Lawfulness of Secession. The Lost Cause doctrine endlessly asserted that secession was a constitutional right. Moreover, because it was lawful, those supporting it were not rebels or traitors; there had not been a rebellion or revolution.[26] The premise of this contention was that because the Constitution was silent on the issue, withdrawal from the Union was permitted. It was argued that the states had entered into a compact from which they had the right to withdraw.

The Saints Go Marching In. Another characteristic of the Lost Cause legend appears in its characterizations of Southern military leaders. These men, at least the successful ones, are not evaluated simply in terms of their military and leadership skills and combat effectiveness. Although they are surely given such credit, they are also presented as remarkable and saintly creatures, supermen. Generals Lee and Stonewall Jackson are the primary examples of this phenomenon. The Lee hagiography is surely well known. Douglas Southall Freeman, his leading biographer, whose treatment has been highly influential with all other Lee writers, goes to great lengths to picture Lee as Christlike. Lee's supreme, God-like status was established almost immediately after the war. As early as 1868 he was described in a Southern publication as "bathed in the white light that falls directly upon him from the smile of an approving and sustaining God."[27] The apotheosis had advanced by 1880, when John W. Daniel, who had served on Lt. Gen. Jubal Early's staff, wrote that: "The Divinity in his bosom shown translucent through the man and his spirit rose up to the god-like."[28] A group of twentieth-century writers including Gamaliel Bradford, Clifford Dowdey, and Freeman have carried this image of Lee well into our own time.

Stonewall Jackson is also presented as more than an effective soldier. Early Lost Cause writers like Robert Lewis Dabney and John Esten Cooke presented him as a deeply religious, mystical, eccentric, and brilliant military leader of Olympian proportions. This was also the thrust of Englishman G. F. R. Henderson's writing in 1898. The neo-Confederate writers of the Lost Cause in this century—people like James I. Robertson Jr.—are, if anything, more elaborate in their tributes to Jackson than were his early biographers. Robertson's 1997 biography describes Jackson as a "spiritual prince," "standing alone on a high pedestal," and he says that Jackson's devotion to God, duty, and country "remain treasured legacies of the American people just as they are inspirations to people everywhere." This work approvingly quotes the following tribute paid by one of Jackson's subordinate officers: "He was indeed a soldier of the cross."[29]

National Park Service personnel conduct a tour of the grounds at Guiney Station, Virginia, including the building in which Jackson died. These affairs are in the nature of pilgrimages, with candlelight and lugubrious readings of accounts of the general's death, not unlike the reading of Christ's Passion and death on Palm Sunday at a Roman Catholic mass.

Currently, a third Confederate general officer, Nathan Bedford Forrest, is in the midst of his apotheosis in the hands of contemporary neo-Confederates and the merchants who sell Civil War materials. God, it seems, also had him by the hand.

As pointed out hereafter, the Lost Cause characterizations of Confederate generals also had a negative category reserved for those like Longstreet who did not fit the myth.

Civil War History

Slavery as the Sectional Issue

The assertion by the Lost Cause spokesmen of the insignificance of slavery in the sectional conflict seems outrageous and disingenuous in the light of nineteenth-century American political history, of which Southern spokesmen were and are well aware. Although muted in the early years of the United States, the sectional slavery disagreement emerged full-blown prior to 1820 in connection with the issue of admitting Missouri to the Union. In the midst of a fierce national debate, Congress passed the Missouri Compromise in 1820. This legislation admitted Missouri as a slave state, Maine as a free state, and prohibited slavery in the territory north of Missouri's southern boundary, that is, latitude 36°30'.[30] At an increasingly accelerated pace during the years between 1820 and Lincoln's election in 1860, the issue of slavery divided the sections in a long series of political crises ranging from the location of a transcontinental railroad to the Wilmot Proviso, which would have prohibited slavery in territory acquired in the Mexican War. These crises also concerned such issues as the Mexican War itself, the congressional gag rule, the admission of other states to the Union, slavery in the District of Columbia, popular sovereignty and the Kansas-Nebraska territory, the Compromise of 1850, the rise of a sectional political party, the sectional division of the Democratic Party, the dispute over the admission of Kansas as a state, and the increase of rhetorical and physical violence between representatives of the sections. Indeed,

Don E. Fehrenbacher does not exaggerate in asserting that the prewar "tendency of nearly all public controversy to fall into line with the slavery question bespeaks the power with which that question gripped the minds of the American people."[31]

Also plainly contradicting the Lost Cause assertion of the irrelevancy of slavery are the prewar statements of the Southern leaders themselves. Jefferson Davis had frequently spoken to the United States Senate about the significance of slavery to the South and had threatened secession if what he perceived as Northern threats to the institution continued.[32] In 1861, Confederate Vice President Stephens in his famous Charleston speech characterized the "great truth" of slavery as the "foundation" and "cornerstone" of the Confederacy.[33] The Confederate Constitution also disclosed the role of slavery. It contained many verbatim repetitions of the Constitution of the United States but also included marked departures from the national document in Article 1, Section 9, and Article 4 by providing for protection of "the right of property in slaves."[34] In spite of these facts, the Southerners' contention that slavery had nothing to do with the war was widely accepted in the postwar North and became part of the Civil War legend in the popular mind. This belief was advanced by such prominent twentieth-century historians as Charles and Mary Beard, Avery Craven, and James G. Randall, influenced surely in part by their own racism. Others also set slavery aside as the critical concern of the Confederacy and critical issue of the war.[35]

Recent scholarship seems at last to acknowledge the pervasive role of slavery in secession and the war. Thus Bertram Wyatt-Brown describes the "desperate commitment of Southern whites to hold black Americans forever in their power." On the other hand, in Fehrenbacher's words, the North "insisted on the value and sanctity of the union" and "there was a growing opinion of the Northern people that slavery was inconsistent with the destinies of the republic." D. W. Brogan, the United Kingdom commentator, has concluded that "the South was demanding of the North what it was less and less willing to give—theoretical and as far as possible practical equality for the peculiar institution." The Southerners, he concluded, "seceded over one thing and fought over one thing, slavery."[36]

The Abolitionists

It is doubtless true that the Abolitionists were difficult. Reformers are always painful people, simply because they will not "go along" and they demand the reluctant attention of those who are going along, frequently provoking an unpleasant sense of guilt among the latter. But it is now early in the twenty-first century. An overwhelming majority of Americans have long believed in Lincoln's words that "If slavery is not wrong, nothing is wrong." The substantial point would seem to be that the Abolitionists were right one hundred fifty years ago. In a historical sense, there would seem to be no excuse for their lingering negative reputation.

The South Would Have Given Up Slavery

This contention overlooks a number of plain historical facts, including the mid-century agitation for the acquisition of Cuba and the filibustering about Central and South American territories. It also overlooks the increasingly more restrictive provisions that the slave states enacted affecting the institution of slavery. In the interest of protecting slavery at all costs, Southern states struck down such American constitutional premises as freedom of speech, freedom of the press, and similar assumptions like privacy of the mails.[37] In regard to free speech and the First Amendment, for example, Virginia in 1849 made it a criminal offense to *state* "that owners had not the right of property in their slaves." And Missouri prohibited the publication of antislavery materials.[38] It appears that Allan Nevins spoke accurately when he said: "The South, as a whole, in 1846–61 was not moving toward emancipation but away from it. It was not relaxing the laws which guarded the system, but reinforcing them. It was not ameliorating slavery, but making it harsher and more implacable. The South was further from a just solution of the slavery problem in 1830 than it had been in 1789. It was further from tenable solution in 1860 than it had been in 1830."[39]

There is simply no evidence tending to show that the South would have voluntarily abandoned slavery. The evidence is that the Southern states had openly abridged the Constitution of the United States, especially the Bill of Rights, in behalf of the institution.

The Nature of the Slaves

In order to respond to the image of the faithful slave and happy darky portrayed in the legend, one may start with the *Official Records*. One of the biggest problems facing Federal logisticians was how to handle the slaves fleeing in wholesale numbers to the Federal lines as those lines advanced southward. As early as December 4, 1861, Secretary of State William H. Seward was forced to instruct Maj. Gen. George B. McClellan that "Persons claimed to be held to service or labor under the laws of the State of Virginia frequently escape from the lines of the enemy's forces and are received in the lines of the Army of the Potomac and are received with the military protection of the United States."[40]

Further contradiction of the myth appears in the numerous accounts by Federal soldiers of assistance rendered to them by slaves in the field. And Benjamin Quarles, Dudley Cornish, and others have reminded us that approximately 180,000 African Americans, mostly former slaves, were enlisted in the armies of the United States and many of them fought and died for this country.[41]

The Nationalistic/Cultural Difference

Kenneth Stampp has commented on this fiction. "Fundamentally," he writes, "the Confederacy was not the product of a genuine southern nationalism. Indeed, except for the institution of slavery, the South had little to give it national identity, and the notion of a distinct southern culture was largely the figment of the romantic imagination of a handful of intellectuals and pro-slavery propagandists."[42] Grady McWhiney and other of today's historians share this opinion.[43]

The Military Analysis

The suggestion that somehow the South was not defeated is, of course, counterfactual. In fact, Federal armies seized the ports and major cities of the Confederacy, decimated its armies in battle, destroyed its logistical facilities, and ultimately roamed at will through the Confederacy. There was no magic or hocus-pocus in the Confederacy's military defeat. Nor do serious historians credit the contention that the defeat of the Confederates was a foregone conclusion.

Historians concede the North's advantage in population and the capacity to make war but reject the inevitable loss tradition and its premise in regard to men and material wealth. Historians today generally believe that the South could have won the Civil War. In 1956, the leading Southern historian, Bell I. Wiley, wrote the following:

> In the years since Appomattox, millions of southerners have attributed Confederate defeat to the North's overpowering strength. This is a comforting conclusion and is not without a substantial basis of fact. . . . But the North also faced a greater task. In order to win the war, the North had to subdue a vast country of nine million inhabitants while the South could prevail by maintaining a successful resistance. To put it another way, the North had to conquer the South while the South could win simply by outlast-

ing its adversary. By convincing the North that coercion was impossible or not worth the effort. The South had reason to believe that it could achieve independence; that it did not do so was as much, if not more, due to its own failings as to superior strength of the North.[44]

A 1960 volume edited by David Donald contained the opinions of other distinguished professional historians who also argued that the defeat of the South was not a foregone conclusion and that it could have won.[45] More recently, Richard Beringer, Herman Hattaway, Archer Jones, and William Still expressed the same view. They note that "No Confederate army lost a major engagement because of a lack of arms, munitions or other essential supplies," and summarize the case as follows:

> By remarkable and effective efforts the agrarian South did exploit and create an industrial base that proved adequate with the aid of imports to maintain suitably equipped forces in the field. Hence the Confederate Army suffered no crippling deficiency in weapons or supplies. Their principal handicap would be numerical inferiority. But to offset this lack Confederates fought the first major war in which both sides armed themselves with rifles and had the advantage of a temporary but very significant surge in the power of the tactical defensive. In addition, the problem of supply in a very large but thinly settled region was a powerful aid to the strategic defensive. Other things being equal, Confederate military leadership were confident that if the Union did not display Napoleonic genius, the tactical and strategic power of the defensive could offset the Northern numerical superiority and presumably give the South a measure of military victory adequate to maintain its independence. In short, the task of the North was literally gigantic. It was the task of organizing and harnessing its superior resources and committing them to warfare on a financial scale that was historically unprecedented. The South too had a similar organizing job to do but inertia was on the South's side and would have been fatal to the North. The North had the necessity to conquer. The South could have won simply by not being conquered. It did not have to occupy a foot of ground outside its own borders.[46]

With further reference to the military claims of the Lost Cause, the "Longstreet-lost-it-at-Gettysburg" thesis is based on the concept of the "high tide at Gettysburg": The Confederate loss at Gettysburg decided the war. This, too, is a myth; it disregards the remaining almost two years of fighting as well as Vicksburg, Missionary Ridge, Nashville, and

Sherman's March to the Sea. Jeffry Wert responds in this volume to the scapegoating of Longstreet regarding Gettysburg. And the Jackson death thesis is also invalid. His death was clearly a blow to the Confederacy, but to point to that single 1863 event as decisive apart from the conduct of the war as a whole is simply unreasonable.

The Idealized Home Front

The typical moonlight and magnolias view of Southern society is highly distorted from a historical standpoint. Bertram Wyatt-Brown accurately notes that the Edenic view of the antebellum South ignores what he calls the "darker side of honor."

> Individuals and sometimes groups spoke out against popular forms of injustice and honor—duels, summary hangings, mob whippings. These efforts at reform seldom received public acclamation and support. Even historians, whether native to the South or not, have not seen these expressions of public will and private esteem as part of a total cultural pattern. Instead they have been labeled tragic aberrations, or techniques by which the planter class manipulated lesser, more virtuous folk. Gentility, the nobler, brighter feature of Southern ethics has been a more congenial topic. Certainly it was the model that Southerners have publicly revered and exalted.[47]

The last three chapters of Wyatt-Brown's *Southern Honor* discuss some of the dark sides of the Southern ethos under the suggestive titles "Policing Slave Society: Insurrectionary Scares," "Charivari and Lynch Law," and "The Anatomy of a Wife-Killing."[48] Contrary to the legend's picture of a unified and committed Southern people, we also know today that the South was bitterly divided politically on issues like the Confederate military draft, control of the Southern armies, and requisition of supplies for the armies. Furthermore, there was a high degree of strife and conflict that marked the political culture, the military establishment, and the personal relationships of Confederate leaders. Wiley remarks that "strife was the Confederacy's evil genius and no major organization or activity escaped its crippling influence."[49]

The Idealized Confederate Soldier

The historical records simply do not bear out the idealized picture of the Confederate common soldier. Piston notes that "Desertions reached nightmare proportions during and after the [Antietam] campaign. Perhaps as many as 20,000 men left the army either before it crossed the

Potomac or prior to the fight at Antietam. Significantly, desertions increased after the Confederates returned to Virginia."[50] Lee's communications confirmed these typical soldier problems. Writing to Jefferson Davis from Hagerstown, Maryland, on September 13, 1862, before Sharpsburg, Lee stated: "One great embarrassment is the reduction of our ranks by straggling, which it seems impossible to prevent with our present regimental officers. Our ranks are very much diminished—I fear from a third to one half of the original numbers." Lee described the state of the army after the battle in a letter dated September 21: "Its present efficiency is greatly paralyzed by the loss to its ranks of the numerous stragglers. . . . A great many men belonging to the Army never entered Maryland at all; many returned after getting there, while others who crossed the river kept aloof. The stream (of stragglers) has not lessened since crossing the Potomac." The next day Lee advised Davis that "A great deal of damage to citizens is done by stragglers, who consume all they can get from the charitable and all they can take from the defenseless, in many cases wantonly destroying stock and property."[51] What Douglas Southall Freeman calls "mass desertion" was a source of losses to Lee's army after Gettysburg as well. Reporting to President Davis on July 27, 1863, Lee stated that "There are many thousand men improperly absent from this army."[52] Less than a month later Lee informed Davis that "General Imboden writes that there are great numbers of deserters in the valley, who conceal themselves successfully from the small squads sent to arrest them." On the same day, August 17, Lee ordered Imboden to collect and send back deserters from the valley in northwest Virginia and Lee reported that according to reports that he was receiving from North Carolina, there was "an organization of deserters . . . a formidable and growing evil there." These men, according to Secretary of War James A. Seddon, were engaged in "dangerous combinations and violent proceedings." Desertions from the Confederate Army of Tennessee in the western theater "climbed at an alarming rate" after the Confederate victory at Chickamauga.[53]

The Lawfulness of Secession

The Northern people did not, of course, concede the Southern contention regarding the legality of secession. Lincoln addressed the question in his first inaugural speech: "I hold, that in contemplation of universal law, and the Constitution, the Union of the states is perpetual. Perpetuity is implied, if not expressed, in the fundamental law of all national governments." On the issue of a compact of sovereign states, he said: "Again, the United States would not be a government proper but an association of states in the status of a contract merely, can it, as a contract be peaceably unmade by less than all of the parties who made it? One party to a contract may violate—break it, so to speak, but does it not require all to lawfully rescind it?"[54] But the issue could not be reduced to a theoretical, abstract argument or be legalistically resolved. In practical terms, the South was asserting a right to revolution, a right Americans acknowledged. But the North in practical terms was unwilling to allow the nation to perish. The real issue regarding secession was whether, under the circumstances, it was just or unjust.

The Saints Go Marching In

The legend's image of Lee is at odds with the facts. He was not anti-slavery as the image claims; he was a strong believer in the institution. His secession, following Virginia, was not inevitable, but a calculated act of will in highly ambiguous circumstances. His aggressive, offensive generalship cost his army disproportionate, irreplaceable, and excessive casualties, which led to his being caught in a fatal siege. Contrary to the legend of his magnanimity, he was hateful and bitter toward the North during and after the war. His persistence in continuing the war after he realized the South was defeated was costly in the lives of his men as well as the Yankees and not necessarily a creditable act. In the postwar period, he was less of a healer than he was a conventional advocate of Southern positions.[55]

Historically, Jackson was clearly an effective soldier. He was also fanatical, like Oliver Cromwell among the Irish, killing people zestfully for the glory of God. He was zealously pietistic, but advocated a no prisoners, black flag war, seriously proposing this to Virginia's governor and proposing that he embark on such a campaign himself.[56]

In many ways Forrest, although an able soldier, seems a strange hero for twentieth-century Americans. His personal fortune resulted from slave trading. He looked on as his troops helped massacre black Union soldiers at Fort Pillow after they had surrendered. After the war he became a prominent Ku Klux Klan leader.[57] To a thoughtful or humane person, he seems an anomalous hero.

The Lost Cause Legacy to History

Taken together, the elements of the Myth of the Lost Cause created the Southern image that was sought. Slavery and the slavery disagreement were excluded from that image. There had been a distinctive and superior Southern culture, benign and effective in its race relations. That culture was led by wise and superior men who seceded because they sought freedom from an oppressive Northern culture, an effort that failed because of overwhelming Northern power. The warfare itself was a contest of honor and martial glory in which the chivalrous and valorous Southerners pursued a sort of Arthurian tournament, seeking Southern independence.

The Lost Cause version of the war is a caricature, possible, among other reasons, because of the false treatment of slavery and the black people. This false treatment struck at the core of the truth of the war, unhinging cause and effect, depriving the United States of any high purpose, and removing African Americans from their true role as the issue of the war and participants in the war, and characterizing them as historically irrelevant. With slavery exorcised, it appeared that the North had conducted itself within the Union so as to provoke secession and then bloodily defeated the secessionists in war so as to compel them to stay in the Union against their will.

The historical image of the war is, of course, quite different. It says that the seceding states were dominated by a cruel and wrongful slavery. As evidenced by the prewar political discord, the nature of the compromise efforts on the eve of Fort Sumter—all of which concerned the legal status of slavery—and the prewar statements of Southern political leaders, slavery was *the* sectional issue. Southern political leaders led their states out of the Union to protect slavery from a disapproving national majority. Although slaveholders constituted a distinct minority of Southern people, a majority of these people were committed to the institution for African Americans. The North went to war to defeat secession. The Civil War, therefore, presented three issues: (1) however flawed the circumstances, human freedom was at stake; (2) the territorial and political integrity of the United States was at stake; and (3) the survival of the democratic process—republican government of, by, and for the people—was at stake.

Secession was not therefore heroic—it was mean and narrow and a profound mistake. Its leaders were wrong and authored a major tragedy for the American people. Dismantling the United States in 1861 would not have benefited either the North or the South. On the contrary, it would have led to constant conflict over such things as access to the Mississippi River and the rights of the two nations to the territories, and it would have established the precedent that a loser in a democratic election may successfully resort to warfare, as Lincoln discussed in his Gettysburg Address. The warfare itself, in which African Americans participated in behalf of the North, was cruel and terribly destructive to the people of both sides.

Confederate sympathizers today contend that the secessionists acted in good faith; this presumably means that they thought that they were doing the right thing. It would seem that this is neither here nor there in a historical sense. Leaders of all kinds of destructive causes—causes with wholly negative values—have thought they were right. It would be inflammatory to identify examples of this in modern times, but surely they occur to us. The historical question is whether, in good faith or bad, the movement that was led was positive or negative, humane or inhumane?

The Lost Cause treatment of the role of slavery in the war and its view of African Americans as subhumans not to be taken seriously formed the prelude to the myth of Reconstruction, another historical legacy of the Lost Cause. As portrayed in D. W. Griffith's *Birth of a Nation* and its updated Margaret Mitchell version, the Reconstruction myth identified the freedmen variously as shiftless fools, corrupt political connivers, or despoilers of the virtues of white women. Reconstruction was pictured as a cynical exploitation of African Americans by cynical schemers. The Ku Klux Klan existed as the shield of justice and the virtue of Southern women. This Negrophobic Reconstruction myth has been so dominant that a man as intelligent and humane as Shelby Foote commented negatively about Reconstruction in Ken Burns's Civil War television series.

The Political Legacy

The political legacy of the Lost Cause had two signal aspects. On one hand, its development facilitated the reunification of the North and South. Ex-Confederates saw the acceptance of the myth by Northerners as "signs of respect from former foes and Northern publishers [which] made acceptance of reunion easier. By the mid-80s, most southerners had decided to build a future within a reunited nation. The North had . . . acknowledged the heroism and nobility of the Confederate effort, the honor of the South" so that "Southerners would be totally at ease in the union."[58]

The second aspect of the political legacy concerned the status of African Americans. The virulent racism that the North shared with the South, in spite of Northern antislavery views, was a premise of the Lost Cause and the principal engine of the North's acceptance of it. The reunion was exclusively a white man's phenomenon and the price of the reunion was the sacrifice of the African Americans. Indeed, the reunion of the white race was expressly at the expense of the freedmen. The Compromise of 1877 gave the presidential election to Rutherford B. Hayes and the Republicans on the promise that Federal troops—the blacks' only shield—would be withdrawn from the South. The blacks were abandoned, the states of Confederacy were "redeemed" by the empowerment of the former Confederate political leadership, and Articles

XIV (equal protection of the law) and XV (voting rights), constitutional products of the war, were permitted to atrophy for a hundred years. In short, the success of the teachings of the Lost Cause led to the nation's abandoning even its half-hearted effort to protect African Americans and bring them into the United States as equal citizens. Jim Crow, lynch law, and disfranchisement followed.[59]

Epilogue

As has been said, the Lost Cause legacy to history is a caricature of the truth. This caricature wholly misrepresents and distorts the facts of the matter. Surely it is time to start again in our understanding of this decisive element of our past and to do so from the premises of history unadulterated by the distortions, falsehoods, and romantic sentimentality of the Myth of the Lost Cause.

Having swept away the counterfactual Myth of the Lost Cause, a historian may briefly state the history of the Civil War as follows.

The eleven states that seceded and became the Confederate States of America did so in order to protect the institution of African slavery from a perceived political threat from the majority of the people of the United States who disapproved of the institution. Although slaveholders were a minority in each of the Confederate states, the slaveholding planter class dominated the politics and culture and tastes of those states and led them into secession and armed rebellion against the United States.

African slavery was an inhumane, reactionary, uneconomic labor system, disapproved of by the civilized people of the world. Most of the slaves disliked their status and took any opportunity to escape slavery, despite the fact that if caught they risked flogging, branding, and other severe punishments or death. The slave states before the war effected legal provisions that plainly violated the United States Constitution's Bill of Rights in an effort to secure the institution of slavery. Furthermore, prior to secession, Southern people who objected to slavery were isolated, silenced, and driven out of the slave states.

Having seceded, the eleven states raised armies and claimed the property and institutions of the United States that were within their borders. If the United States failed to surrender those properties voluntarily, the Confederates seized them by force of arms. When the United States in 1861 refused to surrender Fort Sumter in Charleston Harbor, the fort was attacked and taken by Southern arms. This started the war. Under the leadership of President Abraham Lincoln, an unusually skilled and inspirational politician, the United States defended itself against the Confederate rebellion over the next four years and ultimately reclaimed the territory of the eleven seceded states by military force.

The war was cruel, costly, and devastating, killing in excess of six hundred thousand American men, Northern and Southern, and wounding many, many more. It also was highly destructive to the Southern economy. African Americans also participated in the war; many escaped slavery; 180,000 of them fought in the United States military forces and thousands of others assisted the United States in logistical and supporting ways and in sheltering and taking care of Federal soldiers in Confederate territory. As a consequence of the war, slavery was abolished and constitutional amendments were effected which prohibited slavery (the Thirteenth), guaranteed equal protection of the law (the Fourteenth), and provided for universal male suffrage (the Fifteenth). At the conclusion of the war, the eleven states resumed their places in the Union. There occurred a brief period during which the United States attempted to reform Southern political life by drawing into it the freed slaves and protecting them from persecution and discrimination. The Southern people persistently opposed these efforts, often pursuing cruel and violent acts against the freed people. White Northerners, who were also intensely racist, ultimately abandoned the effort to ensure the protection of the freed people. The United States soldiers were withdrawn from the South. The Confederate leadership returned to power in the former Confederate states and succeeded in institutionalizing the discriminatory and violent treatment of the freed people and excluding them from political life.

Appendix

Because *Gone with the Wind,* both the book and the movie, has been so popular and so widely known and I have been negative about them, I should explain my view. I do not require the reader to choose between Abraham Lincoln and Clark Gable, but I offer examples of Mitchell's great story as very bad history, essentially a Lost Cause statement:

The Slaves. In the story, they are pictured as unintelligent, passive, and faithful to the always indulgent "Old Massa." The implication is that the war was not about slavery and the message is also that the slaves were well treated, happy, and did not care whether they were slaves or free people. As has been pointed out, the fact is that the war was all about slavery—the South seceded to protect slavery—and the slaves knew this and were overwhelmingly supportive of the North.

The Yankee Soldier. The reader may recall the scene in which a snaggle-toothed, evil-looking Federal soldier has entered Tara to steal. Scarlett shoots him on the steps to protect herself from his rather obvious intent to assault her. The implication is that the Yankees were bush-whackers or guerilla warriors—bad people who were gratuitously and randomly upsetting the genteel and benign Southern culture. There were, of course, atrocities committed during the Civil War, as is true in all wars, but such activity was relatively insignificant and, more to the point, there were Southern perpetrators of atrocities in the North as well as in the South, just as there were Federal perpetrators. A particularly interesting fact concerns Pennsylvania as Lee's army was en route to Gettysburg. The Confederate soldiers captured black people, including children and free blacks, and sent them South into slavery.[60]

The Southern Armies. The reader may recall pictures of the ragged, forlorn Southern army, marching through the streets of Atlanta in its attempt to defend the city. The myth is that the defeat of the South was inevitable, that it was simply overwhelmed by massive Northern materiel and manpower and could not have won the war. The consensus among serious historians today discredits this myth. A recent study by a group of professional historians makes this observation: "No Confederate army lost a major engagement because of lack of arms, munitions or other essential supplies."[61]

The Vigilantes. There is a scene in which Leslie Howard, as Ashley Wilkes, and his fellow Southern protagonists secretly go out armed immediately after the war to "clean out" the encampment of homeless former slaves. Howard is wounded in the struggle. This, of course, is the nascent Ku Klux Klan, and it is presented in a manner wholly sympathetic to the idea of vigilantes and the necessity of their existence in order to protect good white people from the former slaves, who are bad black people.

After the War. As indicated by its title, the book extends into the early period of Reconstruction. It depicts the freed black people as arrogant and crude and the Southern whites who cooperated with the social revolution of the war as vicious and evil. The implication again is that the Yankees had replaced the chivalrous and benign Southern people with evil Southern people. Reconstruction was, in fact, a flawed process, but it had its idealistic side. Moreover, the failures were caused by Southern intransigence as much as by Northern errors.[62]

Notes

1. Samuel Eliot Morison, *The Oxford History of the American People* (New York: Oxford University Press, 1965), 725.

2. James M. McPherson, *Ordeal by Fire* (New York: Alfred A. Knopf, 1982), 149.

3. Gaines M. Foster, *Ghosts of the Confederacy: Defeat, the Lost Cause, and the Emergence of the New South, 1865 to 1913* (New York: Oxford University Press, 1987), 117.

4. D. W. Brogan, "Fresh Appraisal of the Civil War," in *The Open Form,* ed. Alfred Kazin (New York: Harcourt, Brace, and World, 1965), 174.

5. McPherson, *Ordeal by Fire,* 476.

6. Foster, *Ghosts of the Confederacy,* 4.

7. E. A. Pollard, *Southern History of the War* (New York: C. B. Richardson, 1866), 562.

8. Michael C. C. Adams, *Our Masters the Rebels* (Cambridge, Mass.: Harvard University Press, 1978), 3.

9. Ibid., 4.

10. *Southern Historical Society Papers* 8, no. 4 (April 1880).

11. Douglas Southall Freeman, *The South to Posterity* (New York: Charles Scribner's Sons, 1951), x, xi.

12. Kenneth M. Stampp, *The Imperiled Union* (New York: Oxford University Press, 1980), 268.

13. Robert F. Durden, *The Gray and the Black* (Baton Rouge: Louisiana State University Press, 1972), 3.

14. James L. Roark, *Masters Without Slaves: Southern Planters in the Civil War and Reconstruction* (New York: W. W. Norton, 1977), 195.

15. Thomas J. Pressly, *Americans Interpret Their Civil War* (New York: Free Press, 1965), 124, 132–33; David Donald, *Lincoln Reconsidered* (New York: Alfred A. Knopf, 1956), chap. 2, 19ff.

16. William Garrett Piston, *Lee's Tarnished Lieutenant: James Longstreet and His Place in Southern History* (Athens: University of Georgia Press, 1987), 158.

17. U.S. War Department, *The War of the Rebellion: A Compilation of the Official Records of the Union and Confederate Armies,* 127 vols., index, and atlas (Washington, D.C.: Government Printing Office, 1886–87) (hereafter cited as *OR;* unless otherwise stated, all references are to ser. 1), ser. 2, 5:807, 808.

18. Piston, *Lee's Tarnished Lieutenant,* 157–58.

19. *Southern Literary Messenger* 30 (June 1860): 401–409.

20. Richard E. Beringer, Herman Hattaway, Archer Jones, and William N. Still Jr., *Why the South Lost the Civil War* (Athens: University of Georgia Press, 1986), 76.

21. Piston, *Lee's Tarnished Lieutenant,* 157–58.

22. Rev. J. William Jones, "Within a Stone's Throw of Independence," *Southern Historical Society Papers* 12 (March 1884): 111–12.

23. Piston, *Lee's Tarnished Lieutenant,* 157–58.

24. Foster, *Ghosts of the Confederacy,* 117–19.

25. Piston, *Lee's Tarnished Lieutenant,* 157–58.

26. Foster, *Ghosts of the Confederacy,* 117–18.

27. Fanny Downing, "Perfect through Suffering," *The Land We Love* 4 (January 1868): 193–205.

28. Rev. J. William Jones, D. D., *Army of Northern Virginia Memorial Volume* (Richmond: J. W. Randolph and English, 1880), 122.

29. James I. Robertson Jr., *Stonewall Jackson: The Man, The Soldier, The Legend* (New York: Macmillan, 1997), vii, viii, xvi.

30. Morison, *Oxford History of the American People,* 405.

31. Don E. Fehrenbacher, *Lincoln in Text and Context* (Stanford, Calif.: Stanford University Press, 1987), 47.

32. William C. Davis, *Jefferson Davis: The Man and His Hour* (New York: HarperCollins, 1991), 127, 177, 208, 212–13, 214, 216.

33. Frank Moore, ed., *Rebellion Record: A Diary of American Events with Documents, Narratives, Illustrative Incidents, Poetry, Etc.,* 11 vols. and supplement (New York: D. Van Nortrand, 1861–68), 844–46.

34. Durden, *The Gray and the Black,* 3–7.

35. Pressly, *Americans Interpret Their Civil War,* chaps. 5 and 7.

36. Bertram Wyatt-Brown, *Southern Honor: Ethics and Behavior in the Old South* (New York: Oxford University Press, 1983), 24; Fehrenbacher, *Lincoln in Text and Context,* 69; Brogan, "Fresh Appraisal of the Civil War," 187.

37. Kenneth M. Stampp, *The Peculiar Institution* (New York: Alfred A. Knopf, 1963), 210–17; Dwight Lowell Dumond, *Antislavery: The Crusade for Freedom in America* (Ann Arbor: University of Michigan Press, 1961), 204–10; See also Stampp, *Imperiled Union,* 235–37; Clement Eaton, *Freedom of Thought in the Old South* (Durham, N.C.: Duke University Press, 1940), chaps. 7, 12.

38. Stampp, *Peculiar Institution,* 211.

39. Allan Nevins, *The Emergence of Lincoln,* 2 vols. (New York: Charles Scribner's Sons, 1950), 2:468.

40. *OR,* ser. 2, 1:783; see also ser. 3, vols. 1–5, and ser. 4, vol. 3; see also Robert Manson Myers, ed., *The Children of Pride: A True Story of Georgia and the Civil War* (New Haven, Conn.: Yale University Press, 1972).

41. Dudley Taylor Cornish, *The Sable Arm* (New York: W. W. Norton, 1966), 288; Benjamin Quarles, *The Negro in the Civil War* (Boston: Little, Brown, 1953), 199; Ira Berlin et al., *Freedom: A Documentary History of Emancipation, 1861–1867,* vol. 1, ser. 2, *The Black Military Experience* (New York: Cambridge University Press, 1983).

42. Stampp, *Imperiled Union,* 255, 265.

43. Grady McWhiney, *Southerners and Other Americans* (New York: Bass Books, 1973), 3–4.

44. Bell I. Wiley, *The Road to Appomattox* (Memphis: Memphis State College Press, 1956), 77.

45. David Donald, ed., *Why the North Won the Civil War* (Baton Rouge: Louisiana State University Press, 1960).

46. Beringer et al., *Why the South Lost*, 16.

47. Wyatt-Brown, *Southern Honor*, 493.

48. Ibid., pt. 3, chaps. 15, 16, and 17.

49. Wiley, *Road to Appomattox*, 78–99.

50. Piston, *Lee's Tarnished Lieutenant*, 174.

51. *OR*, ser. 2, 19:606; ser. 1, 19:143; ser. 2, 19:597, 617–18, 626–27.

52. Douglas Southall Freeman, *Lee's Lieutenants*, 3 vols. (New York: Charles Scribner's Sons, 1942–44), 3:217; *OR*, ser. 3, 27:1041.

53. *OR*, ser. 2, 29:650–51, 692, 768–69. Peter Cozzens, *The Shipwreck of Their Hopes* (Urbana: University of Illinois Press, 1994), 28, 29.

54. Abraham Lincoln, *The Collected Works of Abraham Lincoln*, Ray R. Basler, ed., 9 vols. (New Brunswick, N.J.: Rutgers University Press, 1953–55), 4:264–65.

55. Alan T. Nolan, *Lee Considered* (Chapel Hill: University of North Carolina Press, 1991).

56. Charles Royster, *The Destructive War* (New York: Alfred A. Knopf, 1991), 40–42.

57. James M. McPherson, *Battle Cry of Freedom* (New York: Oxford University Press, 1988), 748; Stewart Sifakis, *Who Was Who in the Civil War* (New York: Facts on File, 1988), 224.

58. Foster, *Ghosts of the Confederacy*, 63, 66.

59. David W. Bright, *Frederick Douglass' Civil War* (Baton Rouge: Louisiana State University, 1989); C. Vann Woodward, *Reunion and Reaction* (Boston: Little, Brown, 1951).

60. W. P. Conrad and Ted Alexander, *When War Passed This Way* (Greencastle, Pa.: A Greencastle Bicentennial Publication, 1982), 253–54.

61. See note 39 above.

62. Eric Foner, *Reconstruction* (New York: Harper and Row, 1988); George C. Rable, *But There Was No Peace: The Role of Violence in the Politics of Reconstruction* (Athens: University of Georgia Press, 1984).

Two

Jubal A. Early, the Lost Cause, and Civil War History
A Persistent Legacy

Gary W. Gallagher

Jubal Anderson Early understood the power of the printed word to influence perceptions of historical events. One of Robert E. Lee's principal lieutenants during the Civil War, he sought to create a written record celebrating the Confederacy's military resistance. Early hoped future generations would rely on this record, the essence of which can be distilled into a few sentences. Lee was a heroic soldier who led an outnumbered army of Confederate patriots against a powerful enemy. With "Stonewall" Jackson initially at his side, he faced Northern generals of minimal talent who later lied in print to explain their failures. Against these men and later against Ulysses S. Grant, a clumsy butcher who understood only that vast Northern resources of men and materiel must be expended freely, the Confederate commander worked his magic across a Virginia landscape that functioned as the cockpit of the war. Lee and his Army of Northern Virginia set a standard of valor and accomplishment equal to anything in the military history of the Western world until finally, worn out but never defeated, they laid down their weapons at Appomattox. If the youth of the white South and succeeding generations of Americans and foreign readers accepted his version of the war, believed Early, ex-Confederates would have salvaged their honor from the wreck of seemingly all-encompassing defeat.

These ideas constitute part of what has come to be called the Myth of the Lost Cause, an explanation for secession and Confederate defeat propagated in the years following the Civil War. Early's role as a leading Lost Cause warrior has been explored by several talented historians, all of whom portray him as so violently anti-Northern that he eventually

isolated himself from the Southern white mainstream. Resolutely unreconstructed, goes the common argument, Early watched disapprovingly
as proponents of the New South gained increasing power and ultimately
rendered him a crabby anachronism long before his death in 1894.[1] This
interpretation neglects Early's long-term impact on the ways in which
Americans have understood the Civil War. Clear-eyed in his determination to sway future generations, Early used his own writings and his
influence with other ex-Confederates to foster a heroic image of Robert
E. Lee and the Southern war effort. Many of the ideas these men articulated became orthodoxy in the postwar South, eventually made
their way into the broader national perception of the war, and remain
vigorous today. To put this phenomenon within the context of current
historical work, Early understood almost immediately after Appomattox
that there would be a struggle to control the public memory of the war,
worked hard to help shape that memory, and ultimately enjoyed more
success than he probably imagined possible.[2]

Before examining Early's largely persuasive efforts in this regard, it
is worth noting that many of his other ideas found little favor in the
postwar South. A conservative Whig who venerated property and rule
by the slaveholding class during the antebellum period, he had resisted
changes to the existing order.[3] After Appomattox, Early remained a self-
styled conservative Whig who never relinquished his elitist conception
of how society should be organized. While other white Southerners
trimmed their ideological sails to suit changed times, he clung tena-
ciously to every element of his antebellum worldview.[4] Gaines M. Foster
has shown that most Southerners displayed little inclination to embrace Early's elitist and nostalgic views. They preferred instead to follow John Brown Gordon and others whose vision of the New South permitted them to acknowledge that the war had altered their world while
still honoring the leaders of the Confederacy and the motives that had
brought secession. Foster likens Early and those who agreed with him
to the Native American Ghost Dancers of the late nineteenth century:
"They appeared captivated by a dream of . . . a return to an undefeated
Confederacy. This aspect of their historical vision does not appear very
different from another revitalization movement of the late nineteenth
century, the Ghost Dance among the Plains Indians. . . . They clung to
the past, defended old values, and dreamed of a world untouched by
defeat." In the end, adds Foster, very few white Southerners "joined the
ghost dance."[5]

Because of Early's passionate interest in how the future would judge
the Confederacy, however, it is a mistake to see him as looking only to the
past. He began work on his memoirs a few months after Appomattox—

well before most former commanders even thought about writing their reminiscences. His opinions about Confederate military history, which he hoped would have force among subsequent generations, earned a very receptive hearing across the postwar South.

Before turning his attention to interpreting wartime events, however, Early left the United States. A much maligned figure in the Confederacy after his army suffered utter defeat against Philip H. Sheridan's forces in the Shenandoah Valley during the fall and winter of 1864–65, Early was relieved of command in March 1865 and missed the surrender of the Army of Northern Virginia at Appomattox. Upon hearing of Lee's capitulation, he traveled westward with the hope of joining Confederates in the Trans-Mississippi theater. He learned en route that they also had surrendered and decided, as he put it, to leave the United States "to get out from the rule of the infernal Yankees. . . . I cannot live under the same government with our enemies. I go therefore a voluntary exile from the home and graves of my ancestors to seek my fortunes anew in the world." Traveling first to Havana, then to Mexico, and eventually settling in Canada, Early spent four years abroad before returning to Virginia in 1869. From Canada he followed events in the United States with mounting bitterness, declaring at one point, "I have got to that condition, that I think I could scalp a Yankee woman and child without winking my eyes."[6]

While in Mexico during the winter of 1865–66, Early crossed pens with his old foe Sheridan in a newspaper exchange that anticipated in tone and focus his later writings about the war. At dispute were the strengths and casualties of the forces in the Shenandoah campaign. Sheridan asserted that Early had lost nearly twenty-seven thousand men killed, wounded, and captured; Early countered that his force had consisted of fewer than fourteen thousand men and could not have suffered the losses claimed by Sheridan. Early's numbers were more accurate, but winning this argument constituted only a means to the larger end of compiling a written record aimed at both contemporaries and future readers. By insisting that he had commanded far fewer men than Sheridan, Early cast his own performance in a better light and sustained the honor of hopelessly outnumbered Confederates. "Sheridan's letter has furnished another evidence of the propriety of my caution to all fair minded men of other nations," insisted Early, "to withhold their judgments upon the reports of our enemies until the truth can be placed before them."[7]

Robert E. Lee figured prominently in Early's crusade to establish the Confederate side of the war's military history. Early had exhibited unbounded admiration for Lee even before the Civil War, agreeing with other Virginians that Lee's record during the conflict with Mexico marked him as a brilliant soldier. In the spring of 1862, a witness noted that Early, who habitually criticized Confederate civilian and military leaders, never spoke negatively about Lee. "For Lee he seemed to have a regard and esteem and high opinion felt by him for no one else," remarked this man.[8] Lee in turn appreciated Early's talents as a soldier and displayed personal fondness for his cantankerous and profane lieutenant. Only Stonewall Jackson among Lee's corps commanders received more difficult assignments from Lee, a certain indication of the commanding general's high regard.

Lee ensured his subordinate's utter devotion with a gentle handling of Early's removal from command in the spring of 1865. He expressed regret at having to replace Early but noted that defeats in the Shenandoah Valley had alienated that vital region's citizens and raised doubts among Early's soldiers. "While my own confidence in your ability, zeal, and devotion to the cause is unimpaired," stated Lee, "I have nevertheless felt that I could not oppose what seems to be the current of opinion, without injustice to your reputation and injury to the service." Lee closed with thanks for "the fidelity and energy with which you have always supported my efforts, and for the courage and devotion you have ever manifested in the service of the country."[9]

In late November 1865, Early received a letter from Lee that likely inspired him to begin work on his memoirs. Lee explained that he intended to write a history of the Army of Northern Virginia, but the loss of official papers during the chaotic retreat from Richmond to Appomattox left him without sufficient information about the period 1864–65. Would Early send whatever materials he had relating to that last phase of the conflict? Seven and a half months earlier Lee had spoken of the Union's "overwhelming resources and numbers" in his farewell order to the Army of Northern Virginia. Now he specifically asked Early for information about Confederate strengths at the principal battles from May 1864 through April 1865. "My only object," concluded Lee in language Early would echo many times in his own writings, "is to transmit, if possible, the truth to posterity, and do justice to our brave Soldiers."[10]

Lee sent Early another request in March 1866 for "reports of the operations of your Commands, in the Campaign from the Wilderness to Richmond, at Lynchburg, in the Valley, Maryland, &c." Lee wanted all "statistics as regards numbers, destruction of private property by the Federal troops, &c." because he intended to demonstrate the discrepancy in strength between the two armies and believed it would "be difficult to get the world to understand the odds against which we fought." "The accusations against myself," Lee wrote in reference to various newspaper accounts, "I have not thought proper to notice, or even to correct misrepresentations of my words & acts. We shall have to be patient, & suffer for awhile at least. . . . At present the public mind is not prepared to receive the truth."[11]

Three months after he received Lee's first letter, Early completed a draft of his wartime memoirs. He published the last section of this manuscript—the first book-length reminiscence by any major Civil War commander—in late 1866 as *A Memoir of the Last Year of the War for Independence, in the Confederate States of America.* Lee's March 1866 letter can be read as an outline for Early's book, which covered precisely the period the letter defined, strongly emphasized the North's advantage in numbers, and detailed Federal depredations in the Shenandoah Valley. A desire to satisfy Lee's request for information about the conflict's final year may have prompted Early to hurry this portion of his larger narrative into print. The fact that he never published the whole memoir suggests that he contemplated revisions and printed only the chapters that would serve Lee's most immediate needs (as well as place his own controversial activities in the Shenandoah Valley in the best possible light).[12]

Early also may have read Lee's March 1866 letter as an unintentional summons to champion his old commander against all detractors. Distressed by the mention of attacks on Lee, Early may have decided to persuade the public to "receive the truth" about the general—to spell out in vigorous detail, and with an attention to evidence befitting Early's years of experience as a lawyer, a case for the greatness of both Lee and his army.

Early discussed the need to tell the Confederate side of the war in a letter to Lee in late November 1868. Decrying the proliferation of errors in everything he had read about the conflict, Early urged Lee not to "abandon your purpose of writing a history of the operations of the Army of Northern Virginia." In one passage Early got to the heart of his concern about the published record: "The most that is left to us is the history of our struggle, and I think that ought to be accurately written. We lost nearly everything but honor, and that should be religiously guarded."[13]

Apart from his concern about future perceptions of Lee and his army, Early also sought to guard his own long-term reputation. "According to my view," he wrote to another former Confederate officer, "the most important books of all are those put into the hands of the rising generation." One new schoolbook implied that Early should have captured Washington during his raid across the Potomac in the summer of 1864.

"It is by no means a pleasant reflection that I am to be held up in that light before not only the rising generation of this day," groused Early, "but all those to come hereafter." He warned that former Confederates must try to get the correct version of the war into print immediately because "We all know how hard it is to eradicate early impressions."[14]

In lectures, writings, and personal correspondence over the last twenty-five years of his life, Early sought to place his impressions of the war on record. He took an active role in publishing the *Southern Historical Society Papers*, wherein former Confederates reexamined old battles and assessed both comrades and enemies. Thomas L. Connelly, Gaines M. Foster, William Garrett Piston, and other historians have explored this aspect of Early's postwar career in detail. Although some of their conclusions are open to debate, the focus of this essay must remain elsewhere. It is enough to note that Early achieved a position in the South as a leading arbiter of questions relating to Confederate military history. He orchestrated the effort to isolate James Longstreet—Lee's senior subordinate throughout the war—as a pariah because he had dared to criticize Lee in print. Other former Confederates took notice. If Early could savage a soldier of Longstreet's wartime accomplishments and reputation, scarcely anyone could be safe criticizing Lee. Robert Stiles, a former Confederate artillerist who wrote a much-quoted volume of recollections, commented about Early's influence among ex-Confederates who wrote about the war: "[A]s long as 'the old hero' lived," stated Stiles, "no man ever took up his pen to write a line about the great conflict without the fear of Jubal Early before his eyes."[15]

Early interpreted key military events and personalities in a series of publications between 1866 and 1872. His major points can be summarized quickly: (1) Robert E. Lee was the best and most admirable general of the war; (2) Confederate armies faced overwhelming odds and mounted a gallant resistance; (3) Ulysses S. Grant paled in comparison to Lee as a soldier; (4) Stonewall Jackson deserved a place immediately behind Lee in the Confederate pantheon of heroes; and (5) Virginia was the most important arena of combat.

Lee towers above all other Civil War figures in Early's writings. The preface to *A Memoir of the Last Year of the War* unabashedly announced Early's "profound love and veneration" for Lee. In an address at Washington and Lee University in 1872, which was widely distributed as a pamphlet and stands as a classic Lost Cause tract, Early hoped to help the audience form "a really correct estimate of [Lee's] marvellous ability and boldness as a military commander." Defending his subject at every turn, Early explained Gettysburg as an instance where Lee's subordinates (especially Longstreet) failed to execute a sound plan of battle. The public misunderstood the campaign only because Lee's magnanimity had prevented his revealing the true causes of that defeat. Early explained the fall of Richmond in April 1865 and the surrender of Lee's army as "consequences of events in the West and Southwest, and not directly of the operations in Virginia." In rendering this judgment that failures elsewhere had undone Lee, Early professed to shun invidious comparisons between his hero and Confederate leaders in other theaters. He closed with an affirmation of Lee's personal and professional greatness, insisting that his hero had no equal during the Civil War or among earlier military figures.[16]

Northern numerical superiority rendered Lee's successes all the more remarkable to Early. He repeatedly stressed the unequal pools of Confederate and Federal manpower, heaping scorn on Northern officers who overestimated Lee's strength. Northern attempts to play down Grant's advantage in manpower over Lee elicited an especially strident reaction. When Adam Badeau, Grant's military secretary during 1864–65, placed Union and Confederate numbers in early May 1864 at 98,000 and 72,000 respectively, Early characterized the article as part of "a persistent and systematic effort to falsify the truth." Addressing his reply to the editor of the *London Standard*, he gave the numbers as 141,000 and 50,000 (Grant actually outnumbered Lee by about two to one). Again with an eye on history's verdict, Early pointed out that a people "overpowered and crushed in a struggle for their rights" had but one resource upon which to rely for vindication—an appeal to "foreign nations and to the next age."[17]

Early found only honor in the Confederate performance against daunting odds. In his scenario, a band of noble Confederates led by the peerless Lee held off a mechanistic North blessed with inexhaustible reserves of men and materiel for nearly three years. Exploiting an array of scientific breakthroughs applicable to military use and relentlessly piling in men, the Federals "finally produced that exhaustion of our army and resources, and that accumulation of numbers on the other side, which wrought the final disaster." The Army of Northern Virginia "had been gradually worn down by the combined agencies of numbers, steam-power, railroads, mechanism, and all the resources of physical science." Early repeatedly juxtaposed steadfast Confederates against craven Northern soldiers who manipulated numbers to rationalize their defeats at the hands of Lee's smaller army. A passage from an address to the South Carolina Survivors' Association in late 1871 typifies Early's tendency to question the virility of Federal officers and their men: "I might multiply the instances of the attempts of our enemies to falsify the truth of history," he said after discussing George B. McClellan's habit of grossly inflating Lee's strength, "in order to excuse their manifold failures, and to conceal the inferiority of their troops in all the elements of manhood, but I would become too tedious."[18]

Early cast Ulysses S. Grant as the principal agent of Northern power, a butcher who threw unending ranks of his hapless soldiers against Lee's veterans. His analysis contained no hint of Grant as a master of maneuver whose willingness to take breathtaking risks and ability to rebound from reverses brought victory at Vicksburg, Chattanooga, and elsewhere. Unwilling to concede anything to Grant, Early insisted that he "had none of the requisites of a great captain, but merely possessed the most ordinary brute courage, and had the control of unlimited numbers and means."[19] Were Grant to publish a work on strategy, the appropriate title would be "The Lincoln-Grant or Pegging-Hammer Art of War."[20]

Stonewall Jackson rather than Grant received Early's nod as the second superior military leader of the war. Lee was the unsurpassed chief, Jackson the peerless subordinate who "always appreciated, and sympathized with the bold conceptions of the commanding General, and entered upon their execution with the most cheerful alacrity and zeal." Early often linked Lee with Jackson, urging fellow white Southerners to "be thankful that our cause had two such champions, and that, in their characters, we can furnish the world at large with the best assurance of the rightfulness of the principles for which they and we fought." Always conscious of the need to influence future generations, Early counted on this team to garner sympathy for the Confederacy: "When asked for our vindication, we can triumphantly point to the graves of Lee and Jackson and look the world square in the face." The pious Lee and sternly Calvinist Jackson easily lent themselves to religious imagery, which Early employed in calling on Virginians "to remain true to the memory of your venerated leaders. . . . Let the holy memories connected with our glorious struggle, afford stronger incentives to renewed efforts to do our duty."[21]

With Lee and Jackson so important to his vision of the Confederate experience, Early inevitably defined the war as predominantly a Virginia phenomenon. He only occasionally mentioned events west of the Appalachians and usually avoided overt criticism of the Confederacy's western leaders and their armies. Yet his writings consistently identified Richmond as the ultimate target of Northern military planning and credited Lee and his soldiers with extending the war through their dogged defense of the Confederate capital.[22]

The *Southern Historical Society Papers*, whose contents Early influenced to a greater degree than anyone else, were published in Richmond and leaned very heavily toward topics associated with Lee and the eastern theater. This bias prompted some ex-Confederates who had fought elsewhere to find other forums for their writings about the war. *The Southern Bivouac* and the *Confederate Veteran*, begun respectively in Louisville and Nashville in 1882 and 1893, paid a great deal of attention to campaigns and leaders outside Virginia but never approached the *Southern Historical Society Papers* in terms of influencing historians.[23]

At a Southern Historical Society (SHS) convention held in August 1873, Early explained the organization's goals. "The history of our war has not been written," he said in the keynote address, "and it devolves upon the survivors of those who participated in that war, to furnish the authentic materials for that history." A flyer subsequently circulated by the SHS announced that "generations of the disinterested must succeed the generations of the prejudiced before history, properly termed such, can be written. This, precisely, is the work we now attempt, to construct the archives in which shall be collected . . . memoirs to serve for future history." Ever since the SHS first described its purpose, legions of historians and other writers have mined the fifty-two volumes of its papers for material on the Confederate war effort.[24]

Disseminated by Early and other former Confederates through publications including the SHS's *Papers*, Lost Cause interpretations of the war gained wide currency in the nineteenth century and remain remarkably persistent today. The longevity of many of these ideas can be attributed in considerable measure to their being grounded in fact. Robert E. Lee *was* a gifted soldier who inspired his army to accomplish prodigious feats on the battlefield. The Army of Northern Virginia and other Confederate forces consistently fought against serious disadvantages in numbers and materiel. A number of Northern newspapers as well as some soldiers in the Army of the Potomac joined Confederates in complaining about Grant's "hammering" tactics in 1864. Stonewall Jackson won his reputation honestly and served Lee as a superb lieutenant. Most people at the time—Northern, Southern, and European—looked to Virginia as the crucial arena of the war, as have a number of historians since. The distortion came when Early and other proponents of the Lost Cause denied that Lee had faults or lost any battles, focused on Northern numbers and material superiority while ignoring Confederate advantages, denied Grant any virtues or greatness, and noticed the Confederacy outside the eastern theater only when convenient to explain Southern failures in Virginia. With these thoughts in mind, I will turn to a brief review of recent scholarly and popular literature, fiction, documentaries and films, and the thriving market in Civil War art that reveals trends that almost certainly would bring a smile to Jubal Early's lips.

A striking irony of the Civil War is that the rebel Lee rather than the Union's protector Grant has joined Lincoln as one of the conflict's two great popular figures.[25] Frederick Douglass complained of friendly treatments of Lee in the North as early as the aftermath of the general's death in October 1870. "Is it not about time that this bombastic laudation of the rebel chief should cease?" asked the nation's most famous black leader. "We can scarcely take up a newspaper . . . that is not filled with *nauseating* flatteries of the late Robert E. Lee." Douglass surely would lament the fact that the United States government, whose sovereignty Lee nearly compromised, has honored the Confederate leader on five postage stamps and made his antebellum home at Arlington a national memorial. Douglas Southall Freeman's Pulitzer Prize–winning *R. E. Lee: A Biography* was issued to a chorus of praise in the mid-1930s and cemented in American letters an interpretation of Lee very close to Early's utterly heroic figure. In the annotated bibliography for *R. E. Lee,* Freeman acknowledged his debt to the *Southern Historical Society Papers* by stating that they contain "more valuable, unused data than any other unofficial repository of source material on the War Between the States."[26]

Anyone writing about Lee since the mid-1930s has labored in Douglas Southall Freeman's immense shadow. Historians such as Thomas L. Connelly and Alan T. Nolan have discovered that challenging the heroic Lee triggers a response reminiscent of Early's attacks on James Longstreet. Nolan's *Lee Considered: General Robert E. Lee and Civil War History,* which appeared in 1991, followed a trail blazed in 1977 by Connelly's starkly revisionist *The Marble Man: Robert E. Lee and His Image in American Society.* Questioning several elements of what he labeled "the Lee tradition," Nolan argued that Lee's famous victories came at so high a cost in manpower that they probably shortened the life of the Confederacy. Many academic reviewers welcomed Nolan's study, but the book took a severe beating from Lee's admirers. One historian called it an "anti-Lee" book that used "always-perfect hindsight" to reach flawed conclusions. A prominent student of the Army of Northern Virginia termed Nolan "a bootless revisionist" with "a total lack of perspective of historical time and sense." Even more to Jubal Early's taste would have been the plea mailed to Civil War scholars from a retired military officer: "I call upon every true student of the Civil War, every son and daughter of the veterans of that war both North and South, and every organization formed to study, research, reenact, perserve [*sic*] and remember our Civil War heritage not to purchase Nolan's book. . . . If you have it already, burn it as it is not worth recycling."[27]

Although a number of recent works have essentially restated Connelly's and Nolan's arguments about Lee's generalship, readers who prefer Lee as Early's icon have found much to applaud in recent literature. A pair of works published in the early 1990s that reached wide audiences through book clubs and paperback editions typify this phenomenon. Paul D. Casdorph's *Lee and Jackson: Confederate Chieftains* bluntly claimed that Lee forged "the foremost military career in the American saga." Describing Grant as "the Yankee Goliath" who outnumbered Lee two to one in the spring of 1864, Casdorph judged Lee "nothing short of brilliant in the campaign of attrition that followed." At Lee's side through most of Casdorph's book is Stonewall Jackson, whose "eagerness to undertake independent orders had insured Lee's great successes throughout the battles of 1862." In his study of the Chancellorsville campaign, Ernest B. Furgurson invoked superlatives in describing Lee and Jackson, claiming that "American history offers no other pair of generals with such perfect rapport, such sublime confidence in each other" (this view overlooked the obvious tandem of Grant and William Tecumseh Sherman).[28]

Winston Groom's *Shrouds of Glory: From Atlanta to Nashville, The Last Campaign of the Civil War* also illustrated that Lost Cause arguments remain current. Although Groom treated a campaign far removed from the eastern theater, his narrative included numerous references to Lee and Jackson and to Grant's inability, despite superior manpower, to subdue his wily opponent. Grant had introduced "a new kind of war, a grinding nightmare of armed embrace in which the victorious dog never turns loose of his victim, but pursues him relentlessly, attacking whenever he can." Earlier in Virginia, Confederates had learned that their "esprit tended to offset federal superiority in numbers and manufacturing. . . . Northern armies, on the other hand, had come to rely on their overwhelming numbers to wreck the Confederates' logistics system, then simply grind their armies down by attrition." Grant's strategy against Lee in 1864 earned him "a reputation in certain quarters on both sides as a 'butcher' or 'murderer' rather than a general. . . . Deserved or undeserved as such sobriquets might have been, the fact was that the North was becoming war wearier by the day." Greeted by generally favorable reviews, selected by book clubs, awarded a prize within weeks of its publication, and beneficiary of its author's wide name recognition because of his success with the novel *Forrest Gump, Shrouds of Glory* seemed destined to reinforce Lost Cause images among thousands of readers.[29]

The wide availability of hundreds of reprinted older titles also keeps Early's Lost Cause arguments current. Paperback editions of books by Clifford Dowdey illustrate this point. A gifted writer who inherited Douglas Southall Freeman's mantle as the principal chronicler of the Army of Northern Virginia, Dowdey published between 1958 and 1964 a biography of Lee and studies of the Seven Days, Gettysburg, and Overland campaigns. "Out of the crucible of the Seven Days," Dowdey wrote of Lee, "he molded an army that would be man for man the greatest fighting force ever on the continent." By the time Lee perfected his organization of the Army of Northern Virginia, however, he faced an impossible task: "[H]e would no longer be fighting off only another army, or even other armies. Lee's Army of Northern Virginia," concluded Dowdey in language reminiscent of Early's address at Washington and Lee University, "was a personally designed, hand-wrought sword fending off machine-tooled weapons that kept coming in immeasurable, illimitable numbers." The most important fact about Lee's image, argued Dowdey elsewhere, "is that the legendary aspects were always present. There was no later building of the legend, no collections of sayings or anecdotes; the Lee of the legend emerged full-scale, larger than life, during his command of the army."[30] Here Dowdey reinforced Early's interpretation of Lee—while at the same time ignoring the postwar efforts by Early and many other Lost Cause writers to burnish Lee's image and defend it against any assailants.

During the 1860s and 1870s, Jubal Early exhibited special interest in how successive generations of young people and foreign readers would view the Confederate struggle. Lost Cause writings have carried great weight with both audiences in the twentieth century. Books on the Civil War for young readers in the 1950s and 1960s emphasized Lee and his campaigns within an interpretive framework substantially attuned to the writings of Early and Freeman.

The roster of ninety titles in Random House's Landmark Books on American history included four relating to the military side of the Civil War—all of which featured Lee as a major actor. Hodding Carter's *Robert E. Lee and the Road of Honor* affirmed that Lee should be admired "so long as men respect and remember courage and high purpose and a sense of duty and honor." Visitors entered Lee's burial crypt at Lexington, Virginia, "as if it were a hallowed place," wrote Carter, and "[t]hat is as it should be." Jonathan Daniels's *Stonewall Jackson* lauded the virtues of Lee and his lieutenant as soldiers and men, and MacKinlay Kantor's *Gettysburg* praised Lee and described units of the Army of Northern Virginia "as the most capable troops ever to go into action." The Landmark series offered neither a biography of Grant (or of Sherman or any other Union general) nor a narrative of any of his victories in the western theater. Only MacKinlay Kantor's *Lee and Grant at Appomattox* devoted appreciable attention to Grant, and it followed conventions far more favorable to Lee than to Grant. Kantor's Grant was a "silent, shabby, stubborn" man who liked animals more than people: "Maybe it is necessary to be like that, if one is to squander a thousand lives through some mistake of judgment during a battle." For Lee, who had a "grave magnificence," Kantor chose knightly and religious allusions: "You could imagine him in the wars of long ago, in polished armor. You could imagine him in the wars of Biblical times, proud in his chariot, facing the Philistines."[31]

Houghton Mifflin's North Star Books for children also ignored Grant but offered Jonathan Daniels's appreciative *Robert E. Lee*. Daniels's penultimate sentence could have been written by Jubal Early. "He went almost as though he rode into eternity," wrote Daniels of Lee's death, "again at the head of a column—a long gray line, ragged and barefoot, lean and hungry, but on its certain way to glory of which no power on earth could deprive it."[32]

No foreign nation has manifested more interest in the Civil War than Great Britain, whose authors generally have followed Lost Cause interpretive contours. Field Marshal Viscount Garnet Wolseley, Arthur James Lyon Fremantle, and Francis C. Lawley, all of whom spent time with Lee as observers or reporters, wrote very favorably about the Confederate leader and his soldiers between 1863 and 1890.[33] George Francis Robert Henderson's *Stonewall Jackson and the American Civil War*, first published in England in 1898 and reprinted there and in the United States numerous times in the twentieth century, marked a milestone of laudatory British writing about the Confederacy. Douglas Southall Freeman remarked in 1939 that no author before or after Henderson "succeeded so well in capturing in print the spirit of the Army of Northern Virginia. . . . The reception of *Stonewall Jackson* by old Confederates was, needless to say, enraptured." In 1933, Maj. Gen. J. F. C. Fuller departed from these earlier British historians in *Grant & Lee: A Study in Personality and Generalship*, wherein he dismissed Henderson's biography of Jackson as "almost as romantic as Xenophon's *Cyropaedia*." Fuller also questioned Lee's strategic grasp and accused him of too often taking the tactical offensive. "[I]n several respects," stated Fuller, Lee "was one of the most incapable Generals-in-Chief in history."[34]

The most renowned British author to write seriously about the Civil War was Winston S. Churchill, whose assessments echoed Henderson rather than Fuller. In the late 1950s, Churchill told readers that Lee's "noble presence and gentle, kindly manner were sustained by religious faith and exalted character." Lee and Jackson formed a brilliant partnership that faced awful odds: "Against Lee and his great lieutenant, united for a year of intense action in a comradeship which recalls that of Marlborough and Eugene, were now to be marshalled the overwhelming forces of the Union." Churchill's Grant also filled a typical Lost Cause role. Mentioning "Grant's tactics of unflinching butchery" during the Overland campaign, Churchill observed that "[m]ore is expected of the high command than determination in thrusting men to their doom." The former prime minister also touched on the theme of honor so important to Early and other Lost Cause advocates. "By the end of 1863 all illusions had vanished," claimed Churchill. "The South knew they had lost the war, and would be conquered and flattened. It is one of the enduring glories of the American nation that this made no difference to the Confederate resistance."[35]

Two imperfect but highly suggestive measures of Lee's triumph over Grant as a popular figure can be found in late-twentieth-century Civil War fiction and art. Lee and his army have been central to a number of successful novels. Harry Turtledove's *The Guns of the South* presented Lee with the tantalizing prospect of overcoming Northern numbers and superior military hardware by acquiring modern automatic weapons from time-traveling South Africans (who hope to gain a twentieth-century ally by helping the Confederacy win its independence). Douglas Savage's *The Court Martial of Robert E. Lee* posited a scenario wherein Lee faced charges from his own government for the defeat at Gettysburg, M. A. Harper's *For the Love of Robert E. Lee* detailed the process by which a woman in the 1960s became infatuated with Lee and imagined the details of his life, and Richard Adams's *Traveller* followed the Confederate commander from the perspective of his favorite horse. Lee's victory at Second Manassas served as the backdrop for Tom Wicker's sprawling *Unto This Hour,* Bernard Cornwell's *Battle Flag,* and a significant portion of Thomas Keneally's *Confederates*—all of which included long sections devoted to Stonewall Jackson. Jackson predictably loomed large in another novel titled *A Bullet for Stonewall,* the literary merits of which could be exhausted in a brief sentence.[36]

By far the most widely read of Civil War novels published in the last quarter century was *The Killer Angels,* which featured Lee as one of the six characters around whom author Michael Shaara built his narrative. This Pulitzer Prize–winning novel—as well as *Gettysburg,* the sprawling four-hour film based closely on its text—would by turns delight and upset Lost Cause adherents. The primacy of the eastern theater shines through both the novel and the screenplay, which understandably defined Gettysburg as the decisive moment of the conflict. "I think if we lose this fight," remarks Union colonel Joshua Lawrence Chamberlain at one point, "the war will be over." Early and other Lost Cause writers also treated Gettysburg as the most important battle, repeatedly reexamining it in the *Southern Historical Society Papers* and other publications. If only Longstreet had obeyed Lee's orders more expeditiously, they insisted, Gettysburg would have been a great victory and Confederate independence a reality. So Early would have approved of a film devoted to Gettysburg, and appreciated as well Shaara's tribute to an Army of Northern Virginia that maintained a jaunty confidence despite being outnumbered and outgunned: "It is an army of remarkable unity, fighting for disunion. . . . They share common customs and a common faith and they have been consistently victorious against superior numbers. They have as solid a faith in their leader as any veteran army that ever marched." Elsewhere, the novelist stated that Lee's army was "unbeatable, already immortal." Shaara's portrayal of Lee as an aging and ill lion, blindly insistent on attacking despite James Longstreet's sagacious advice to the contrary, would have riled Lee's nineteenth-century champions, however, and Early would have seethed at Shaara's description of his own conduct at Gettysburg as timid and motivated by concern for reputation and position.[37]

Jeff Shaara's *Gods and Generals: A Novel of the Civil War* represented a distant aftershock of his father's novel about Gettysburg. Set in the period September 1859 to June 1863, it served as what the film and television industries, with typical disregard for the English language, would call a "prequel" to *The Killer Angels*. Once again Lee was one of the main characters, and the younger Shaara's treatment of the Confederate hero virtually never departed from Lost Cause orthodoxy. Lee literally sheds tears when he decides he must go with Virginia and against the Union in April 1861, achieves strategic brilliance at Second Manassas and Chancellorsville, and enjoys a magnificent military relationship with Stonewall Jackson. In the wake of Chancellorsville, with Jackson dead, Lee knows Union numbers are lengthening the odds against the Confederacy. "[I]f we are to end this war," he tells Longstreet in May 1863, "we must *win* this war, and I believe it [an invasion of the North] is the only way." The book closes with Lee and his army on the march northward in June 1863, thus anticipating the clash at Gettysburg that so fascinated Early and other Lost Cause writers. Shaara followed up the considerable success of *Gods and Generals* with another novel titled *The Last Full Measure*, which carried the story forward from the ending point of *The Killer Angels* to Appomattox and once again featured Lee as a central character.[38]

What of Grant? He appeared along with Lee in Richard Slotkin's

The Crater, a masterful evocation of the botched Federal attempt to breach the Confederate lines at Petersburg in July 1864, as well as in Shaara's *The Last Full Measure.* Shaara's treatment was on the whole very favorable, but Grant shares the stage equally with Lee. The Union commander was also the protagonist in Robert Skimin's *Ulysses: A Biographical Novel of U. S. Grant.* Offered to a largely indifferent reading public in 1994, *Ulysses* gave a mixed reading of Grant as a man and a general. In the opening two sentences, however, Skimin adopted a tone entirely absent from novels that sketched Lee: "As he looked blearily into the cracked mirror, Grant tried to recall his foray, but only glimpses returned. His hands shook, his eyes were blood red, and his filthy uniform reeked of whiskey and vomitus." Far more sympathetic was Ted Jones's *Grant's War: A Novel of the Civil War,* the dust jacket of which alerted readers to be prepared for a tone "shockingly different" from the typical portrayal of Grant "as a butcher who coldly, unimaginatively, and methodically sent tens of thousands of his countrymen to their deaths in futile frontal assaults."[39]

No successful novels have been built primarily around Grant, his campaigns, or the armies he led. The fact that the Confederate commander's horse has gotten almost as much attention as the general-in-chief of the United States armies in recent novels offered by mainline publishers delineates the chasm separating Lee and Grant in fiction (the notion that someone might write a novel about Cincinnati, Grant's favorite horse, is beyond imagining). Novelists admittedly have portrayed Lee in different ways, some sketching military limitations and others falling closer to Jubal Early on the interpretive scale.[40] Interpretations aside, however, Lee's presence dwarfs that of Grant in novels published during the last twenty-five years.

The same pattern holds true in Civil War art. The past decade has witnessed a proliferation of artists who cater to the Civil War market. Their advertisements adorn the pages of leading popular magazines devoted to the subject, a perusal of which leaves no doubt that Jubal Early's heroes have dominated the war on canvas and in clay to a degree they never achieved against the Union armies. Lee far outstrips Grant as a subject for prints, sculptures, and other items. During 1998–99, for example, *Blue & Gray Magazine* ran advertisements for a half dozen items with Lee as the primary subject and none for works highlighting Grant (the Union commander did appear with Lee in a pair of ads). In *Civil War: The Magazine of the Civil War Society,* the totals were eleven for Lee, one for Grant, and three featuring both generals. The magazine with the largest circulation in the field is *Civil War Times Illustrated.*

Items featuring Lee in its issues for 1998–99 included seven prints, a pewter statuette, two busts, two commemorative plates, a commemorative medallion, an "Official Collectors Knife," a seminar, and a tour. Advertisements for a reenactment and a chess set highlighted Lee and Grant. Grant also appeared in ads for a videocassette on the battle of Shiloh, a military history series on a cable channel, and one print.[41]

A brochure describing a special edition of *Jackson & Lee: Legends in Gray*, a coffee-table book featuring seventy-five paintings by Mort Künstler and a narrative by Civil War historian James I. Robertson Jr., included language that echoed Jubal Early's writings. "In the pantheon of American soldiers, none stands taller than Confederate generals Thomas J. 'Stonewall' Jackson and Robert E. Lee," reads one passage. Another affirms that "these two Southern generals forged the greatest partnership in command in American history." Although they fought for a cause that would have dismembered the United States, Lee and Jackson are described as men who "epitomized the virtues of duty, valor and honor that patriotic Americans hold so dear."[42]

Grant has been the subject of no such book—for the apparent reason that despite *his* sense of duty, unquestioned valor, and unmatched contributions to Union victory, there is no comparable market among Civil War enthusiasts for works of art devoted to him. What explains this situation more than 130 years after he extended generous and honorable terms of surrender to Lee at Appomattox? Part of the answer probably lies in the often repeated stories about Grant as a drunkard and prewar failure that contrast so dramatically with descriptions of Lee as a devout Christian who made self-denial and self-control cardinal elements of his personal philosophy. Grant's scandal-ridden presidency also influenced his later reputation. Another major factor must be Grant's enduring image—carefully nurtured by Jubal Early and other Lost Cause writers—as an unimaginative officer who bludgeoned the Army of Northern Virginia into submission.

In 1987, Mark E. Neely, Harold Holzer, and Gabor S. Boritt published *The Confederate Image: Prints of the Lost Cause*, a superb analysis of nineteenth-century prints depicting Lost Cause themes. They concluded that by the end of the century, "throughout the South, and particularly in the iconography of the Lost Cause, Robert E. Lee had emerged as first in war, first in peace, and first in the hearts of his countrymen." Stonewall Jackson also inspired a number of nineteenth-century prints, and "one of the most enduring" of all Lost Cause images was an engraving of E. B. D. Julio's "The Last Meeting of Lee and Jackson"—a subject that has been painted repeatedly by modern artists.[43] Current Civil War art demonstrates that, if anything, Lee and Jackson are more dominant than in the heyday of the original Lost Cause writers.

Apart from their penchant for depicting Lee and Jackson, modern artists select topics using other criteria that conform to Early's framework for understanding the war. For example, Confederate topics outnumber Union ones by two or three to one (and, according to price sheets for prints and sculpture, typically appreciate more rapidly). Subjects associated with the eastern theater are painted four or five times as often as those relating to all other theaters combined. Modern artists and the Civil War public to which they cater clearly join Early in considering the arena of Lee's activities the most important of the conflict.[44]

On October 30, 1865, Early composed his last letter to Robert E. Lee before leaving the country for self-imposed exile. "I have brought away with me feelings of the highest admiration and respect for yourself," wrote Early, "and I am satisfied history will accord to you the merit of retiring from the struggle with far more true glory than those who, by overwhelming numbers and resources, were enabled to thwart all your efforts in defence of the liberties and independence of our unfortunate country." Almost precisely five years later, Early struggled to come to terms with news of Lee's death. "The loss is a public one," he remarked, "and there are millions of hearts now torn with anguish at the news that has been flashed over the wires to all quarters of the civilized world." Early wanted to honor Lee and asked a former comrade what he considered a "suitable mode by which the officers who served under General Lee can give expression to their sentiments, and manifest to the world their appreciation of his talents, his virtues, and his services."[45] Deciding that Lee's memory could be served best through attention to the written record of the war, Early worked tirelessly in the vineyards of Lost Cause advocacy. He proved himself a devoted lieutenant of Lee to the end of his life—and together with other Lost Cause authors helped demonstrate that the victors do not always control how historical events are remembered.

As much as anyone, then, Jubal Early constructed the image of the Civil War that many Americans North and South still find congenial. To explain why they do so would require another essay far longer than this. It would have to address the degree to which Lost Cause warriors wrote accurately about their war against the Union, what subsequent generations of Americans really wanted when they called for states' rights, how conservatism and race fit into the equation, and why the ultimate goals of Union and freedom for which more than a third of a million Northern soldiers perished often have figured only marginally in the popular understanding of the conflict.

Notes

1. The most influential interpretations of Early as a Lost Cause figure have been Thomas L. Connelly, *The Marble Man: Robert E. Lee and His Image in American Society* (New York: Alfred A. Knopf, 1977), and Gaines M. Foster, *Ghosts of the Confederacy: Defeat, the Lost Cause, and the Emergence of the New South, 1865 to 1913* (New York: Oxford University Press, 1987). Also useful are William Garrett Piston, *Lee's Tarnished Lieutenant: James Longstreet and His Place in Southern History* (Athens: University of Georgia Press, 1987), and Thomas L. Connelly and Barbara L. Bellows, *God and General Longstreet: The Lost Cause and the Southern Mind* (Baton Rouge: Louisiana State University Press, 1982). Each of these books depicts Early as a soldier of limited talent who worked out his personal and professional frustrations after the war by championing Robert E. Lee—an interpretation open to revision but beyond the scope of this essay to examine.

2. A useful introduction to the subject of historical memory is David Thelen, ed., *Memory and American History* (Bloomington: Indiana University Press, 1990). See also Michael Kammen's *Mystic Chords of Memory: The Transformation of Tradition in American Culture* (New York: Alfred A. Knopf, 1991), especially pt. 2.

3. Jubal A. Early, "To the Voters of Franklin, Henry & Patrick Counties," July 20, 1850, Scrapbook, Jubal A. Early Papers, Library of Congress, Washington, D.C. [repository hereafter cited as LC]. See George H. Reese, ed., *Proceedings of the Virginia Secession Convention of 1861*, 4 vols. (Richmond: Virginia State Library, 1965), 1:428, for Early's description of himself as a Whig in 1861.

4. For an example of Early's describing himself as a Whig after the war, see Jubal A. Early to J. Randolph Tucker, August 8, 1884, Tucker Family Papers, Southern Historical Collection, Wilson Library, University of North Carolina, Chapel Hill [repository hereafter cited as SHC]. Early's obituary in the March 3, 1894, edition of the *Lynchburg News* described him as "a lifelong Whig, of the most conservative type." See Jack P. Maddex Jr., *The Virginia Conservatives, 1867–1879: A Study in Reconstruction Politics* (Chapel Hill: University of North Carolina Press, 1970), and James Tice Moore, *Two Paths to the New South: The Virginia Debt Controversy, 1870–1883* (Lexington: University Press of Kentucky, 1974), for some of the debates that revealed how Early's prewar conservatism carried over into the postwar years.

5. Foster, *Ghosts of the Confederacy*, 60–61.

6. Jubal A. Early to John Goode, June 8, 1866, Early Papers, LC; Jubal A. Early to R. E. Lee, October 30, 1865, Mss3 L515a, Virginia Historical Society, Richmond [repository hereafter cited as VHS]; Jubal A. Early to John C. Breckinridge, March 27, 1867, collection of William C. Davis (who kindly granted permission to quote from the document).

7. Philip H. Sheridan to Editors of the *New Orleans Daily Crescent*, January 8, 1866, and Jubal A. Early to Editor of the *New York News*, February 5, 1866, newspaper clippings in Scrapbook, Early Papers, LC.

8. John S. Wise, *The End of An Era* (Boston and New York: Houghton Mifflin, 1899), 228.

9. R. E. Lee to Jubal A. Early, March 30, 1865, reproduced in Jubal A. Early, *Lieutenant General Jubal Anderson Early, C.S.A.: Autobiographical Sketch and Narrative of the War Between the States* (Philadelphia: J. B. Lippincott, 1912), 468–69.

10. R. E. Lee to Jubal A. Early, November 22, 1865, George H. and Katherine Davis Collection, Howard-Tilton Memorial Library, Tulane University, New Orleans [repository hereafter cited as TU]; R. E. Lee, General Order No. 9, April 10, 1865, in R. E. Lee, *The Wartime Papers of R. E. Lee*, ed. Clifford Dowdey and Louis H. Manarin (Boston: Little, Brown, 1961), 934.

11. R. E. Lee to Jubal A. Early, March 15, 1866, George H. and Katherine M. Davis Collection, TU.

12. Jubal A. Early to John Goode, June 8, 1866, Early Papers, LC. The first edition of *A Memoir of the Last Year of the War* was printed in Toronto by Lovell and Gibson. Subsequent editions, each slightly revised, were published in 1867 in New Orleans; Lynchburg, Virginia; and Augusta, Georgia. Early's full memoir, edited by his niece Ruth H. Early, was published eighteen years after his death under the title *Lieutenant General Jubal Anderson Early, C.S.A.: Autobiographical Sketch and Narrative of the War Between the States*. For Early's sending Lee portions of his manuscript devoted to campaigns prior to May 1864, see R. E. Lee to Jubal A. Early, October 15, 1866, George H. and Katherine M. Davis Collection, TU; and Jubal A. Early to R. E. Lee, November 20, 1868, box 25, folder titled "Introductory Chapter (Notes & Pages of a Rough Draft) I," John Warwick Daniel Papers, Alderman Library, University of Virginia, Charlottesville [repository hereafter cited as UVa].

13. Jubal A. Early to R. E. Lee, November 20, 1868, Daniel Papers, UVa.

14. Jubal A. Early to Charles Venable, June 9, 1871, Charles Scott Venable Papers, SHC.

15. Robert Stiles, *Four Years Under Marse Robert* (New York and Washington: Neale, 1903), 190–91. On Early's stature as a Confederate historian, see Virginia General Assembly joint resolution quoted in the *Lynchburg News*, March 4, 1894.

16. Early, *A Memoir of the Last Year of the War*, vii; Jubal A. Early, *The Campaigns of Gen. Robert E. Lee. An Address by Lieut. General Jubal A. Early, before Washington and Lee University, January 19th, 1872* (Baltimore: John Murphy, 1872), 3–4, 29–33, 40–41, 45.

17. Jubal A. Early, "Address of General Jubal A. Early," in *Proceedings of the Third Annual Meeting of the Survivors' Association, of the State of South Carolina; and the Annual Address by Jubal A. Early, Delivered before the Association, November 10, 1871* (Charleston: Walker, Evans and Cogswell, 1872), 20–21; Jubal A. Early, *The Relative Strength of the Armies of Genl's Lee and Grant. Reply of Gen. Early to the Letter of Gen. Badeau to the London Standard* (n.p.: n.p., 1870), 1–2, 5.

18. Early, *Campaigns of Lee*, 40; Early, "Address of General Jubal A. Early," 31–32. Many other former Confederates also stressed the disparity in numbers. Walter H. Taylor of Lee's staff spent more time than any other ex-Confederate attempting to show that the Federals vastly outnumbered Lee. See especially his *Four Years with General Lee: Being a Summary of the More Important Events Touching the Career of General Robert E. Lee, in the War between the States; Together with an Authoritative Statement of the Strength of the Army which He Commanded in the Field* (1877; reprinted several times, most recently in a paperback edition by Indiana University Press [Bloomington, 1996]).

19. Early, "Address of General Jubal A. Early," 33; Early, *Campaigns of Lee*, 39.

20. Early, *A Memoir of the Last Year of the War*, 34–35; Early, *Campaigns of Lee*, 44.

21. Early, *Campaigns of Lee*, 27, 31, 44, 47.

22. Ibid., 39.

23. Gaines M. Foster correctly noted that the *Veteran* enjoyed a far wider circulation than the *Papers* but did not address the question of which publication wielded greater influence on the writing of Confederate military history (Foster, *Ghosts of the Confederacy*, 106).

24. *The Proceedings of the Southern Historical Convention, Which Assembled at the Montgomery White Sulphur Springs, Va., on the 14th of August, 1873; and of the Southern Historical Society, as Reorganised, with the Address by Gen. Jubal A. Early, Delivered before the Convention on the First Day of Its Session* (Baltimore: Turnbull Brothers, [1873]), 37–38; Southern Historical Society, *Official Circular* ([Richmond]: [Southern Historical Society, 1876]), 3. A measure of the enduring influence of the fifty-two volume *Southern Historical Society Papers* (J. William Jones and others, eds. [Richmond: The Southern Historical Society, 1876–1959]) is that it has been reprinted twice in the past two decades.

25. The best examination of the process by which Lee became a national hero is Connelly's *The Marble Man*, chaps. 4 and 6. Readers should approach this work, which combines insights and distortions in about equal mea-

sure, with an understanding that Connelly grossly underestimated Lee's stature as the preeminent hero in the Confederacy from early 1863 through the close of the war.

26. David W. Blight, *Frederick Douglass' Civil War: Keeping Faith in Jubilee* (Baton Rouge: Louisiana State University Press, 1989), 229; Douglas Southall Freeman, *R. E. Lee: A Biography*, 4 vols. (New York: Charles Scribner's Sons, 1934–35), 4:558. Freeman summed up his interpretation of Lee as a man and a soldier in chaps. 11 and 28 of vol. 4. The five stamps appeared in 1937 (Lee and Stonewall Jackson with Stratford Hall in the background), 1949 (Lee and George Washington with Washington and Lee University in the background), 1955 (a bust of Lee), 1970 (Lee with Jackson and Jefferson Davis on the Confederate memorial at Stone Mountain, Georgia), and 1995 (a three-quarter-length portrait of Lee). Pictures of the five stamps are in U.S. Postal Service, *The Postal Service Guide to Stamps*, 23d edition (Crawfordsville, Ind.: R. R. Donnelley and Sons, 1996).

27. Reviews of *Lee Considered* by James I. Robertson Jr., in the Richmond *News Leader* (May 29, 1991), Robert K. Krick in the Fredericksburg (Va.) *Free Lance-Star* (July 20, 1991), and Dennis E. Frye in *Blue & Gray Magazine* 9 (February 1992), 26; Brig. Gen. (Ret.) M. H. Morris to "Dear Civil War Scholar," April 28, 1992 (copy in author's files). For a positive reaction by an academic historian, see Drew Gilpin Faust's review, page 18 of *The New York Times Book Review*, July 7, 1991.

28. Paul D. Casdorph, *Lee and Jackson: Confederate Chieftains* (New York: Paragon House, 1992), 403, 401, 400, 194; Ernest B. Furgurson, *Chancellorsville 1863: The Souls of the Brave* (New York: Alfred A. Knopf, 1992), 146. For a review of recent work that is critical of Lee, see Alan T. Nolan, "Historians' Perspectives on Lee," *Columbiad: A Quarterly Review of the War between the States* 2 (Winter 1999): 27–45. For more positive recent scholarship on Lee's generalship, see Joseph L. Harsh, *Confederate Tide Rising: Robert E. Lee and the Making of Southern Strategy, 1861–1862* (Kent, Ohio: Kent State University Press, 1998); Harsh, *Taken at the Flood: Robert E. Lee and Confederate Strategy in the Maryland Campaign of 1862* (Kent, Ohio: Kent State University Press, 1999); Charles P. Roland, *Reflections on Lee: A Historian's Assessment* (Mechanicsburg, Pa.: Stackpole, 1995); and chap. 3 of Gary W. Gallagher, *The Confederate War* (Cambridge, Mass.: Harvard University Press, 1997).

29. Winston Groom, *Shrouds of Glory: From Atlanta to Nashville, The Last Great Campaign of the Civil War* (New York: The Atlantic Monthly Press, 1995), 8–9, 11. On the reception of Groom's book, see "'95 Kirkland Book Award Goes to Winston Groom," *The Civil War News*, August 1995, 24. For a dissenting view, see my review in *The New York Times Book Review*, April 16, 1995, 23.

30. Clifford Dowdey, *The Seven Days: The Emergence of Lee* (1964; reprint,

Lincoln: University of Nebraska Press, 1993), 358; Dowdey, *Lee's Last Campaign: The Story of Lee & His Men Against Grant—1864* (1960; reprint, Lincoln: University of Nebraska Press, 1993), 5–6.

31. Hodding Carter, *Robert E. Lee and the Road of Honor* (New York: Random House, 1955), 174, 176; Jonathan Daniels, *Stonewall Jackson* (New York: Random House, 1959); MacKinlay Kantor, *Gettysburg* (New York: Random House, 1952), 19; MacKinlay Kantor, *Lee and Grant at Appomattox* (New York: Random House, 1950), 26–27, 32–33. Each of these titles went through many printings in the 1950s and 1960s. The Landmark Books also included two titles on Abraham Lincoln.

32. Jonathan Daniels, *Robert E. Lee* (Boston: Houghton Mifflin, 1960), 180.

33. See Garnet Wolseley, *The American Civil War: An English View*, ed. James A. Rawley (Charlottesville: University Press of Virginia, 1964), which collects Wolseley's writings about the Civil War; A. J. L. Fremantle, *Three Months in the Southern States: April–June 1863* (Edinburgh: W. Blackwood and Sons, 1863; reprinted in New York and Mobile, Ala., 1864); and Francis C. Lawley, "General Lee," *Blackwood's Edinburgh Magazine* 101 (January 1872):348–63. Lawley's piece and Wolseley's "General Lee" are reprinted in Gary W. Gallagher, ed., *Lee the Soldier* (Lincoln: University of Nebraska Press, 1996).

34. Douglas Southall Freeman, *The South to Posterity: An Introduction to the Writing of Confederate History* (New York: Charles Scribner's Sons, 1939), 165; J. F. C. Fuller, *Grant & Lee: A Study in Personality and Generalship* (1933; reprint, Bloomington: Indiana University Press, 1957), 8. Longman's, Green, and Company of London published the first edition of Henderson's *Jackson*.

35. Winston Churchill, *The American Civil War* (New York: Dodd, Mead, 1961), 39, 41, 123, 119. This book is a reprint of the chapters on the Civil War from vol. 4 of Churchill's *A History of the English Speaking Peoples: The Great Democracies*, 4 vols. (New York: Dodd, Mead, 1958). Echoes of Early's unflattering interpretation of Grant also can be found in William S. McFeely's Pulitzer Prize–winning *Grant: A Biography* (New York: W. W. Norton, 1981).

36. Harry Turtledove, *The Guns of the South: A Novel of the Civil War* (New York: Ballantine, 1992); Douglas Savage, *The Court Martial of Robert E. Lee: A Historical Novel* (Conshohocken, Pa.: Combined Books, 1993); M. A. Harper, *For the Love of Robert E. Lee* (New York: Soho, 1992); Richard Adams, *Traveller* (New York: Alfred A. Knopf, 1988); Tom Wicker, *Unto This Hour* (New York: Viking, 1984); Bernard Cornwell, *Battle Flag* (New York: HarperCollins, 1995); Thomas Keneally, *Confederates* (New York: Harper and Row, 1979); Benjamin King, *A Bullet for Stonewall* (Gretna, La.: Pelican, 1990). Other recent novels set in the eastern theater that feature the Army of Northern Virginia include Bernard Cornwell's *Copperhead* (New York: HarperCollins, 1994) and *The Bloody Ground* (New York:

HarperCollins, 1996); Harold Coyle's *Until the End* (New York: Simon and Schuster, 1996); and Donald McCaig's *Jacob's Ladder: A Story of Virginia during the Civil War* (New York: Norton, 1998).

37. Michael Shaara, *The Killer Angels: A Novel* (New York: David McKay, 1974), 33, ix, 85. "Gettysburg" debuted in theaters in 1993 and later was shown on television in an expanded version. Almost all of the film's dialogue came directly from the novel. Like Jubal Early, Union hero Joshua Lawrence Chamberlain understood the power of the printed word. His publications rank among the most evocative by any veteran and have impressed generations of historians and other writers. Shaara's fascination with Chamberlain prompted him to make the Maine soldier a key character in *The Killer Angels*, which in turn helped convince the public that Chamberlain was perhaps the best regimental commander on the field at Gettysburg. Visitation at the site on Little Round Top where Chamberlain and his 20th Maine fought at Gettysburg increased dramatically following publication of *The Killer Angels* and again after the release of the film *Gettysburg*. (Telephone conversation between Kathy Georg Harrison [historian at Gettysburg National Military Park] and the author, August 11, 1995.)

38. Jeff Shaara, *Gods and Generals: A Novel of the Civil War* (New York: Ballantine, 1996), 487; Shaara, *The Last Full Measure* (New York: Ballantine, 1998).

39. Richard Slotkin, *The Crater* (New York: Atheneum, 1980); Robert Skimin, *Ulysses: A Biographical Novel of U. S. Grant* (New York: St. Martin's, 1984), xi; Ted Jones, *Grant's War: A Novel of the Civil War* (Novato, Calif.: Presidio, 1992). Like Harry Turtledove, Slotkin is a professional historian.

40. Douglas Savage, for example, credited the writings of Douglas Southall Freeman, Thomas L. Connelly, and Alan T. Nolan for influencing his portrait of Lee. One advertisement for the book included a blurb from William Garrett Piston calling it "a remarkable accomplishment."

41. See, for example, advertisements in the May 1999 issue of *Civil War Times Illustrated* for a pewter statuette of Lee (p. 14), a commemorative medallion of Lee (p. 19), a two-day seminar on "The Military Career of Robert E. Lee" (p. 63), and a "life size bronze bust" of Lee (p. 74). Grant appears just once, opposite Lee in an ad for a 135th anniversary battle reenactment (p. 18).

42. The brochure was produced by The Easton Press of Norwalk, Connecticut. The book was first published in 1995 by Rutledge Hill Press of Nashville, Tennessee. Künstler also published a book titled *Gettysburg: The Paintings of Mort Künstler*, with text by James M. McPherson (Atlanta: Turner Publishing, Inc., 1993). Issued in conjunction with the release of the film *Gettysburg*, this book included eight depictions of Lee at Gettysburg.

43. Mark E. Neely Jr., Harold Holzer, and Gabor S. Boritt, *The Confederate Image: Prints of the Lost Cause* (Chapel Hill: University of North Carolina Press, 1987), 168, color plate 11. On Lee and Jackson, see especially chaps. 6, 10, and 11. Julio's famous interpretation of "The Last Meeting" remains available in a variety of prints as well as in one bas-relief version.

44. These comparative figures were compiled from advertisements in *Civil War Times Illustrated, Civil War: The Magazine of the Civil War Society,* and *Blue & Gray Magazine.* The data on prices come from sheets listing out-of-print works by Don Troiani, Dale Gallon, Mort Künstler, Don Stivers, and other leading Civil War artists.

45. Jubal A. Early to R. E. Lee, October 30, 1865, Mss3 L515a, VHS; Jubal A. Early to William Nelson Pendleton, October 13, 1870, William Nelson Pendleton Papers, SHC.

Three

"Is Our Love for Wade Hampton Foolishness?"
South Carolina and the Lost Cause

Charles J. Holden

What did he do to always be a hero?

In the early 1940s, John A. Rice recalled his childhood days at the turn of the century in Columbia, South Carolina, seeing on occasion an aged Wade Hampton. These chance meetings left a lasting impression on young Rice, who wrote later, "I wanted deep down in me to be like Wade Hampton, mutton-chop whiskers and all." Rice imagined it would be a thrill to be looked upon by "ordinary folks" as "sometimes general, sometimes governor, sometimes senator, but always hero."[1] The different facets to Hampton's career offered South Carolinians several avenues for admiration. Rice's assumption that Wade Hampton was "always hero" reflects a common belief held by South Carolinians by the mid-twentieth century. Unquestioned adoration does not accurately tell the story of Hampton's life in postwar South Carolina, however. The rise and fall and rise again of the Hampton legend after the Civil War paralleled the state's bitter political struggles. While the rancor did not cease, a specific and politically charged image of Wade Hampton no longer figured in debates after the turn of the century. Instead, a range of interpretations opened up within the state's numerous Lost Cause ceremonies that led Rice to assume by mid-century that all South Carolinians regarded the old general as having been "always hero."[2]

While Carolinians held the expected reverence for Robert E. Lee, Wade Hampton rivaled Lee as the focus of the Lost Cause in South Carolina. As a lieutenant general, Hampton was South Carolina's highest-ranking Confederate officer. His place in the state's experience of the Lost Cause can be organized into four phases that trace the evolution of Hampton's image from a narrow, self-constructed symbol for traditional conservative values to a representation open to the public for diverse interpretations. For the first decade after the war, Hampton and his aristocratic associates forged an interdependent relationship. The general promoted traditional conservative values of elite rule and local government. His friends, in turn, promoted the general as a symbol of post-Confederacy hope and unity in their successful campaign against a Reconstruction government virtually all white South Carolinians abhorred.

In the second phase of Hampton's place in the Lost Cause, the old general found new opposition from a surprising source. Rid of the Yankees and unsettled by a new free labor economy, leaders of the politicized, non-elite segment of the white population began to point out that Hampton represented not just brave battlefield deeds and the overthrow of Reconstruction, but a reestablished aristocratic class as well. (Before the war, Hampton owned more than three thousand slaves and ranked among the wealthiest men in the South.) From 1878 to the early 1890s, some anti-aristocratic, white South Carolinians expressed second thoughts about their participation in the war and openly questioned the worthiness of former Confederate leaders. In the same vein, poorer Carolinians resented the presumption to rule of the Hampton-led, conservative government. The anti-elite forces first followed Martin W. Gary, himself a former Confederate general, until his death in the early 1880s. Their dissent climaxed in 1890 when "Pitchfork Ben" Tillman's followers overthrew Hampton's conservative political allies and unceremoniously turned Hampton himself out of the United States Senate.

The conservatives countered their political defeat with a series of public ceremonies through the 1890s that either celebrated Hampton himself or featured him as the keynote speaker. These ceremonies kept the virtues of an older conservatism, symbolized by Hampton, very much before the public eye. Conservatives' efforts in this third phase of the Hampton legend succeeded in making the old general extremely popular again, but they did not completely reverse their political fortunes. The overwhelmingly high regard given to Hampton in the early 1900s, combined with the general's death in 1902, opened the way, finally, to multiple meanings of his place in the state's history. Poorer whites found a champion of segregation, seeing Hampton as the founder of white rule in a free South Carolina. Struggling farmers in the 1920s based their call for action against creditors on a legend of white unity from Hampton's days. By the 1930s, Wade Hampton came to represent white South Carolina's often violent insistence on maintaining independence from an increasingly powerful federal government. Over the years Hampton's essential conservatism, rooted in an antidemocratic, elitist outlook, was lost as he, like Robert E. Lee, became "what others wished him to be."[3]

Following the war, Wade Hampton played prominent roles in the state's political reorganization and earliest memorial efforts.[4] At an 1870 unveiling of a memorial to the fallen Confederates in the Washington Light Infantry, Hampton proclaimed it his duty to the dead to "vindicate their motives, to praise their patriotism, to commend their example, and to protect their memory." The general urged his former Confederates not to be "misled by that unmeaning jargon, which tells you that . . . the sword has decided that cause against you." Military conquest, he continued, could never take the place of an established truth or a just cause. Victory on the field could "make might take the place of right; but it can never reverse the immutable laws of God, and make what is evil appear right in His sight."[5]

In political pamphlets published during the immediate postwar years, Hampton clarified exactly what he meant by "the cause." In addition to countering new black political strength (an African American majority rare among the former Confederate states) and the federal government's control of the state, traditional conservatives like Wade Hampton resumed a longer struggle against the national forces for democracy and simple majority rule.[6] With other conservative Carolinians, Hampton co-authored petitions to both the United States House of Representatives and Senate protesting the proposed postwar state constitution that would eliminate property requirements for the vote and make freedmen and propertyless white males participants in the political system. Conservative Carolinians would resist, they wrote, until they had "regained the heritage of political control handed down to us by an honored ancestry." The former slave was "entitled to all the civil rights that are enjoyed alike by all classes of the people." But voting was another matter. The writers revealed that it was not simply black suffrage that concerned them. The vote, they contended "is not a political right nor a civil one for man, either white or black, but it is a *trust,* a delicate trust, to be conferred by the State." Still, the former slave remained the topic of the day and the solution conservatives proposed recognized freedmen "as an integral element of the body politic . . . entitled to a full and equal protection under the State Constitution and laws." When "we have the power," they added, conservatives would "grant them, under proper qualifications as to property and intelligence, the right of suffrage."[7]

When the first Reconstruction Acts passed in March 1867, Hampton spoke at a ceremony sponsored by the Union Brotherhood Society, a group of African American leaders recently formed to support the

"Military Universal Suffrage Bill." At the March 18 ceremony Hampton and other conservatives stressed openly that political systems required safeguards of some sort and that "all, white as well as black, who do not possess these qualifications shall be excluded" from the vote.[8] As Hampton wrote privately, the state needed its conservative leadership to check the momentum toward a new, expanded democracy in South Carolina: "If we cannot direct the wave it will overwhelm us."[9] Hampton's appeal to the "best men" of white and black South Carolina did not prevent the 1868 state constitution from mandating universal male suffrage.

Hampton was out of the state for much of the late 1860s and early 1870s. He still had vast landholdings in Mississippi and lived for a time in Baltimore, where he served as an officer for a company that made mechanical cotton pickers. He remained active in national politics, wielding what influence he could toward relieving the restrictions placed on former Confederates. Hampton also kept himself very visible within the early Lost Cause efforts. He communicated with the founders of the Southern Historical Society and made much of his last meeting with Robert E. Lee, where legend has it the Confederate hero uttered his famous "I only did what duty demanded. I could have taken no other course without dishonor." His 1871 memorial address on the life of Lee, delivered to former Confederate soldiers and sailors in Baltimore, was published as a pamphlet and further linked the two generals symbolically. Eventually Hampton found drumming up support for Southern Historical Society literature frustrating and perplexing. "I know the people are poor," he wrote to organization leader Dabney Maury, "but they find money to buy Northern journals and I have been discouraged by the apathy shown."[10]

As the 1876 gubernatorial campaign neared, state leaders of the Democratic Party turned to Hampton to run. With Hampton as the nominee, white South Carolinians realized that the chance to regain political power was at hand. Hampton, meanwhile, ran a campaign for conservative rule—the type of traditional conservative rule that believed the white race to be superior to the black, but which also believed in elite rule over all. He fully expected that his victory would enable him to install such a conservative regime. Conservative themes pervade the collection of Hampton's campaign pledges published as a pamphlet entitled *Free Men! Free Ballots! Free Schools!* He made a concerted effort to woo black voters and made it a central theme of his campaign that, if elected, "I shall know no party, nor race, in the administration of the law . . . not one single right enjoyed by the colored people to-day shall be taken from them. They shall be the equals, under the law, of any man in South Carolina."[11] Hampton's endorsement of black suffrage did not require him to reject his understanding of the Lost Cause. Instead, his conservative philosophy, in which he assumed that black voters would be naturally inclined to follow the political guidance offered by the traditional white ruling elite, fit neatly with what Thomas L. Connelly and Barbara L. Bellows described as the "Inner Lost Cause"—a philosophy that was popular among former Confederates during those years. The "Inner Lost Cause" rested on a firmly held belief that Confederates like Hampton were "still the *better men*." In his memories of his fighting past, as well as in his outlook on the critical present, the notion of being "the better man" came easily to Wade Hampton.[12]

During the campaign, Hampton and his captains reached an uneasy accord with the more aggressively racist beliefs and actions of fellow Democrats like Martin W. Gary. Gary recently had been impressed by the tactics used for "redemption" in the 1875 campaign in Mississippi, where whites had employed violence and intimidation against black voters. Gary and his followers urged white South Carolinians to adopt the same strategy. George Brown Tindall has accurately described the relationship between the two Democratic factions in the 1876 election as a "dual campaign." Working separately, Hampton sought black voters willing to cross over to the Democratic Party by guaranteeing their civil rights, whereas Gary and his band intimidated black Republican voters and anyone else who crossed them.[13]

Both Hampton and Republican incumbent Daniel H. Chamberlain claimed victory in a campaign marred by violence, intimidation, and suspected fraud. After several tense weeks, newly elected president Rutherford B. Hayes put his influence behind the claims of Hampton and the state's Democrats. Morrison R. Waite, chief justice of the United States Supreme Court, who happened to be in the state at the time, wrote that with Hampton's victory white Carolinians had "gone back to their original idols."[14] While the white North satisfied itself that South Carolina was safely back in the hands of those who knew its special problems best, and while white South Carolinians celebrated the withdrawal of the Chamberlain government and federal troops, Wade Hampton openly sought to reestablish conservative rule. In his victory address, Hampton, speaking as the "representative of the conservative party," declared that "a great task is before the conservative party of this state." That task included ensuring that "all citizens of South Carolina, of both races and of both parties, should be recognized as equals in the eyes of the law; all to be protected in the enjoyment of every political right now possessed by them."[15]

Portents of future problems for Hampton and the traditional conservatives surfaced in the 1878 state elections. While Hampton's reelection was not in doubt, Democrats in some counties yearned to eliminate black voters brought into the ranks by Hampton's conservatism. Gary's Edgefield County led the movement away from Hampton's comparatively conciliatory policies regarding race. He had no interest in sharing the Democratic party with black voters: "I suppose we shall next hear of '*dining*' or *dancing* with the colored brothers and sisters as events the natural result of Hampton Democracy."[16] (*The Nation* characterized Gary's outburst as "simply childish confusion of the social and political aspects of the negro question."[17]) The Garyite opposition became surprisingly personal. After Hampton blasted the decision by Edgefield Democrats to eliminate black voters from their primary, the Garyite Democrats responded in kind. A letter from "One of the People" to the *Edgefield Advertiser* claimed that they had not gone back on the promises of 1876; rather it was Hampton who "stabbed himself by . . . pandering to Northern sentiment" regarding black voters. Hampton would regret taking on the Edgefield Democrats, who had faithfully nominated and elected him "in spite of himself." Edgefield, he continued, would "not be intimidated by Hampton . . . into swallowing the negro." The author accused Hampton of ingratitude toward his Edgefield supporters from 1876. He also mocked the pledges that Hampton made to lure black voters during the campaign and claimed instead that intimidation did the trick: "The negroes voted our ticket, some through fear, but mostly because they dreaded to lose their homes and work, which our people threatened in the event of Chamberlain's election." Another Edgefield writer noted that "Our Northern Republican brethren thus 'bulldoze' their factory operatives; and what is good for them is good for us. . . . " The Edgefield Democrats, he boasted, were "intimidators to that extent in 1876, and Gov. Hampton may—nay, '*has made the most of it.*' For it we thank him, but it seems he doesn't thank us." Hampton's charges hurt, he conceded, but "the wound, though painful—coming whence it does, is not mortal."[18]

Hampton and his conservative allies carried the 1878 elections handily. His followers pointed to the essential conservatism of Hampton as the key to success. Johnson Hagood, a former Confederate general and Hampton follower who became governor in 1880, likened the election of 1878 to that of 1876 and attributed their success to their "wise conservatism." E. W. Moise urged voters to accept the Hampton policy: "we must be conservative and secure the colored vote."[19] Hampton himself noted the next year that "As the negro becomes more intelligent, he naturally allies himself with the more conservative of the whites."[20] The results of the 1878 election confirmed what Hampton's opponents had suspected: that Wade Hampton was, first and foremost, the leader of an elite ruling regime. This left them little choice but to attack Hampton as they had attacked the old conservative regime.

While they admitted privately that the 1876 and 1878 campaigns were sordid affairs of corruption and intimidation, traditional conservatives assured themselves that, for the moment, the ends justified the ugly means. Back in power, conservatives addressed the persistence of the election unruliness that seemed to characterize the expanded democracy of postwar South Carolina. They feared that both social instability and majority rule contained "the chaotic seeds of their own undoing," as E. Culpepper Clark writes. By 1880 the same conservatives who had accepted the violence of 1876 had become "the harbingers of moderation, stability, and order."[21] In 1879 the General Assembly voted to send Hampton to represent South Carolina in the United States Senate. Hampton had recently suffered a terrible fall from a mule and broken his leg severely enough to require amputation. George Tindall has argued that hopes for South Carolina to continue its difficult course toward a biracial society were lost with Hampton's physical impairment combined with his move to Washington, D.C. As the angry, if still isolated, uprising in Edgefield proved, there was open discontent against Hampton among white South Carolinians. Martin Gary complained of being "gagged" in 1878 and explicitly spelled out the political battle lines being drawn between white South Carolinians: "the action of certain leaders has been to declare that *they* and not the people shall rule the party. They assert the spirit of autocracy, and the people reassert the principles of Democracy. The autocratic and aristocratic leaders will be driven to the wall whenever the issue is made up between them and the masses of the people. They will then find out that this is a Government of the people, by the people, and for the people."[22] Hampton's conservative allies were up for the challenge.

Led by former Confederate colonel Edward McCrady Jr., the assembly in 1880 considered legislation that would impose reading qualifications and a small poll tax on the right to vote. Through the "eight box law," a voter needed the ability to read the names of the candidates and offices in order to place the correct ballot in the corresponding ballot box. McCrady, an attorney from an old, wealthy Charleston family, mounted his campaign through a series of pamphlets outlining his position. Adhering to the traditional conservative principles upon which he had been reared, McCrady advocated a form of literacy test that would be applied to both black and white voters. When opponents pointed out that this measure would disfranchise perhaps thousands of white voters, McCrady replied candidly: "we care not if it does. . . . To them, too, we say the schools are open."[23]

Poor whites responded angrily and raised the issue of the Lost Cause to attack McCrady and the Hampton forces. South Carolina in the 1880s, therefore, offers a contrasting story within the development of the Lost Cause from the trends noted by Gaines Foster for the South as a whole. Foster found that the 1880s marked a time of transition toward a more unified, celebratory theme regarding the war.[24] In South Carolina, rival political factions introduced war memories to sharpen the divisions among white voters. One writer, "B," wrote to the *Charleston News and Courier* angry that "it is too often a certain class of leaders are indignant when their views are opposed." McCrady's proposals offended poorer whites who had "followed (contrary to his better convictions) his leaders in the late war and fought the whole four years' term with all its sacrifices." He predicted its passage would be "the crushing straw that broke the camel's back." New restrictions on white suffrage "will act as a cleaver that will divide the Democratic party in South Carolina . . . and then if Mahoneism steps in and usurps the power I guess you will understand who was to blame."[25] The author's reference to "Mahoneism" no doubt rankled conservatives and former Confederates such as McCrady and Hampton. It refers to Virginia's brief, but highly controversial, anti–elite, biracial political movement of the mid-1870s led by former Confederate general William Mahone.

A watered-down version of the "eight-box" bill passed the assembly in 1882, giving election officials discretion over enforcement of the new requirements. The episode is significant, however, because "B" dared to question whether poor whites had been wise in supporting the Confederacy, or at least its elite officer corps. It dangerously undermined the myth of Confederate unity crucial to Hampton's associates, many of whom were antebellum and wartime leaders. By suggesting that poorer whites had been ill-advised in following their leaders into war, the way was now clear to go their own way in peace. By attacking the myth of Confederate unity, "B" struck at the heart of the conservative philosophy and at Hampton's self-image, both of which held that all of South Carolina society was better off under their rule.

Remarks from Greenville's Thomas Woodward captured the struggle within the hearts and minds of many white South Carolinians— especially former Confederates—during those years. Woodward admired Hampton greatly for his war record and for his service to the state in 1876. But time and again Woodward found himself at odds with Hampton's elitist politics. In an 1878 address Woodward detailed his opposition to Hampton's appointments and policies and then concluded, "But, sir, despite all this, and more that can be alleged, I honor and love this man."[26] In the same year, Massachusetts newspaper editor E. P. Clark queried South Carolinians regarding Hampton's philosophy toward governing. He noted ominously that he had "put this question to a good many people: 'How . . . many Democrats . . . would support any other man carrying out the same policy?' . . . One very intelligent Republican said, not one in ten; several agreed in saying, not a majority."[27] In the postwar, expanded democracy of South Carolina, the majority mattered, as Hampton and his associates soon learned.

Antielite sentiments again erupted in the mid-1880s, this time with a startling fury. "Pitchfork Ben" Tillman launched his vitriolic campaign against the state's traditional rulers in 1886 and the old conservative regime never fully recovered. He blasted the conservative presumption to rule for the good of all and instead charged that the elite "intend in the future, as in the past, to get all they can, and keep all they get." Tillman worked to wrest control of the Democratic Party from Hampton's allies, promising that "a Legislature in sympathy will naturally follow."[28] Traditional conservatives simply could not believe that Tillman and his allies could succeed by attacking *them*, the elite—especially with Hampton as their titular head. Hampton, however, had a sense that real trouble was afoot. In 1888 he wrote Jefferson Davis complaining that life in the political arena had become "very irksome and I would gladly exchange it for that of a planter."[29]

By 1890 Tillman had mustered enough support to seek the Democratic nomination for governor, the winner of which was assured election. During this tumultuous campaign Tillman repeatedly confounded the conservatives with personal attacks on them as a class and Hampton individually. Reminiscent of Gary's attacks, he noted that "whenever a champion of the people has attempted to show them their rights . . . an aristocratic oligarchy has bought him with an office, or . . . turned loose the floodgates of misrepresentation and slander."[30] Tillman also skillfully exploited the division within the ranks of the Lost Cause. He asked his followers if they could continue to leave the state "in the hands of those wedded to ante-bellum ideas, but possessing little of ante-bellum patriotism and honor?"[31] He ridiculed those politicians who came to Columbia ready to do the farmers' work, but having breathed "the polluted atmosphere" returned home "intent on doing something for himself. The contact with General This and Judge That and Colonel Something Else who have shaken him by the hand and made much of him, has debauched him."[32]

During the same summer that former Confederates wept and cheered over Richmond's unveiling of the new Robert E. Lee statue, General Hampton and South Carolina's conservatives were fighting for their political lives. Hampton himself took to the campaign trail to speak on behalf of the conservative candidates. At a rally in Columbia he employed unifying Lost Cause themes, taking the crowd to task for a recent incident involving the "howling down" of anti-Tillmanite and former Confederate officer John Bratton. "When I saw that a South Carolina audience could insult John Bratton," Hampton wailed, "I thought, good God! have the memories of '61 or '65, have they been obliterated?" Hampton refuted the charge that he headed an exclusive ruling class: "I don't know what an aristocracy is, God knows I do not know." Tillman then took the podium and struck back viciously, calling Hampton and Bratton "innocent lambs" and repeating mockingly, "they never saw an aristocrat!" He concluded daringly, sneering in Hampton's direction on the platform: "The grand mogul here who ruled supremely and grandly cannot terrify me. I do not come from any such blood as that."[33]

Hampton's followers left the meeting stunned. Judge Andrew Crawford wrote following the incident: "In the very presence of Hampton, I have heard this man strike with poisoned tongue at the vitals of our civilization. It is incumbent upon us to take this man by the throat and choke him until his lips are livid and until he retracts his infamous insinuations."[34] The situation worsened three days later when Hampton arrived to address a campaign crowd in Aiken. He took the podium amidst jeers and hisses. As he began to speak, the abuse only intensified and forced an incredulous Hampton to abandon the effort and take his seat. The old general and the savior of '76 had himself been "howled down."[35]

After Tillman's election, the news only got worse for Hampton. Tillman's forces swept the statehouse and by December rumors swirled that the General Assembly would vote to send someone to replace Hampton in the Senate. Again the conservative press and Hampton's allies simply could not believe this was possible. By December 8 the ardently pro-Hampton *Charleston News and Courier* had reached an almost frantic tone in its support of their hero. "Who is Wade Hampton?" the headlines asked, with the subtitle, "A Startling Question for South Carolina to Consider." The paper devoted two front page columns to letters to the editor invoking Lost Cause themes to support Hampton.[36] In D. E. Huger Smith's defense of Hampton, the general's importance grew directly from his service during the war. "Blot out Hampton from the history of thirty years," wrote Smith, "and you blot out South Carolina." Lamenting that he lived in "a very new South Carolina,"

Huger Smith added, "The old Carolina is dead . . . the death agony has been a long one—from 1865 to 1890." But it was "absurd to call useless now that great man who . . . towered over the State." Meanwhile "the infantile new Carolina sucks its thumb and smiles at its rattle, it yet will some time think and reason, and look with contempt on the man who thrusts out Hampton."[37] A writer who signed as "Cavalry" voiced the belief that the situation gave Carolinians a chance to prove that "gratitude is, with us, not an obsolete sentiment, a forgotten thing, but a vital factor in our lives, an ever-present duty." He challenged "every true Confederate, who was near enough to the front" to consider his decision carefully. Another writer, "Citizen," noted "that the finest characteristic of a gentleman is that he never forgets an obligation." No one could question the obligation under which Carolinians lived to Hampton. He was, after all, the "the old soldier, the patriot, the peerless Carolinian."[38]

The *News and Courier* ran editorials from other Carolina papers supporting Hampton's reelection. The *Colleton Press* asked: "Who has a more brilliant record than the man who, whether upon the crimson battlefields, on the hustings or in the councils of his country, has shown the most exalted heroism, the sublimest virtue and the purest patriotism?" Will Tillman's government "go back on the old war horse?" the authors wondered. "We think not." The *Abbeville Press and Banner* also mined the martial memories to support Hampton. The Abbeville paper had not always been in Hampton's corner in recent political contests. But when the issue was Hampton himself, the matter was clear: "Pardon the old hero for whatever may have seemed amiss," they urged. "Hampton is now an old man, and in reverence for his age, and in giving due respect to a beloved old soldier, we trust no Confederate soldier in the General Assembly can find it in his heart to vote against the noblest Roman of them all. . . . Soldiers of the Lost Cause, let us honor him."[39]

Naturally the *News and Courier* weighed in with its own editorials, which likewise employed a heavy Lost Cause theme. The paper predicted rejection of the "new principle in the politics of South Carolina" that disregarded one's previous military service as a "suitable test for the bestowment of public rewards." The *News and Courier* continued to place the war as central to the matters at hand. "We do not believe that the old memories of the past have been forgotten," the editorial writers continued, adding their certainty that the "old soldiers in the Legislature," where it counted most, would not forget Hampton's importance either. As the day of the vote neared, however, the *News and Courier* again revealed that it was, in fact, not simply Hampton the general or Hampton the redeemer that they cherished. It was Hampton the conservative. As they continued to sing the praises of his past deeds, the paper also wondered whether there was anyone who would be more "faithful, conservative, just and honest" than Hampton.[40] The elite presumption to rule, central to the traditional conservatism, offended the Tillmanites time after time. This point continued to elude the conservatives. (For example, Tillman's supporters no doubt took offense to comments like Charlestonian James G. Holmes's Bourbon-style reference in the *Confederate Veteran* to the "loved and honored Hampton [derided now by the *sans coulottes* and ingrates."])[41] As the prospect of Hampton's removal loomed, the *News and Courier* confessed simply, "We hardly know what to say about it."[42] When the General Assembly met on December 11, the representatives voted to send to the Senate J. L. M. Irby, a young man who was seven years old when the Civil War began.

Hampton's defeat dealt traditional conservatives a thunderous blow. "The agony is over," the *News and Courier* wrote on December 12. In defeat, the *News and Courier* continued to tie the present to a Lost Cause past: "A change seems to have come over the spirit of our dreams, and we have seen a South Carolina Legislature, composed very largely of Confederate soldiers, seeking to degrade a Confederate soldier. Perhaps it means that the Confederate soldier must go, and that the war, with all its memories, is over at last." The paper quoted at length John Esten Cooke's *Surrey of the Eagle's Nest* depicting gallant deeds and ending with the realization that the narrator had been dreaming. So it was for South Carolina. The *News and Courier* indulged in a maudlin conclusion:

> The war is over in South Carolina. . . . Take the old grey coat out of the closet and look at it for the last time before it is thrown into the rag bag—it represented something and meant something twenty years ago. Throw the battered old canteen into the ash barrel—it meant something twenty years ago. Unfold the tattered old battle-flag, under whose glorious folds you, perchance, followed Hampton into the very jaws of death—look at it for the last time and let the flames consume it. All these things are but dust and ashes. . . . There are no longer any "rebels" and "traitors." The Confederate soldier has outlived his days in South Carolina. "It was only a dream."[43]

Not surprisingly, Hampton felt the sting from the rejection by former Confederates. He wrote Matthew C. Butler, a longtime political ally, "I am hurt that the old soldiers turned against me, for I did not expect that at their hands."[44]

Ironically, while Hampton and his fellow conservatives feared that the issues, memories, and glory of the war were finally in the past, the

Lost Cause was becoming increasingly popular and institutionalized. The formation and emergence of groups such as the United Confederate Veterans (UCV) created new outlets for Lost Cause commemorations. South Carolina quickly became a hotbed for UCV chapters and activities. Hampton, living in Washington, D.C., through most of the 1890s, served as the UCV commander of the Army of Northern Virginia.[45] Within the more organized structure for Lost Cause commemoration, South Carolina's traditional conservatives suddenly found a new opportunity to keep Hampton, and through him their values, in the public eye.[46] Lewis Pinckney Jones writes that during the 1890s, Columbia's *The State* gave ample coverage to the Confederate memorial efforts and to Hampton's life in particular. "Any time two Confederate veterans got together," Jones notes, "copious columns described the event (all veterans being 'our gallant heroes'), and if Wade Hampton made public utterance, the whole front page seemed to renew its frequent efforts to beatify the General."[47] During the 1890s Hampton became transformed into a symbol not unlike Gaines Foster's description of Robert E. Lee after 1871. As an active political figure, Hampton had become, like Lee, "dead and perfect" and therefore very useful for symbolic purposes in the ongoing political battle against Tillman's allies controlling the state assembly.[48]

The canonization began within five months of his removal from the Senate. In May 1891, Hampton gave the keynote address celebrating Columbia's centennial. According to the press coverage, the day nearly turned into an exclusive celebration for the general rather than the city. "This was strictly Hampton's Day," *The State* proclaimed. The "grand old warrior" led a procession of "battle-scarred and worn veterans who stepped behind the gallant old hero with an elasticity of step and radiance of countenance that indicated the warm love that burned in their hearts." With Tillman among the honored guests on the platform, the mayor of Columbia, F. W. McMaster, introduced Hampton in glowing terms. After recounting Hampton's place in the state's history, McMaster announced grandly: "Fellow citizens, behold the patriot, the hero, the gentleman. An honor to the State, to the Confederate States, the United States, and to mankind." *The State* reported that Tillman sat near Hampton during the address and "remained perfectly quiet for the whole time, except for an occasional smile."[49]

Hampton's address contained a pointed reference to his recent political defeats and the new Tillman regime. As he recounted his career for the crowd, he noted that "No public office, however high, can of itself confer honor. It is only honorable as an evidence of the good will, the esteem and confidence of those who bestow it. That obtained by falsehood, or misrepresentation, or trickery, frauds its possessor with dishonor." *The State* plainly relished reporting on Hampton's reception in the very presence of Governor Tillman. "The gathering at yesterday's great meeting," the paper reported, "was decidedly more representative of South Carolina than our 'reform legislature.' Wade Hampton would not have had many votes cast against in that crowd."[50] *The State* kept up the drumbeat in the next day's paper, comparing Tillman's reputation to Daniel H. Chamberlain's, the last "carpetbag" governor. "Yesterday, for the first time since the Reconstruction period, a Governor of South Carolina, riding at the head of the State troops through the heart of the city of Columbia in the sight of twenty thousand people did not have a cheer raised for him by even one voice," the article's author noted. He added that "It was a very significant circumstance when it is considered that the visitors to the Centennial were among the very best men in South Carolina."[51]

Historians David D. Wallace and Francis B. Simkins have noted that Tillman's power peaked between his reelection in 1892 and his election to the Senate in 1894. South Carolina, meanwhile, suffered from the dislocating effects of an industrializing economy. State elections remained fractious and bitter, and by the mid-1890s pressure mounted to follow Mississippi's precedent of disfranchising black voters in the name of political stability. In the midst of deep economic uncertainty the symbol of Hampton continued to serve as a potent vehicle for promoting the return of conservative political leadership.

In May 1895 the Camp Moultrie division of the South Carolina Sons of Confederate Veterans (SCV) along with the Charleston Chapter of the United Daughters of the Confederacy (UDC) invited Hampton to be the main orator at their first joint meeting. This event, too, quickly became referred to as Hampton Day and turned into a citywide festival honoring the old general with extensive coverage provided by the staunchly conservative *News and Courier.* Speeches from the day mixed conservative themes from the war and the election of 1876 with little differentiation. The speakers also displayed an acute awareness of more recent political battles, those of 1890 especially. The *News and Courier*'s coverage pulled out all the stops to portray the day in a flattering light to Hampton and the conservative cause. The paper tugged at heartstrings by touching on Hampton's mortality and noting the thousands of children seeing "the face of Hampton for the first time and all perhaps for the last." There was, in addition, the "pathetic motive in the hearts of the few hundred Veterans who had followed Hampton on the battlefield and were about to see Hampton again perhaps for the last time on earth."[52]

The day began with a massive parade down Meeting Street and around the Battery—the heart of what is today historic Charleston. The *News and Courier* reported that "Cheer after cheer was sent heavenward in honor of the old hero, the greatest son of Carolina" and that more cheers "followed the hero of the Lost Cause." Following the parade and morning ceremonies, Hampton spent the rest of the day receiving guests, gifts, and floral arrangements that included "a beautiful wreath of laurel with the name of 'Hampton' in the centre."[53]

The *News and Courier* used its coverage of Hampton's day to briefly theorize on the importance of heroes. The "hero" remained worthy of adoration and emulation even though "reverses and adversity may follow." The "hero" was that figure "in whom ebbs and flows and centres that patriotic fervor and national reverence." For South Carolina's traditional conservatives, the hero occupied that vital, symbolic center between the past and present and future. The values for which he was famous, the editorial continued, "may slumber in the ashes of a new condition of things, or it may smoulder in quiescence while other issues are tried and other causes proven," but the potential for their return yet existed until "a spark will set it aflame again." This was Hampton's role as "The State's greatest chieftain and typical hero," and Charleston's love for Hampton and for "all that he is, all that he has represented, *and all that he does represent,* burst the bands of conventionality and enveloped the city in an enthusiasm which was boundless."[54]

That night, at the Academy of Music, the local SCV and UDC chapters held their joint meeting. The "meeting" amounted to little more than a celebration of their honored guest. With the playing of "Hail to the Chief," Hampton entered the Academy of Music hall at 9 P.M. through a door draped by the Confederate and South Carolina flags. When the honored guests took their seats on the platform, Theodore G. Barker, a Charlestonian and ardent conservative, introduced Hampton. Making the expected references to Hampton's valor during the war and his vital role in ending Reconstruction, Barker also made a pointed reference to the Tillman regime. Building toward a dramatic finish, Barker readied the crowd to receive their hero as, among other things, "the stone which the political builders of 1890 refused."[55] With that, Hampton rose to thundering applause to address the crowd.

While Southern conservatism is often seen in the light of resistance to all things modern, it did in fact accept change as a part of life. Southern conservatives believed, moreover, that the principles and values that dominated an older society could, with care, be transmitted into a new society for a new era.[56] William D. Porter assured his fellow Charlestonians in 1871 that while much had changed with defeat, "all is not changed."[57] In 1876, South Carolina historian William J. Rivers still invoked the values and the memory of the Old South and urged the state's elite to "infuse her nature" into the new order.[58] Hampton, meanwhile, assured the UCD and SCV members that adherence to the old principles would continue to hold Southern society together. Let slip away that reverence, he warned, and South Carolina would be unable to "escape the doom which awaits the people who sacrifice principle for subservient expediency; who abandon their ancient virtues to adopt the vices of their conquerors, who are willing to barter for gilded servitude." As he summed up, he asked pointedly, "Will history vindicate us, if we condemn ourselves?"[59]

Hampton then recounted for his adoring audience "the proudest day in my life" in 1877 when "I announced to our people . . . that the Federal troops would be withdrawn from the State House, and that Carolinians, the rightful rulers of the State, would resume their hereditary authority, so long denied them." Hampton, significantly, was speaking just months before the state effectively disfranchised its black population through a constitutional convention. While rumors about the proposed constitutional convention swirled through the state, Hampton reminded his audience that the struggle in 1876–77 was not simply for white rule—in fact he made no specific mention of white rule at all.[60] His battle was for the traditionally conservative values of "home rule, for personal liberty and States' rights."[61] Hampton's speech ended with a burst of applause and an ensuing "floral bombardment" of the stage.

The next day's press coverage contained a glowing report from "The Women of Carolina." Under the title "Sans Peur, Sans Reproche," the "women of Carolina" explained that as a "hero worshipping people," adulation for Hampton came easily. "Ah! how the very name thrills us," the women continued, recounting Hampton's exploits. Shortly after the war, Hampton once again put on the gray uniform for his daughter's wedding, where he "put her hand in the left hand of a man whose right arm was buried in Virginia."[62] The women then traced Hampton's enduring qualities through 1876 and up to the 1890s. They noted how "The Greeks banished Aristides, poisoned Socrates, degraded Epaminondas," and how, in reference to Tillman's followers, "the mob of South Carolina put aside Wade Hampton." As a result, "these are dark days for the State." But, they hoped, there was "yet a future for Wade Hampton," adding, "and the men and women who love him and all he represents." "All that he represents" was precisely the point behind much of the Hampton celebrations during those years and into the early 1900s. "Is our love for Wade Hampton foolishness?" the women of Charleston asked. It certainly was not from the conservative perspective. It is clear that what Hampton represented within the context of South Carolina was not simply the fighting Confederate or rebel, but traditional conservative values of elite rule and order against the rise of mass democracy represented by Tillmanism.[63]

The State used Hampton's presence at the UDC/SCV celebration in Charleston to address the recent constitutional developments in the Tillman-led regime of Gov. John Gary Evans and Sen. J. L. M. Irby. "Between Hampton in Charleston and Tillman, Evans and Irby in Columbia, what an appalling abyss!" an editorial screamed: "In Columbia were Hampton's successors in office and power, without a welcome, without honor—conspiring in corners to perfect the destruction of that peace and liberty which Hampton gave to South Carolina." By May 1895, the Tillman forces had revealed their intentions to disfranchise black voters through the constitutional convention. Tillman himself weighed in with the ominous reminder that while legal machinations regarding the black vote had come and gone in the past, "the shotgun has not gone away."[64] *The State* decried this development as sending a message of "hatred and strife." The government, the paper charged, "seeks to arouse against the hapless race which Hampton pledged protection in 1876 the passions of the mob . . . [and] calls for vengeance upon the white men who stand on the Hampton platform by which the State was won. It is utterly unworthy and degrading." The editorial concluded passionately, "Ah! what a contrast—what a pitiful shameful contrast! How far we have fallen in the five years which span between the old and new orders in South Carolina!"[65] Nonetheless, the convention came off as planned and Tillman persuaded a number of conservatives to help steer the new statutes regarding suffrage past the Fifteenth Amendment.[66]

In the first decade of the 1900s, the Hampton celebrations reached their peak. The culmination came with the general's death in 1902 and the dedication of the Hampton statue near the statehouse in 1906. Following a week of boosterism from Charleston's Commerce Exposition, the headlines of the April 12, 1902, papers took a somber turn with the announcement of Hampton's death on the eleventh. The papers devoted massive coverage to the details of his death. Hampton's final words, "All my people, black and white,—God bless them All," received special attention, testifying to the paternalistic values that conservatives still trumpeted. *The State* made explicit use of Hampton's death to further the conservative cause against Tillmanism. "Most of his contemporaries of 1877 had passed away," the paper reported. "Political revolutions had come and gone, his fortunes had varied greatly, and the old story of 1877 had lapsed from many memories; but the news of Hampton dying,

Hampton dead, reawakened remembrance of his great performance of a great trust and thrilled through a new South Carolina the sentiment of the old." *The State* could not resist taking a shot at those who still followed the antielite path to political power successfully taken by Ben Tillman. "'All my people,'" the paper reiterated, "There are white men, and prominent ones, upon whom these words will fall like the stroke of a lash." *The State* did not envy those "who compassed the retirement of Wade Hampton from the high post he held . . . who almost broke his heart with the thought that the people had repudiated him."[67]

South Carolina's conservatives achieved a partial political comeback at the turn of the century. They sent an anti-Tillman senator to Washington in 1896 and, as Francis Simkins notes, by the 1900s, Tillman himself had aligned his views more consistently with traditional conservatives. In 1902, South Carolina elected rice planter Duncan Clinch Heyward governor (with Tillman's support). By 1906, the image of Wade Hampton in South Carolina remained no longer tied to a specific conservative construction. But while the interpretations of Hampton became more diverse in the early 1900s, they consistently avoided, or dealt lightly with, the political difficulties of the 1880s and early 1900s.

The ceremonies surrounding the memorial statue dedicated to Hampton near the statehouse give the first indication of the loosening interpretations regarding the general. Commissioned in 1904 by Governor Heyward, the statue depicts Hampton in a gallant pose riding an impressive mount. Old conservative stalwarts Gen. Matthew C. Butler and Theodore G. Barker served as the keynote speaker and chief marshal respectively. On November 20, 1906, three Hampton granddaughters and one great-granddaughter unveiled the statue to the roar of the crowd.[68] The headline story from the November 20 edition of *The State,* which ran adjacent to an article reporting a lynching near Newberry, struck a theme commemorating Hampton's fight for white supremacy. While the paper noted that the ceremony blended all South Carolinians for the day into "the party of Hampton," it further recounted how the statue celebrated "white men freed from the despotism of outnumbering aliens, freed because Wade Hampton led them." This marked a significant shift in the interpretation of Hampton. For decades, conservatives such as Hampton had referred very explicitly to the 1876 election as a conservative victory for good government and law and order.[69]

The image of an almost pathetic Hampton also emerged from the coverage of the statue's unveiling. One article depicted Hampton as a relic. Military valor and political conquest remained praiseworthy, the paper noted, but it was his "uncomplaining fortitude" in the hour of his devastating 1899 house fire that made the old general "more a hero" to the new generation. Meanwhile, the editorial continued, "he was and is yet the ideal of the generation passing away." At the article's conclusion, the writer noted that "The good old feudal days were destined to end, but in ending they proved that the Southern gentleman was a graceful loser, and that in every phase of fortune his was an example to be followed."[70]

In the years after the statue's dedication, the image of Hampton continued to pass into the more general patriotic lore that fit the needs of almost any occasion or cause. During World War I the UDC sponsored hospital beds in France dedicated to Wade Hampton's name to demonstrate their nationalist fervor.[71] In their programs for "Children of the Confederacy," they selected February to be Wade Hampton's month, and UDC literature listed questions on Hampton's life as part of the organization's historical education efforts. The questions asked students to discuss Hampton's life as a "gentleman planter of the Old South and his paternal care of his slaves, whose affection he held to the day of his death"; his opposition to secession; his wartime heroics; and the "signal service" to South Carolina "ridding her of the carpetbag element."[72] Like most accounts of Hampton during the 1900s, the UDC literature made no mention of the open dissent against the elite and against Hampton personally in the 1880s and 1890s.

The last grand celebration dedicated to Hampton came on the fiftieth anniversary of his 1876 victory over Daniel Chamberlain. On December 10, 1926, Gov. Thomas G. McLeod gave his official proclamation that the fourteenth would be a state holiday to commemorate the anniversary of Hampton's victory.[73] The 1926 Hampton celebration lacked a specific political core or purpose. "This is Hampton's Day," The State proclaimed. Upon further reflection the paper added more generally that "It is really Hampton's Year and Era. He means for us infinitely more than the span of any single day, no matter how glorious, how shining with golden memories." "Hampton came," the editorial concluded dramatically, "in the evening twilight of the gods."[74]

Despite The State's willingness to place Hampton among the deities, other South Carolinians used the legend of the general's exploits for more earthly pursuits. Not unlike the legend of Robert E. Lee in the 1920s, Hampton came to symbolize a diverse range of causes and purposes. The South Carolina National Bank used the occasion for advertising purposes, grandly billing itself as "A Banking Institution Old Enough to Tell the Glories of 1876." Meanwhile, longtime newspaperman Alfred B. Williams, who had already begun his career as a journalist by 1876, wrote that the "Spirit That Won in '76 Can Defeat Today's Ills." Specifically, Williams was referring to the depth of economic depression already crippling the state's farmers, a group notorious for their dislike of bankers. His solution was to instill unity among white farmers from a legend of white unity in 1876. "Growl as some of us may, and as some of us have right to do, over present conditions," the state's farmers still had the legacy of 1876 to lead them on to better days and "to rescue for themselves fair returns from what they produce."[75]

Admiral Samuel McGowan Jr., son of Confederate general Samuel McGowan, stayed closer to the Hampton's historical record by offering to pay the expenses of any surviving black Democrats who had supported the general in 1876. "For a Negro to be a Democrat in 1876, and to be known and to act as such, was mighty risky business," McGowan wrote. "If they were good enough, and brave enough, to ride side by side with our fathers, then, I think they ought to be in the parade tomorrow; not as servants, but as 100 per cent South Carolina participants."[76] The paper reported the next day that three black South Carolinians responded. The *Columbia Record* reported that one African-American supporter of Wade Hampton, Wyatt McMaster, was readying himself for the grand day. He told the paper that his "old Prince Albert coat is being pressed" and that his wife was "shining up his beaver hat." Apparently McGowan's words of blacks' equal bravery eluded the parade organizers in consideration of McMaster. He may have "ridden side by side" with white South Carolinians in 1876, but Wyatt McMaster's parade assignment in 1926 was to drive the "Carriage of '76" for other "honor guests."[77]

The parade itself showed the flexibility that had grown regarding the meaning of Wade Hampton. Four former South Carolina governors rode together, ranging from aristocratic planters Duncan Clinch Heyward and Richard Irvine Manning to John Gary Evans, the 1890s Tillmanite leader. (The demagogue Coleman L. Blease was invited to ride with the other former governors, but the paper did not report his presence at the parade.) Parade goers wore the popular button of the day, which featured triple portraits of Hampton, Matthew C. Butler, and Martin W. Gary, all Confederate generals and leaders of the Democratic campaign to end Reconstruction. The commemorative button of the three generals thus paid tribute to both a beloved Lost Cause and a hallowed, yet narrowly interpreted, political victory. The fact that Gary emerged from the celebrated 1876 campaign as a bitter antagonist of Hampton's remained overlooked or conveniently ignored.[78]

An image of Wade Hampton remained useful to white South Carolinians well into the 1930s. White political leaders in the state became increasingly anxious over the reach of New Deal policies, fearing a threat to the South's racial hierarchy. By the end of the decade, some Southern Democrats, like South Carolina's Ellison "Cotton Ed" Smith, broke openly with their Democratic president, Franklin D. Roosevelt. Facing a bitter senatorial primary contest with pro–New Deal governor Olin D. Johnston, Smith depicted himself as a latter-day Wade Hampton, a legacy he interpreted as fending off the long arm of the federal government.[79] On the night of his election, "Cotton Ed" celebrated his hard-fought victory by appearing at the Wade Hampton statue near the statehouse in Columbia wearing the famous red shirt of Hampton's followers in 1876. "We conquered in '76," proclaimed Smith, "and we conquered in '38." Addressing the crowd, which included two hundred red-shirted men from Orangeburg, Smith crowed over his victory: "Boys, the symbol you wear tonight is the symbol we hurled to the world after the Confederate War between the States when negroes and carpetbaggers got control of the state government." Hampton, he explained, "did not agree that our civilization should be threatened by federal bayonets." Roosevelt's campaigning in South Carolina for Johnston suggested a new type of federal invasion. "No man dares to come into South Carolina and try to dictate to the sons of those men who held high the hands of Lee and Hampton."[80]

The issue, however, was not simply the balance of power. "On you rests the responsibility to protect her [South Carolina] from the mongrel breed who would take us back to the horrid days of reconstruction," he challenged the neo–Red Shirts in the audience. The *News and Courier* reported that Orangeburg men wore red shirts and spent Election Day milling around the voting precincts. The *News and Courier* ran an article claiming "No One Hinders Them," in reference to African Americans attempting to vote in South Carolina.[81] Until such time as Roosevelt came to South Carolina and disavowed his intention to allow "hordes of negroes" into the Democratic primaries, or when he came to reassure white South Carolinians that "he and his allies in the Northern cities have no intention of interfering with South Carolina," then and only then "we shall say that the re-adoption of the Red Shirt may not now be necessary." But, the editorial continued, Roosevelt was not about to do either of these, and therefore the "Red Shirt's appearance in Orangeburg heartens South Carolina." A brief article beneath this editorial added that the Red Shirts' appearance was a "timely and wise act, for unless The News and Courier is mistaken the national Democratic party is now resolved to destroy the white man's party in South Carolina."[82]

Toward the end of *The Road to Reunion, 1865–1900,* historian Paul H. Buck analyzed the impact on postwar writing made by the deaths over the years of the war's "lofty actors." Buck set up this discussion by asking his readers, "what would posterity do with them? What traditions cluster around their names?" In line with the book's overall thesis, Buck answered his own questions: "We take our heroes and bend them to our wishes."[83] So it was with Wade Hampton and the Lost Cause in South Carolina. Following his death in 1902, Hampton came to be seen as a symbol of nationalism in World War I, both the hope of poor farmers and a reference point for solid banks in the 1920s, and a forerunner of the resistance to the New Deal in the 1930s. In his 1950 campaign for the United States Senate, Strom Thurmond's opponent attacked the former governor for appointing an African American to a minor post and spoiling "Wade Hampton's era of segregation."[84]

Lost in the various uses of Wade Hampton were the principles to which he and his fellow conservatives clung consistently in the postwar decades. Hampton and South Carolina's conservatives, like their antebellum forefathers, persistently fought to stem the national tide toward mass democracy. Their effort to reconfigure a regime of elite rule over the former slaves and poor whites succeeded in part through their constant promotion of Hampton and his war exploits and his role in the 1876 election. Through Wade Hampton, conservatives' belief in elite rule dovetailed neatly with a wider image of the Lost Cause that held Confederate leaders to be "the better men." But the friction generated by a changing economy and society gradually separated Hampton's wartime and 1876 heroics from his elitism and revealed to all the aristocrat that he truly was. Thus South Carolina in the 1880s and 1890s offers a unique twist in the story of the Lost Cause. At a time when other Confederate military leaders were gradually taking their place in the pantheon of national idols, Hampton faced bitter political opposition at home from resentful former soldiers. Not until the early 1900s, when he was no longer on South Carolina's political stage, did white South Carolinians come once again to see Wade Hampton as, in John Rice's words, "always hero."

Notes

1. John A. Rice, *I Came Out of the Eighteenth Century* (New York: Harper and Brothers, 1942), 91.

2. In the historiography of the Lost Cause, two of the more recent and substantial books take different approaches to the subject. Gaines Foster's *Ghosts of the Confederacy: Defeat, the Lost Cause, and the Emergence of the New South, 1865 to 1913* (New York: Oxford University Press, 1987) exam-

ines how the ceremonies and literature surrounding the Lost Cause helped
the South ease into a new economic and social world. Charles Reagan Wilson's *Baptized in Blood: The Religion of the Lost Cause, 1865–1920* (Athens:
University of Georgia Press, 1980) describes the Lost Cause as a "civil
religion" that provided white Southerners with a bulwark against the
moral uncertainties generated by a rapidly changing society. Each is perti-
nent to South Carolina's history. Wade Hampton figures into the scholarship as a conciliatory figure between the sections in Foster's book. Nina
Silber also notes that Hampton in the 1890s served as a mediator between
the Confederate past and a new industrial age. This essay, however, examines how Wade Hampton's image, as the focus of the Lost Cause, was used
and became subsequently entangled in the often bitter postwar political
struggles within the state and particularly among white South Carolinians.

3. Thomas L. Connelly, *The Marble Man: Robert E. Lee and His Image in
American Society* (New York: Alfred A. Knopf, 1977), xv.

4. Hampton delivered the keynote address at the first Ladies Memorial Association gathering in Charleston in 1866. The Ladies Memorial Association
was one of the first organized efforts at commemorating the war.

5. *Proceedings on the Occasion of Unveiling the Monument, Erected in Memory
of Their Comrades who Died in the Service of the State, June 16, 1870. Oration by General Wade Hampton. Poem by Rev. E. T. Winkler, &c., &c.*
(Charleston, S.C.: Walker, Evans & Cogswell, 1870): 12–15. Hampton's
understanding of the war over the years followed roughly the outline of
Lost Cause interpretation spelled out in Gaines Foster's *Ghosts of the Confederacy.* Foster notes that in the immediate postwar years, most white
Southerners mixed feelings of grief over their losses and defensiveness
about the cause with submission to the results.

6. See especially Eugene D. Genovese, *The Slaveholders' Dilemma: Freedom
and Progress in Southern Conservative Thought, 1820–1860* (Columbia: University of South Carolina Press, 1992) and Drew Gilpin Faust, *A Sacred
Circle: The Dilemma of the Intellectual in the Old South, 1840–1860* (Baltimore: Johns Hopkins University Press, 1977). From the days of John C.
Calhoun to secession, conservative Carolinians had struggled to maintain
elite or local political rule. By the 1830s they had rejected Jeffersonian notions of equality, and their proslavery philosophy gloried in human society's fundamental inequality. Conservatives like James Henry Ham-
mond, William Gilmore Simms, Frederick A. Porcher, and William Henry
Trescot observed warily as the democratic impulses spread throughout the
rest of the nation. Carolinian conservative Christopher G. Memminger
captured their mood toward mass democracy succinctly in 1849 by making
reference to propertyless whites and adding with a sneer, "and every one
of them would have a vote."

7. *The Respectful Remonstrance, on Behalf of the White People of South Carolina, Against the Constitution of the Late Convention of that State, Now Sub-*

mitted to Congress for Ratification (Columbia, S.C.: Phoenix Book and Job Cover Press, 1868), 12–14. Hampton laid out the same themes in a personal letter to President Andrew Johnson. South Carolina's conservatives also tried to make common cause with John Quincy Adams II by corresponding and inviting Adams to Columbia for an address. Hampton's letter to Johnson can be found in Charles E. Cauthen's *Family Letters of the Three Wade Hamptons, 1782–1901* (Columbia: University of South Carolina Press, 1953). See also *An Appeal to the honorable the Senate of the United States, in behalf of the Conservative People of South Carolina, Against the Adoption, By Congress, of the New Constitution Proposed for South Carolina* (Columbia: Phoenix Book and Job Power Press, 1868) and *Massachusetts and South Carolina. Correspondence Between John Quincy Adams and Wade Hampton and Others of South Carolina* (Boston: J. E. Farwell, 1868).

8. *Charleston Daily Courier,* March 23, 1867, 1.

9. Charles E. Cauthen, ed., *Family Letters of the Three Wade Hamptons, 1782–1901,* 142–43.

10. Wade Hampton to Dabney H. Maury, December 10, 1874, Dabney Maury Correspondence, Southern Historical Society Collection, Eleanor S. Brockenbrough Library, Museum of the Confederacy, Richmond, Virginia.

11. *Free Men! Free Ballots! Free Schools! The Pledges of Gen. Wade Hampton, Democratic Candidate for Governor, to the Colored People of South Carolina, 1865–1876,* n.p., 6.

12. Thomas L. Connelly and Barbara L. Bellows, *God and General Longstreet: The Lost Cause and the Southern Mind* (Baton Rouge: Louisiana State University Press, 1982), 22–27.

13. George B. Tindall, *South Carolina Negroes, 1877–1900* (Columbia: University of South Carolina Press, 1952), 13.

14. E. Culpepper Clark, *Francis Warrington Dawson and the Politics of Restoration, 1874–1889* (University: University of Alabama Press, 1980), 70.

15. The *News and Courier* saw fit to reprint Hampton's entire 1876 address in the May 11, 1899, edition as part of their ongoing effort to spark the conservative resurgence through Lost Cause/UCV celebrations. In his policies toward black Carolinians, Hampton had a level of success later forgotten or purposely ignored by the leaders of segregation and conservative descendants in the early 1900s. Thomas Holt observes that Hampton appointed eighty-six African Americans to governmental offices, although he qualifies this by adding that none were prominent positions. Moreover, Hampton did garner thousands of black votes both in 1876 and in his landslide reelection in 1878. Black South Carolinians clearly saw something in the Hampton administration worth their support, even if it was nothing more than an utter lack of better choices. At the same time, Hampton's conservatism and the extent to which he did show fairness and concern for black South Carolinians continued to rankle the element within white South Carolina that had no time for a biracial society and dwindling pa-

tience with the traditional conservative claims to rule. Martin W. Gary, himself a former Confederate general, continued to lead this increasingly fractious segment into the post-Reconstruction years. See Thomas Holt, *Black Over White: Political Leadership in South Carolina during Reconstruction* (Urbana and Chicago: University of Illinois Press, 1977), 211.

16. "A Southern Rebuke of Bourbonism," *The Nation* 27 (September 5, 1878): 140.

17. Ibid.

18. *Edgefield Advertiser*, July 18, 1878. A parody of Bill Arp appeared in the same edition that similarly took Hampton and the conservatives to task for criticizing Edgefield and its antiblack policies. Under the title "Arp's Bill," this writer mocked Hampton openly. Signing off a letter to "Mistur Edyturs," "Arp's Bill" added that "I just learned by tellygraf . . . that Gov. Hampton is losin his memory! He has forgotten which county elected him!!" However, for the time being Hampton was able to assure his friend Armistead Burt that "the opposition has been crushed out." Wade Hampton to Armistead Burt, 24 March 1878, Folder 1, Hampton Papers, Special Collections Library, Duke University, Durham, North Carolina.

19. Both these quotations are in footnotes in Hampton M. Jarrell, *Wade Hampton and the Negro: The Road Not Taken* (Columbia: University of South Carolina Press, 1949), 145 n 66 and 146 n 68.

20. "Ought The Negro to be Disfranchised? Ought He to Have Been Enfranchised?" *North American Review* 128 (March 1879): 241.

21. Clark, *Francis Warrington Dawson*, 71.

22. "Gen. Gary's Speech Before the County Convention," *Edgefield Advertiser*, May 13, 1880, 1. The irony of Gary's invocation of Lincoln's "of the people, by the people, and for the people" as a rallying cry in this struggle between two former Confederate generals apparently prompted no public comment.

23. Edward McCrady, *The Registration of Electors* (Charleston, 1879), 11.

24. Foster, *Ghosts of the Confederacy*, 89.

25. *Charleston News and Courier*, December 9, 1881.

26. Quoted in Jarrell, *Wade Hampton and the Negro*, 128.

27. Ibid., 131.

28. *Charleston News and Courier*, January 23, 1890.

29. Wade Hampton to Jefferson Davis, April 9, 1888, Box 10, Folder 77-6, Jefferson Davis Papers, Museum of the Confederacy, Richmond, Virginia.

30. *Charleston News and Courier*, January 23, 1890.

31. Ibid.

32. Francis B. Simkins, *Pitchfork Ben Tillman* (Baton Rouge: Louisiana State University Press, 1944), 94.

33. Ibid., 159.

34. Ibid.

35. Ibid.

36. *Charleston News and Courier*, December 8, 1890.

37. Ibid.

38. Ibid.

39. Ibid.

40. Ibid.

41. "The Carolina Rifles," *Confederate Veteran*, March 1893, 77.

42. *Charleston News and Courier*, December 10, 1890.

43. Ibid., December 12, 1890.

44. Wade Hampton to Matthew C. Butler, December 13, 1890, Matthew C. Butler Papers, The South Caroliniana Library, University of South Carolina, Columbia.

45. Foster, *Ghosts of the Confederacy*, 106–107. Foster notes that the UCV organized chapters in every county in South Carolina.

46. Conservatives outside of South Carolina used Hampton in the same way. Colonel Charles C. Jones Jr., an unreconstructed Georgian, honored Hampton at an April 1891 meeting of the Confederate Survivors Association. Jones frequently left his law practice in New York City to give blistering pro-Confederate speeches. His introduction of Hampton at this meeting paid tribute to "this distinguished Confederate chieftain, enlightened statesman, genuine patriot, and chivalrous son of the South." Hampton symbolized for Jones fading principles of the Old South. Jones lambasted the "absurd guise of a New South." For Jones, the New South meant, specifically, "flaunting the banners of utilitarianism, lifting the standards of speculation and expediency, elevating the colors whereon are emblazoned consolidation of wealth and centralization of government, lowering the flag of intellectual, moral, and refined supremacy in the presence of the petty guidons of ignorance, personal ambition, and diabolism, supplanting the iron cross with the golden calf." The leaders of the New South sought to convert the South into a "money-worshipping domain" populated by an ungrateful citizenry that, "careless of the land-marks of the fathers, impatient of the remarks of a calm, enlightened, conservative civilization, viewing with indifferent eye the tokens of Confederate valor, and slighting the graves of Confederate dead, would counsel no oblation save at the shrine of Mammon." Charles C. Jones Jr., "Sons of Confederate Veterans," *Southern Historical Society Papers* 18 (1890): 92–97.

47. Lewis P. Jones, *Stormy Petrel: N. G. Gonzales and His State* (Columbia: University of South Carolina Press, 1973), 165.

48. Foster, *Ghosts of the Confederacy*, 52.

49. *The State* (Columbia), May 14, 1891.

50. Ibid.

51. Ibid., May 15, 1891.

52. *Echoes From 'Hampton Day,' May 14th, 1895. Compiled and Arranged for the Camp* (Charleston: Walker, Evans, and Cogswell, 1895), 4–7.

53. Ibid., 8–10.

54. Ibid., 12–14.

55. Ibid., 18.

56. College of Charleston professor Frederick Porcher spoke of this in his 1850 eulogy to John C. Calhoun. Porcher considered Calhoun a "great man" and added that "Greatness is essentially conservative." To the conservative, "existing institutions are sacred in his eyes. He never seeks to change them, but to apply those wholesome correctives which necessity may require, and circumstances indicate." Porcher concluded this thought by reminding fellow conservatives that "he honours himself in honouring the wisdom of his ancestors."

57. *College and Collegians. An Address Delivered by W. D. Porter, Before the Alumni Association of the College of Charleston, on Commencement Day, 28th March, 1871* (Charleston: Walker, Evans, and Cogswell, 1871), 5.

58. *Address delivered before the South Carolina Historical Society on their Twenty-First Anniversary, May 19, 1876, by William J. Rivers* (Charleston: The News and Courier Job Presses, 1876), 24.

59. Ibid., 22.

60. In January 1890, however, Hampton supported a bill that would provide federal funds for African Americans seeking to emigrate. He "recognized as fully as anyone the political rights of our colored fellow-citizens," but believed further in the "maintenance of good government and the perpetuity of republican institutions. . . . In my judgement, these can only be maintained in their integrity by our own race." See Wade Hampton, *Negro Emigration. Speech in the Senate of the United States, Thursday, January 30, 1890* (Washington: n.p., 1890), 5–8.

61. For Southern conservatives like Hampton, "home rule" was often synonymous with elite rule. In the heat of the conservative struggle against Tillman in the late 1880s, Edward McCrady Jr. captured this belief by insisting that "the public business is ours!" See *Address Delivered to the South Carolina Military Academy, at the Annual Commencement, German Military Hall, Charleston, S.C., July 27th, 1887. By Gen'l Edward McCrady* (Charleston: Walker, Evans, and Cogswell, 1887), 4.

62. Ibid., 32–34.

63. Ibid., 39–40, 44.

64. Simkins, *Pitchfork Ben Tillman*, 291.

65. "Hampton," *The State*, May 15, 1895, 4. White South Carolinians reached

an accord on their political state by disfranchising black voters through an 1895 constitutional convention. Conservative South Carolinians gave ground—it was not a stretch to concede to racism—and helped write the constitution to keep it from running afoul of the Fifteenth Amendment, as it was interpreted in the 1890s.

66. George Brown Tindall, "The Campaign for the Disfranchisement of Negroes in South Carolina," *Journal of Southern History* 15 (May 1949): 212–34. The idea of eliminating, or at least containing, the black vote did not originate with the Tillmanites, of course. In the early 1880s, Hampton's allies in the assembly gerrymandered Low Country districts across county lines to confine the black vote to a few districts. Clark, *Francis Warrington Dawson,* 93–96.

67. "Hampton of South Carolina," *The State,* April 12, 1902. Columbia's *The State* and the *Charleston News and Courier* both ran black borders around the paper and through the columns signifying their grief. *The State* found deep significance in the coincidence of Hampton's dying on the twenty-fifth anniversary of his taking the reins of power from the Reconstruction government of Daniel Chamberlain. Not since Thomas Jefferson and John Adams both died on July 4, 1826, had the nation witnessed such a historic and meaningful coincidence, the paper reported.

68. *Final Report of the Commission to Provide For A Monument to the Memory of Wade Hampton* (Columbia: Gonzalez and Bryan, 1906–1907), 16–17.

69. *The State,* November 20, 1906, 1, 4.

70. "Home of the Hamptons," *The State,* November 20, 1906, 10.

71. *Confederate Veteran,* March 1918, 127.

72. Ibid., 130.

73. "Governor Proclaims Hampton Day," *The State,* December 12, 1926, 11.

74. *The State,* December 14, 1926, 4.

75. Ibid., December 15, 1926, 1. The bank advertisement can be found in the *News and Courier,* December 14, 1926, 9.

76. Ibid., December 14, 1926, 10.

77. "Negro Red Shirt to Drive Carriage," *Columbia Record,* December 13, 1926, 1.

78. *The State,* December 15, 1926, 1. South Carolinians eventually erected a statue to Benjamin R. Tillman in 1940. Unlike the stately equestrian pose for Hampton, Tillman is depicted in plain clothes, striking a stubborn pose. Reception to the Tillman statue was dramatically different from the ceremonies devoted to Hampton. South Carolinian and Roosevelt cabinet official James Byrnes gave the keynote address in which he lauded Tillman as the "first New Dealer" by his efforts to use the power of the state government to benefit struggling farmers. *The State* could not resist noting that "Heavy gray clouds . . . threatened" the proceedings (May 2, 1940). The *Charleston News and Courier,* meanwhile, long fierce in its opposition

to Roosevelt, called the reference to Tillman as a New Deal governor "scarcely an original complement." At the same time, the *News and Courier* half-wished that Tillman was still around to "'arouse the masses,' though again he might crush us and those of our way of thinking" (May 2, 1940). Both papers estimated that three thousand attended.

79. V. O. Key Jr., *Southern Politics in State and Nation* (New York: Alfred A. Knopf, 1949), 139–45.

80. "Cotton Ed Dons a Red Shirt, Addresses Red Shirt Crowd," *Charleston News and Courier,* August 31, 1938, 1.

81. Patricia Sullivan's *Days of Hope: Race and Democracy in the New Deal Era* (Chapel Hill and London: University of North Carolina Press, 1996) is the best among the recent scholarship on the struggle to end black disfranchisement in the 1930s.

82. "No One Hinders Them" and "The Signs Are Ominous," *Charleston News and Courier,* September 1, 1938, 4. On the same page as these articles was a letter from W. E. Pearson of Branchville. Pearson expressed his joy at seeing the "spirit of Wade Hampton" at the local voting booths. "There were a lot of men wearing red shirts at the election pools here today," he noted. "I am glad to see that spirit revived. Any man not having an independent spirit is very little better than a slave. My mind is still with the spirit of '76." *The State,* meanwhile, took a less-favorable stand on Smith's tactics and victory. "The Negro issue—if it is an issue—helped Senator Smith," the paper explained, adding insightfully, "But it did not help South Carolina." See "First Thoughts on the Victory of Senator Smith," *The State,* September 1, 1938, 6.

83. Paul H. Buck, *The Road to Reunion, 1865–1900* (Boston and Toronto: Little, Brown, 1937), 248.

84. Quoted in George B. Tindall, *South Carolina Negroes, 1877–1900* (Columbia: University of South Carolina Press, 1952), 306.

Four

"These Few Gray-Haired, Battle-Scarred Veterans"

Confederate Army Reunions in Georgia, 1885-95

Keith S. Bohannon

The 1880s and 1890s witnessed large numbers of white Southerners participating in public ceremonies honoring the memory of the Confederacy. Some of the most ubiquitous activities were the reunions held for Confederate army veterans, events that fulfilled multiple needs in a region beset with political unrest and economic change. The social aspect of these gatherings was important; the old soldiers "delighted to meet in annual reunion to perpetuate the memory of their dead comrades, and to feel the kindly grasp of the hand of those who fought shoulder to shoulder with them." Reunions also helped communities preserve a collective memory of the past, honor local veterans, and teach postwar generations about Confederate history and the sacrifices of their elders.[1]

Remembering and celebrating the Civil War was the major theme at Confederate reunions, but not the only one. Politicians frequently spoke at reunions to gain favor with voters and promote the "New South" ideal of a bustling and wealthy region based on commerce, industry, and scientific agriculture. Although the majority of reunion speakers supported the racial and political orthodoxy of the post–Civil War South, evidence indicates that spokesmen from the Farmer's Alliance or Populist Party were sometimes present to articulate their goals of political and economic change.

This essay focuses on Confederate army reunions held in Georgia during the months of July and August in the years 1885 to 1895. The *Atlanta Constitution*, one of Georgia's most widely circulated newspapers, reported on ninety-two reunions during this period. There were undoubtedly many gatherings of veterans that did not appear in the

Constitution; the majority of those mentioned here took place in Atlanta or small towns located in central and northern Georgia.

Most Georgia Confederate veterans began forming survivors' associations in the mid- and late 1880s. These were probably the earliest organizations to enroll large numbers of rank-and-file ex-Confederates, preceding by several years the better-known United Confederate Veterans. The latter group, formed in 1889, did not gain significant numbers of members until the early 1890s.[2]

Some Confederate survivors' associations enrolled veterans living in a specific locale (e.g., the Sumter County or Crawford County Veterans Association), but most included only members of a specific army unit. Twenty-seven Confederate army commands, including twenty-three infantry units, two cavalry units, and two artillery units, held the reunions examined in this essay. Sixteen of these units served in the Army of Northern Virginia, while eleven fought in the Army of Tennessee.

Annual reunions were the main activities of the survivors' associations. Most gatherings were held in July and August, often coinciding with the anniversaries of important battles. Survivors of the 7th and 8th Georgia Infantry Regiments held their reunions on July 21 to commemorate the battle of First Manassas, where both commands took heavy casualties. The 42d Georgia held its reunions on July 22, the anniversary of the unit's gallant and costly charge in the 1864 battle of Atlanta. There was also a practical reason to hold reunions in July, as pointed out by the popular newspaper columnist Charles H. Smith, better known as "Bill Arp." "Arp" reminded readers that July was "about the time when the crops are laid by and there is plenty of green corn and tomatoes, and spring chickens and sheep, meat and ripe fruit."[3]

Confederate infantry veterans held reunions in different locales every year, usually in the towns where their unit's individual companies had been raised. Since most reunions involved hundreds if not thousands of participants, survivors' associations and local planning committees began preparations many weeks before an event. The organizers' myriad tasks included arranging lodging and contacting railroads to obtain discounted rates for the transportation of ex-soldiers and their families.[4]

Reunion planners often invited prominent individuals to speak, including politicians and ex-Confederate officers such as John Brown Gordon, Clement Evans, and James Longstreet. Longstreet had been highly controversial in the post–Civil War South, but he remained popular among the rank-and-file veterans. When survivors of the 2d Georgia Infantry met in Holland Springs, Georgia, in 1886, they ended their reunion by traveling as a group to visit Longstreet at his home in nearby Gainesville. Three years later at a Confederate reunion in At-

(handwritten margin note: Why write about the aftermath if the title is about Civil War.)

lanta, a reporter noted how battle-scarred veterans hovered around Longstreet and "hung upon every word the old general uttered, and in their eyes . . . [and in] the expression of their faces could be seen the deep respect and true love they bear for their old commander."[5]

The presence of prominent former Confederates like Longstreet was only one of the attractions of veterans' reunions; large barbecues and picnic dinners were another. Local planners often canvassed their counties for weeks before an event asking for contributions of foodstuffs or money. Organizers of the 1886 combined reunion of the 5th and 13th Georgia Regiments in Upson County obtained seventy-one carcasses of pigs and sheep to barbecue, as well as "carloads of bread, cakes, chickens, etc." The planners assured the press that there would be plenty to feed the immense crowds. Citizens in Morgan County also made extensive preparations for the 3d Georgia's 1888 reunion, raising $1,000, obtaining 150 pig and sheep carcasses, acquiring the services of a band from Augusta, and erecting a bandstand.[6]

Planning for large crowds at reunions was important. Throngs of people began pouring into towns early in the morning on the day of a reunion. On the morning of an 1889 reunion in Carollton, the main avenues into town "presented a continuous line of moving humanity—some in wagons, some in buggies, some on horseback and many a-foot." When the 30th Georgia held its reunion in Stockbridge later that summer, the roads became crowded with "carry alls, spring wagons and buggies, filled with men, women, happy children, and sleeping babies." Trains arriving later brought more people from Atlanta and the surrounding towns.[7]

Veterans traveling to reunions by train usually received an official greeting upon their arrival at the town hosting the event. When members of the 3d Georgia Infantry got to Eatonton for their 1887 reunion, a large concourse of people greeted them. The assembly included a local brass band, a military company known as the "Putnam Rifles," and a "baby cannon" firing salutes.[8]

After forming in ranks at the local train station, veterans often received badges identifying their unit and listing the battles in which it had fought. These badges helped identify the veterans among the throngs of people. At least ten of the reunions examined in this essay attracted crowds estimated at between five thousand and ten thousand individuals, while the smallest ones involved at least several hundred people.

Reunions often drew the largest crowds ever seen in towns like Lithonia, Adairsville, Powder Springs, and Acworth. Many events drew several hundred veterans, although individual regimental survivors' associations usually counted only between 50 and 150 members at a reunion. The small size of these groups provided vivid testimony of the toll taken by the war and intervening years on regiments that had numbered between 1,000 and 1,200 men in 1861.[9]

At many reunions, the veterans marched in ranks from the train station to an open grove or churchyard, where they mingled with others. (Reunions held in Atlanta often took place at popular locales such as Grant Park or Ponce de Leon Springs.) On other occasions, the veterans went first to a courthouse or academy. Once inside they started the day's activities with prayer and hymns followed by a message of welcome to the veterans from the mayor or another local official.[10]

The survivors' associations usually began their annual business meetings after thanking local people for their hospitality. The meetings always involved a series of mundane procedures: reading letters of regret from members or invited speakers who could not attend, going over the minutes of the last year's meeting or the association's constitution and by-laws, thanking railroads and hotels for reduced rates offered to veterans and their families, and planning the location of the next reunion. Elections of association officers usually resulted in the unit's wartime officers retaining positions of leadership and authority within the veterans' organizations.[11]

Sometimes business meetings included a reading of unit muster rolls. As the association secretary read the rolls, noted a reporter watching one reunion, there was a long gap between the "heres." The veterans devoted special attention, usually in the form of resolutions or memorials, to those who had died since the last reunion. Association officers often asked veterans for assistance in securing complete lists of the men who had served in their companies; such requests reveal the widespread destruction or loss of Confederate regimental records during the war.

Speeches delivered by association officers usually followed the handling of official business. The oration of ex-governor and former Confederate colonel James M. Smith at the 13th Georgia's 1885 reunion was typical of the talks delivered at countless reunions. Smith spoke at length "of the affection that existed between the members, of the trials and privations they had undergone together, of the many brotherly kindnesses that had been granted by each other" and related a number of wartime anecdotes. Speakers such as Smith seldom if ever referred to topics such as desertion, demoralization in the Confederate army and on the home front, incompetent officers, and poor battlefield performances by their units.[12]

Veterans of the ill-fated Army of Tennessee sometimes mentioned battlefield defeats in their reunion speeches but invariably defended the actions of their individual units. An ex-officer from the 39th Georgia recalled the May 1863 Confederate defeat at Baker's Creek, Mississippi, by reminding his comrades how they "stood shoulder to shoulder a single regiment, and received the charge of a whole division of Federals." Although the regiment broke and ran at Baker's Creek, surrendered at Vicksburg, and performed poorly in several engagements during the Atlanta Campaign, the former officer insisted that "the 39th never failed to come up to the full measure of her duty . . . not one page of her history we would hide from review."[13]

Other western theater veterans emphasized the heroism of individual officers, rather than focusing on their unit's questionable performance in an engagement. At the battle of Resaca, Georgia, on May 15, 1864, Brig. Gen. Marcellus Stovall's brigade, which included the 42d Georgia Infantry, fell apart in an attack when dense thickets threw the command into a state of confusion. Twelve days afterward, one of Stovall's men admitted to his wife that the brigade's "reputation suffered in the fight at Resaca." Twenty-four years later, a speaker at an 1888 reunion praised the 42d's "impetuous charge" at Resaca. He made no mention of the thickets or the unit's collapse, but instead recalled how the field officers of the 42d "covered themselves in glory," several of them falling dead or wounded.[14]

Two months after Resaca, the 42d Georgia participated in an attack during the July 22, 1864, battle of Atlanta, briefly occupying a section of the Union line. Orators at the 42d Georgia's reunions always spoke at length about this assault, praising the gallant performance of the regiment and its commanding officer. Their accounts of the battle invariably rely on a selective recounting of the events; they never mention the eventual retreat of the Confederates or the overall failure of the Southern army to lift Maj. Gen. William T. Sherman's investment of the city.[15]

References to comrades who fell in battle often elicited emotional reactions from veterans. An observer at the 52d Georgia's 1885 reunion noted how the "old battle-scarred confederates . . . would cry like children" at mention of the dead. Tributes honored the fallen in reverential or religious terms. Captain James W. Butts reminded other veterans of the 4th Georgia Infantry that their "four years of heroic endeavor" resulted in "a host of martyrs" from the regiment's ranks. L. L. Knight paid tribute to Brig. Gen. Thomas R. R. Cobb, slain at Fredericksburg in December 1862, by saying that Cobb resembled "Joshua in his courage, . . . St. Paul in the logic of his eloquence and Stephen in the triumph of his martyrdom."[16]

The presence at reunions of regimental flags, torn and blackened in battle, elicited almost as much emotion from veterans as did the mention of dead comrades. When an ex-Confederate officer living in Texas sent the battle flag he had hidden on his body at the surrender back to Georgia, a reporter noted that "one might have expected to hear an old time yell at the sight of that banner, but the boys were too much moved toward tears for such a demonstration." Flags held a prominent place at reunions, appearing at the head of processions and draped behind speakers' stands. The tattered appearance of these banners, like the empty sleeves and pants legs of many veterans, provided graphic reminders of the terrible violence and cost of war.[17]

Confederate battle flags were not the only banners at veterans' reunions. The speakers' rostrums often also included United States flags. At an 1885 reunion, the veterans of the 13th Georgia Infantry draped behind their speaker's stand a captured battle flag that had belonged to the 119th New York Infantry. During the course of the reunion the Georgians appointed a committee to return the Union banner to the former colonel of the 119th.[18]

The return of the 119th New York's flag was indicative of the reunification sentiments felt by many white Southerners in the 1880s. The passage of years, the 1884 election of Democrat Grover Cleveland to the presidency, and the growing signs of respect shown to the former Confederates by Northern veterans and publishers made it easier for Southerners to accept sectional reconciliation. "By the mid-eighties," states Gaines Foster, "most southerners had decided to build a future within a reunited nation."[19]

Confederate veterans also displayed their willingness to "clasp hands across the bloody chasm" by sending delegates to Northern reunions and inviting Union veterans to Southern reunions. Veterans of the 3d Georgia Infantry seemed particularly attached to those of the 9th New York Infantry (also known as Hawkins's Zouaves), the two units having faced each other on several battlefields during the war. On at least two occasions, 9th New York veterans appeared at 3d Georgia reunions. At the 3d Georgia's July 1889 reunion, a crowd of two thousand people greeted a delegation of New Yorkers at the train station in Fort Valley, Georgia. The welcome extended by the Georgians to the New Yorkers, noted a reporter, was "grand, earnest, [and] sympathetic; being filled with the friendliest feelings and fondest embraces, so realistic of the strong brotherly love now existing between the north and the south." The ladies of the New York delegation received a particularly warm welcome from "the fairest ladies and daughters of the sunny south."[20]

Two years later, at the 3d Georgia's reunion in Athens, a former officer of the 9th New York told the crowds that "the northern soldiers entertained the warmest feelings for the confederate veterans and that the slings and slurs from one side to the other never came from the soldiers who met face to face on the field of battle, but from the extreme rear guard." Fanciful statements like this exemplify much of the reconciliation discourse. As Gaines Foster has noted, "time and a tendency while reminiscing to downplay the war's violence and gore . . . helped center the veteran's memory on the courage and camaraderie of battle rather than on its political implications or bloody consequences."

Northern veterans speaking at Confederate reunions offered effusive praise of the South and its white inhabitants but remained silent on issues of substance that might prove controversial. A former Union officer who had moved to north Georgia after the war told how he had been attracted by the spirit of Southerners and the region's "genial clime and boundless resources." The Northerner "spoke feelingly of the generous sympathies between true soldiers, and concluded amidst the hearty cheers of the [Southern] veterans." Another northerner who had moved to Atlanta stated that he found the "southern people . . . to be as hospitable, chivalric and kind as it was possible for any people to be."[21]

Southern speakers likewise made friendly overtures toward their former enemies. At a thirtieth anniversary celebration of the battle of Atlanta attended by Confederate and Union veterans, a Southern clergyman noted how "the blue and gray meet on common ground and shake hands in common fellowship." He continued by praising the Confederate and Union soldiers for having "honest motives and patriotic principles." Georgia congressman Judson C. Clements, himself a Confederate veteran, pointed out at an 1889 reunion how the Northern veterans had "joined hands with their unfortunate but brave Confederate comrades" in rebuilding the South after the war.

Although many ex-Confederates like Clements seemed to welcome sectional reconciliation, Michael Kammen is correct in claiming that "bitterness, vindictiveness, and resentment lay just beneath the surface" in late-nineteenth-century Southern society. Relations between North and South remained fragile, especially when attention shifted from honoring the common soldiers to divisive topics such as the causes and results of the war, the Reconstruction years, and the place of African Americans in white Southern society. Confederate veterans often voiced their opinions on these issues at reunions.[22]

The majority of Southern veterans passionately proclaimed that the Confederacy had gone to war over the issue of states' rights. At an 1887 reunion of the 42d Georgia, Judge William L. Calhoun quoted ex-Confederate president Jefferson Davis on this issue. "The southern states," Calhoun said, "had rightfully the power to withdraw from a union into which they had, as sovereign communities, voluntarily entered." The denial of that right "was a violation of the letter and spirit of the compact between the states, and that the war waged by the federal government against the seceding states was in disregard of the limitation of the constitution and destructive of the principles of the Declaration of Independence."[23]

Other veterans enunciated their belief in states' rights in their own words. J. D. Stewart told his comrades that the Confederacy had fought for "Freedom's cause; a struggle for constitutional rights against aggression, oppression and wrong." S. W. Harris proclaimed that Confederates "fought for the right of local self government, for country and for home." A former private from the 7th Georgia exclaimed that "the south is and always has been opposed to centralization of government." John B. Gordon, one of the South's foremost spokesmen of reconciliation, declared that he was "reared with the idea that liberty in a government like ours is best preserved by restraining central power and giving to the states . . . all the rights which are not distinctly and absolutely conferred upon the central power."[24]

Few reunion speakers attributed the war directly to slavery, but some referred to the threat Northern abolitionism had posed to antebellum Southern society. One veteran remembered how "a cloud charged with the fierce power of sectional hate and fanaticism" loomed in the North in 1861, threatening "the civilization of the south and the purity of our blood and the integrity of our race." Judson Clements made an oblique reference to William H. Seward's famed speech by declaring that the war had been "a grand and immortal protest" by white Southerners against "the oppressive usurpation of a people who would recognize as higher law . . . their ambition and unrighteous prejudices."[25]

Captain Charles K. Maddox of the 7th Georgia was one of a handful of reunion speakers who linked secession with the preservation of slavery. In a "widely praised" speech given in Decatur in 1890, Maddox declared that secession had not been "a question of the union" but "simply fought about 'niggers'!" He reminded listeners that "we fought for the supremacy of the white race in America; for civilization against abolition theories; the cause of truth against abolition prejudice; and the cause of common sense against the foulest errors that will ever astonish posterity."[26]

Ex-Confederates attributed their ultimate defeat solely to the overwhelming force of the Federal armies. Henry L. Wilson stated that "we were overpowered and forced to surrender," and added that "genius and valor went down before brute force." Captain Maddox defiantly noted that his regiment had been ordered to surrender "not by the enemy, but by our own officers." The 7th Georgia, he declared, "had surrendered but was never whipped."[27]

Reconstruction, or "twenty years of Republican misrule," as one veteran called it, presented a "far different struggle" than the war to white Southerners. Many reunion speakers referred to the Reconstruction era in terms more grim than those used to recount the war. Henry Wilson told listeners how the defeated Confederate soldiers had returned home "penniless and without means to begin business" with "nothing but gloom . . . to be seen." Wilson reminded his audience of how "the very horizon seemed to hang over us[,] a dark cloud ready to drop and forever cover our despondency."

Captain Butts noted that during Reconstruction "there was no touch of a comrade's elbow renewing confidence, no thrill of victory atoning for perils, no fever of patriotism inspiring devotion, none of the fiercer passions of war even, to nerve resolutions." During Reconstruction, "the individual heroism of patient endurance" had succeeded "the collective heroism of action of the war." Butts, like most reunion speakers, made no mention of the activities of ex-Confederates in such groups as the Ku Klux Klan. One orator who did refer to that organization claimed that it included not Confederate soldiers but "those that stayed at home and became brave after the enemy was gone."[28]

Sometimes speakers praised "southern character in defeat" even over valor exhibited during the war. At an 1894 Confederate reunion attended by a large contingent of Northern veterans, Georgia governor and ex-Confederate Henry D. McDaniel claimed that "veterans of the confederate armies have a prouder title, if that were possible, to the gratitude and admiration of posterity." McDaniel explained that during Reconstruction "partisan hate offered prescription instead of reconciliation, and sought to degrade states into provinces." White Georgians had "roused themselves to the danger, and maintained their rights under the constitution." Exhibiting a "spirit of forebearance and loyalty to the pledges of their leaders and the principles of their fathers," former Confederates had regained control of their state governments and "rebuilt the social fabric, restored material prosperity, and secured to every citizen of whatever race or color all the rights for which he is entitled."[29]

The vast majority of ex-Confederates believed African Americans were not entitled to vote. Attempts by Northern congressmen in the late 1880s and early 1890s to protect black voters in the South outraged Confederate veterans, and their bitterness emerged at reunions. Orators such as Capt. W. D. Ellis seldom criticized Union army veterans or the Northern people, but focused their philippics on "pusillanimous and cowardly politicians." Georgia congressman Judson Clements, speaking to a large reunion crowd that included Northern veterans, avowed that "all the animosity existing now was that kept up by small politicians who had never commenced to fight until peace gave him a safe place from which to assail their brave fellow-citizens."[30]

Henry Cabot Lodge's so-called force bill, introduced in the U.S. Congress in June 1890 to protect Southern black voters from state disfranchisement measures, exacerbated the anger of former Confederates against Northern politicians. (C. Vann Woodward has noted that the Lodge bill "caused more alarm and excitement in the South than any Federal measure since 1877.") Although ex-Confederates once again considered themselves American citizens, they staunchly opposed federal interference in Southern race relations. Charles Maddox noted that "when I am told that the flag means 'nigger on top,' and that I can't stand under it and cast my ballot without asking a nigger's permission, then I think it is time to rescue the flag from the infamy that threatens it."[31]

Some reunion orators responded to Northern meddling in Southern race relations by calling for continued solidarity among white Southerners. S. W. Harris noted that "upon every hand we are met with the gravest problem that a people ever had to face—the problems of the races." Harris told his listeners to teach future generations "to cling to the traditions of your race." Captain Maddox proclaimed that "we laid down our arms, but we did not lay down our principles, the fight for civilization must go on. . . . Whites alone, must rule America."[32]

Despite racist oratory, African Americans occasionally appeared at Confederate reunions. Although their reasons for attending are unknown, some were perhaps drawn by lifelong associations with former masters. Tom Phillips, a former slave of Col. John B. Wilcoxon, supposedly insisted on accompanying Wilcoxon to the 1893 reunion of Phillips's Legion. A reporter claimed that "if there was an old soldier who enjoyed the day more than this devoted servant, he was not to be found."[33]

Two elderly black men attended an 1886 reunion of the 42d Georgia. When a reporter asked one of the men if he was a veteran, the man replied, "Guess I is, young master. Yer see I went fru de wah wid old marster, an' I tell you I had some skerry speriences." After relating a story about the propensity of Confederate soldiers for stealing chickens, the elderly black man asked the reporter to "gimme a dime to git er watermillion." The presence of former slaves at Confederate reunions reinforced the Lost Cause tradition of the "faithful old-time negro" who knew his "proper place" in postbellum Southern society.[34]

Other African Americans attending reunions assisted in the preparation of food or provided musical entertainment, perhaps for monetary compensation. Black men at the 1885 reunion of the 52d Georgia in Dahlonega received thanks for assisting, in the rain, with transferring tables to the college chapel, with barbecuing, and with transporting ladies in hacks and carriages. At a 23d Georgia reunion in Emerson, the regiment's survivors formed in ranks and marched to the grandstand "preceded by the Acworth colored band." In several other instances, bands composed of African Americans played music at reunions.[35]

An eagerly awaited event at every reunion occurred when the participants broke for dinner. (One veteran said he could talk about his regiment all day long but "can't talk against a barbeque.") The meals involved staggering amounts of barbecued meats and other foodstuffs. The 7th Georgia's 1887 reunion meal included five beef cattle, eight sheep, five hogs, two thousand chickens, plus "breads, butter, milk and coffee." At the 1892 reunion of the 3d Georgia Infantry, four tables totaling a thousand feet in length groaned under the weight of over a hundred gallons of hash and 125 barbecued pigs and sheep.[36]

The methods of serving meals varied. The veterans of Cobb's and Phillips's Legions allowed ladies to seat themselves first, whereas the 3d Georgia reunion featured a more chaotic "grab-as-grab-can method of serving." At a reunion of the 23d Georgia, the veterans formed in line and marched to tables covered with "a bounteous repast." When given the order to charge, the old soldiers "obeyed the order with more alacrity than they did a similar order given them on the attack of Fort Harrison."

One of the biggest meal disasters occurred at a 7th Georgia reunion in July 1889 in Carrollton attended by more than seven thousand people. As Gov. John B. Gordon finished a lengthy oration, "a dark cloud came rapid[ly] from the west, and before the crowd had dispersed, the rain fell in torrents." Although "rapacious hands" carried off most of the barbecued meats, the "bread, cakes, pies, pickles, preserves, and numberless dainties, contributed with loving zeal by our noble women," turned into a "conglomerate mass of mush." Most of the food ended up being "given away to the hogs."[37]

Fortunately disasters like that which befell the 7th Georgia were rare. At most reunions, informal mingling followed the afternoon feast. A member of the 30th Georgia remembered how "it was pleasant to talk over old times, to meet in social converse, to recount the many interesting incidents of the war, to crack jokes and to fight once more." Veterans of the 4th Georgia Infantry talked of "half forgotten incidents—the muffled drum beat that marked the passage of a corps, or the wild rebel yell that marked the passage of Stonewall Jackson." Sometimes the old soldiers organized after-dinner activities. The veterans of Savannah's Oglethorpe Light Infantry had shooting matches, as did the men of the 42d Georgia. Members of the 42d also had a "jumping match" at their 1886 reunion that was undoubtedly a sight worth seeing. It featured Capt. James M. Summers, who tipped the scales at 290 pounds, and Sgt. Moses Martin, who had lost a leg at the Battle of Bentonville.[38]

Following dinner and other activities, the veterans and crowds often turned their attention again to speeches, many of them overtly political in nature. Gaines Foster has written that the United Confederate Veterans prohibited discussion of politics, but added that veterans sometimes violated the ban. No such ban existed at the reunions of Confederate Survivors' Associations, which provided ideal speaking engagements for office seekers and those hoping to stay in office. Many of the politicians were Confederate veterans. Colonel Tyler M. Peeples drew tumultuous cheers at an 1894 Atlanta reunion when he defended "the idea of the veteran office seeker" and "declared that the old soldier racket was not dead." The speeches of such politicians almost always mixed paeans to the Southern soldier and the Lost Cause with discussions of contemporary issues and appeals for votes.[39]

Newspaper accounts indicate that many office seekers were successful in gaining support at reunions. At least two politicians spoke at the 1886 reunion of the 5th and 13th Georgia Regiments. The crowds frequently drowned out one of them, John B. Gordon, with applause and shouts of "three cheers for our next governor." The other orator, a congressman from Macon, convinced his listeners that he should represent them in Washington. Those running for lesser state offices also had success. At a reunion in Crawford County, Col. R. T. Nesbitt, the state agriculturist, convinced listeners that "he was the right man . . . in the right place" and that he would make the Agricultural Department "a source of revenue to the state and of incalculable benefit to the farmers."[40]

Politicians often attempted to win the votes of former soldiers by addressing issues that directly affected them, including support to needy Confederate veterans and their families. Veterans of the 13th Georgia Infantry decided at an 1885 reunion that each Georgia county should establish a league to protect maimed soldiers and soldiers' widows and orphans, claiming that "our strong right arms and liberal hearts shall be a substitute for the pension bureau." Others believed the state should provide pensions, as the federal government did for Union veterans. Captain Joseph W. Woodward told comrades from the 52d Georgia that the state should "pension every one of her soldiers who could give good testimony that they were in good standing at the close of the war."[41]

The great expansion of the federal pension system in the late 1880s and early 1890s undoubtedly rankled many ex-Confederates. Henry W. Grady, editor of the *Atlanta Constitution* and promoter of the New South, tapped into this frustration during an 1889 speech in Americus, Georgia. After praising the courage and heroism of the Confederate soldier, Grady focused his considerable oratorical skill on attacking organized efforts in the North "being made to pension every man who had even a visiting acquaintance with the Union Army during the late war." Grady charged that expanding the federal pension system would "sweep away the surplus of the Federal Treasury, and thus create a demand for a higher and more burdensome tariff." Listeners greeted Grady's oration with immense cheering and a contingent of veterans pinned a fragment of a Confederate battle flag and regimental badge to his breast.[42]

Georgia politicians could not ignore the requests of Confederate veterans for pensions, despite the penchant for strict economy that marked state governments in the post-Reconstruction South. In December 1888, the Georgia legislature provided annual payments to veterans based on their level of disability. As R. B. Rosenburg has pointed out, Georgia's pension payments totaled $5 million by 1899, "representing on average more than 10 percent of the state's total expenditures during the decade."[43]

Many old soldiers also believed the state should open a home for aging and infirm Confederate veterans. This idea may have originated at an August 1887 reunion of the 18th Georgia Infantry, where veterans formed a committee to act with other survivors' associations to establish a Georgia Confederate veterans' home. Another meeting that month in Atlanta involving the Atlanta Ladies Memorial Association and the Fulton County Confederate Veterans Association resulted in a promise of support for a home.[44]

By 1889 Grady was the most important advocate of a Georgia soldiers' home. Grady's involvement with the home stemmed not only from philanthropic desires and a loyalty to the memory of the Lost Cause, but also from a desire to foster his own image. Grady also probably hoped that a campaign to build a soldier's home would win over rural Confederate veterans and their sons, many of whom had joined the growing Farmers' Alliance movement. Building the home might convince these "wool hat boys," as the state's rural yeomen were often called, that Georgia's New South advocates had common interests with the state's farmers.[45]

Despite Grady's death in December 1889 and a series of construction delays and cost overruns, builders completed the Confederate soldiers' home by mid-July 1891, and that summer legislators introduced a bill in the Georgia legislature requiring the state to maintain it. At the same time, several prominent Atlanta veterans began traveling across the state to muster support among veterans for the home. Judge Robert L. Rogers and Capt. John Milledge, the state librarian, spoke at numerous regimental reunions, urging veterans to support the soldiers' home and the pending bill regarding its administration.

Newspaper reports claimed that veterans who heard Rogers and Milledge heartily endorsed state maintenance of the soldiers' home. Despite such support, some legislators opposed state maintenance of the home. Many of these opponents resented the Atlantans who had been the home's strongest advocates; others worried about the home's cost and argued that veterans would rather remain with their families and receive additional pension benefits. Opposition killed the 1891 bill, as well as two later ones. It was 1901 before the state legislature finally voted to accept the home.[46]

Larger issues than the soldiers' home or pensions sometimes occupied the attention of reunion speakers. The Farmer's Alliance and the People's or Populist Party drew many thousands of Georgia's struggling yeomen and small planters into their ranks in the late 1880s and early 1890s. Circumstantial evidence indicates that speakers who were probably Alliance men and Populists articulated the frustrations of these organizations at reunions. At an 1892 gathering in Dahlonega, J. W. Robertson spoke about "the railroads demanding a 25 per cent increase on freight rates, which in Georgia alone, would amount to over $4,000,000." Although the newspaper report failed to elaborate on Robertson's speech, exorbitant railroad rates were a major complaint of the agrarian radicals, and public ownership of the roads was a plank of the Populist Party platform. Another veteran speaking at an 1892 reunion railed against the "centralization of capital," undoubtedly a reference to the Populist disdain for banking corporations and trusts.[47]

When Georgia Populists ran their first candidates for office in the summer of 1892, Democratic leaders in the state went on the attack. Senator John B. Gordon, notes Barton Shaw, was one of the Democratic orators who "seemed to be everywhere, alternately chiding the Populists and crying for a Democratic victory." At a Confederate reunion in southwest Georgia in mid-July 1892, Gordon "spoke with great force" in front of thousands of listeners, "appealing for unity of the white race and asking . . . if the people could expect anything but overwhelming ignominy and shame if we divide among ourselves." Race baiting by Gordon and other Democrats, along with tactics that included intimidation and violence, contributed to the Populist defeat that fall in the polls.[48]

Many conservative Democrats like Gordon utilized the Confederate tradition not only to defeat groups like the Populists, but also to promote their vision of a New South, a region with an economic and social order based on commerce, industry, and scientific agriculture. Praise for the New South creed became a theme at reunions alongside tributes to the Confederate soldier and his chieftains. Judge Walter C. Beeks exemplified this dual allegiance in an 1891 keynote address at a reunion of the 44th Georgia Infantry. After eulogizing the Confederate soldier and his cause and claiming that Robert E. Lee and "Stonewall" Jackson had been two "of the grandest men the world has ever known," Beeks concluded by lauding "the new south, her industries and her patriotic people." However, some veterans disagreed with spokesmen like Beeks about the virtues of the New South. Roland B. Hall criticized the "busy haunts of trade where mammon rules the hour," and urged his comrades to hold their reunions elsewhere.[49]

Confederate veterans exercised great power in Georgia's government and economy in the 1880s and 1890s, yet many worried about their legacy and believed they must educate younger generations about the Confederate tradition. The alternative, the old soldiers warned, was to let Northern writers who "vehemently utter vile misrepresentations, gross exaggerations, and malicious denunciations" distort the facts and "debouch the pages of history with infamous falsehood." Reverend J. William Jones told veterans at an 1889 meeting in the state capitol in Atlanta that "southern schools should use southern histories, and related several instances of the perversions of sentiment and truth by books that were brought from the north."

Numerous veterans voiced concerns about the image of the Confederate soldier presented by Northerners. Judge Calhoun urged his comrades to "make a record of our deeds and preserve their memory that our sons know that they are not the descendants of traitors and cowards, but of patriotic and chivalrous sires." S. W. Harris echoed Calhoun, instructing fellow veterans of the 7th Georgia Infantry to "teach your children that their sires were neither rebels nor traitors, but that they went forth at the call of the sovereign state of Georgia to do battle in Georgia's cause."[50]

Ironically, some Confederate veterans turned to the U.S. government as the arbiter of truth. John B. Gordon lashed out at those who used "rancorous sectional malice to misrepresent the facts and debouch the pages of history with infamous falsehood," but assured his audience of veterans that "the 'Records' were safe in the Capitol at Washington." Judge Robert Falligant told members of the Savannah Confederate Veterans Association in 1893 that "the National Government, with perfect impartiality, is publishing the Federal and Confederate military records." Falligant promised that the *Official Records* would show that "the unselfish loyalty and heroic devotion" of the soldiers towered over "the stupendous wrongs and tragic sorrows of the colossal conflict."[51]

The singing or recitation of poems by young women at reunions undoubtedly assuaged the fears of many veterans that future generations might misinterpret the past or forget them and their sacrifices. While women of all ages prepared the large feasts at reunions, those who entertained the veterans were almost always young and unmarried, often the daughters of veterans or local officials. The girls usually read poems steeped in Lost Cause sentiments with titles such as "The Georgia Volunteer," "The Jacket in Grey," "The Blue and Grey," or Father Abram J. Ryan's popular lament, "The Conquered Banner." One young woman, standing before the veterans of the 35th Georgia, delivered a particularly dramatic rendition of Father Ryan's famous poem by using the remnant of a Confederate battle flag as a prop.[52]

Veterans often sounded their appreciation of the young women's presentations by offering a rendition of the "rebel yell." Occasionally the old soldiers also awarded the girls a gold badge or "adopted" one of them as "the daughter" of the regiment. Such displays, as Gaines Foster has suggested, have several layers of meaning. By honoring these daughters, the veterans indirectly paid tribute to Southern white women who had remained faithful during the war. The presentations also assured the old soldiers that Southern women "loved them despite their defeat," thereby indirectly affirming the veterans' masculinity and role as protectors of white womanhood.[53]

Many reunions ended with the singing of a hymn and prayer. After a day of music, speeches, and the election of officers, the survivors of Brig. Gen. George T. Anderson's brigade joined hands and sang "God Be With You Till We Meet Again." When rain forced veterans of the 23d Georgia into a church, they ended their reunion by listening to the ladies of the town of Emerson, "assisted by a few of the sterner sex," sing "Sweet By-and-By," accompanied by Miss Grace Gilbert at the organ. Such rituals, as Charles R. Wilson has explained, show the interrelation between Christianity and the rhetoric and symbols of the civil religion of the Lost Cause.[54]

The hymn singing and prayer at Confederate reunions, combined with the socializing and the large afternoon meal, reminded some veterans of the camp meetings periodically held by Protestant churches in the South.[55] But beyond the displays of Christian faith and socializing, Confederate reunions served a number of other important functions. By closing businesses and decorating their towns, by planning and fixing enormous feasts, and by preparing their daughters to entertain with poems and songs, white people in late-nineteenth-century Georgia honored the aging Confederate veterans and paid homage to the Lost Cause.

Reunions also gave Confederate veterans a chance to remember the past and their dead and keep strong the bonds of camaraderie forged under fire years earlier. The gatherings also provided a forum for the veterans to instruct younger generations in the "truths" of Southern history and, as Henry McDaniel said, "vindicate our motives and conduct in the judgement of posterity." Although the old soldiers claimed that they assembled with no "rebellious thoughts or feelings of animosity . . . for our old-time enemies," their speeches indicate otherwise. Alongside the sentiments of reconciliation, Confederate veterans revealed in reunion discourse that their views on the important issues related to the Civil War, Reconstruction, and Southern race relations had changed little over the years.[56]

Notes

The author offers his thanks to Dr. William F. Holmes for his assistance with this essay.

1. "The Old Veterans," *Atlanta Constitution,* July 22, 1886; Gaines M. Foster, *Ghosts of the Confederacy: Defeat, the Lost Cause, and the Emergence of the New South, 1865 to 1913* (New York: Oxford University Press, 1987), 127, 135, 136; Richard Starnes, "'The Stirring Strains of Dixie': The Civil War and Southern Identity in Haywood County, North Carolina," *North Carolina Historical Review* 74 (July 1997): 247.

2. Numerous organizations claimed to have held the first Confederate veterans' reunion in Georgia. Members of the Panola Guards, a company of the Cobb's Legion Infantry Battalion, held their first reunion in 1874. The Confederate Survivors' Association of Augusta claimed in 1895 to be the oldest such organization in the state "by many years." "The Veterans Meet," *Atlanta Constitution,* August 20, 1889; n.a., *Address Delivered Before the Confederate Survivors' Association of Augusta, Georgia Upon the Occasion of Its Seventeenth Annual Reunion* (Augusta: Chronicle Job Printing Co., 1895), 4; Foster, *Ghosts of the Confederacy,* 104; William W. White, *The Confederate Veteran* (Tuscaloosa, Ala.: Confederate Publishing Co., 1962), 11–12, 20. For evidence that most regimental survivors' associations held their first meetings in the mid- and late 1880s, see "The Boys in Gray," *Atlanta Constitution,* July 7, 1885; "The Gallant Seventh," *Atlanta*

Constitution, July 21, 1885; "The Third Georgia," *Atlanta Constitution,* August 2, 1885; "The 35th Regiment," *Atlanta Constitution,* August 29, 1885; "The Reunion," *Americus Recorder,* August 15, 1889; and "Meetings of Old Veterans," *Cartersville Courant-American,* September 5, 1889.

3. "The Confederate Reunions," *Atlanta Constitution,* July 31, 1898; "Celebrating Manassas," *Atlanta Constitution,* July 22, 1885; "The Gallant Seventh"; "The Reunion of the 42d," *Atlanta Constitution,* July 23, 1885; "Happy Gatherings," *Atlanta Constitution,* July 22, 1888.

4. "They Meet at Roberta," *Atlanta Constitution,* July 25, 1891; "Old Vets Meet Again," *Atlanta Constitution,* July 22, 1887; "The Bloody Seventh," *Carroll Free Press,* July 21, 1889; "The Forty-Second Georgia," *Atlanta Constitution,* July 14, 1888.

5. William G. Piston, *Lee's Tarnished Lieutenant: James Longstreet and His Place in Southern History* (Athens: University of Georgia Press, 1987), 159–61, 164, 166; "The Second Georgia," *Atlanta Constitution,* August 7, 1886; "Veterans Talking," *Atlanta Constitution,* August 19, 1889; "General Wade Hampton," *Atlanta Constitution,* July 25, 1891. For accounts of Gordon and Evans see, among many, "Old Vets Meet Again"; "Greenville's Great Day," *Atlanta Constitution,* August 8, 1889; "The Bloody Seventh"; "The Third Georgia." William G. Piston plays down Longstreet's participation in Southern reunions, claiming that he "preferred Northern reunions; in the North he met no prejudices."

6. "The Forty-Second Georgia"; "The Third Georgia," *Atlanta Constitution,* July 9, 1888; "Madison's Preparations," *Atlanta Constitution,* July 30, 1888; "The Fifth and Thirteenth Georgia," *Atlanta Constitution,* August 23, 1886; "Military Reunions," *Atlanta Constitution,* August 27, 1886.

7. "The Bloody Seventh"; "A Thrilling Scene," *Henry County Weekly,* August 9, 1889.

8. "Regimental Reunions," *Atlanta Constitution,* August 31, 1887.

9. "Happy Gatherings"; "Reunion of the 52nd Georgia Regiment," *Dahlonega Signal,* July 10, 1885; "Famous Forty-Second," *Atlanta Constitution,* July 23, 1891; "Old Vets Meet Again"; "Met at Lithonia," *Atlanta Constitution,* July 18, 1897; "Meetings of Old Veterans"; "Veterans Meet Again," *Atlanta Constitution,* August 9, 1891. Columnist "Bill Arp" noted "when the few surviving vets have a reunion their children and kinfolks and friends meet with them to make the number look respectable."

10. "The Soldier Boys," *Atlanta Constitution,* July 23, 1886; "A Grand Reunion," *Atlanta Constitution,* July 23, 1887; "The Seventh's Veterans," *Atlanta Constitution,* July 22, 1892; "Veterans' Day," *Atlanta Constitution,* July 23, 1892; "Two Reunions," *Atlanta Constitution,* July 31, 1891; "Veterans' Reunions," *Atlanta Constitution,* July 25, 1891.

11. "The 5th Georgia Reunion," *Griffin Weekly News,* August 28, 1885; "The Third Georgia," *Atlanta Constitution,* July 21, 1892; "The Fourth Reunion

of the Survivors of the Third Georgia Regiment," *Waynesboro True Citizen*, July 31, 1885; "Two Reunions"; White, *The Confederate Veteran*, 23.

12. "A Big Day! The Reunion of the 13th Ga. Regiment of Volunteers," *Griffin Weekly News*, August 21, 1885.

13. The conclusions drawn here and elsewhere are sometimes based on reporter's summaries of reunion speeches, leaving the possibility that veterans discussed topics that never appeared in print. See, for example, "The Old Reb Vets," *Dalton Argus*, August 20, 1887. On the performance of the 39th Georgia at Baker's Creek and in the Vicksburg Campaign, see Edwin C. Bearss, *The Vicksburg Campaign*, 3 vols. (Dayton: Morningside Press, 1986), 2:596–600; *The War of the Rebellion: A Compilation of the Official Records of the Union and Confederate Armies*, 127 vols., index, and atlas (Washington, D.C.: GPO, 1880–1901), ser, 1, vol. 24, pt. 1, 264. For a rare account of a reunion speaker admitting to running in battle, see the humorous remarks of Evan Howell in "The Men in Gray," *Atlanta Constitution*, September 18, 1888.

14. Albert Castel, *Decision in the West: The Atlanta Campaign of 1864* (Lawrence: University Press of Kansas, 1992), 176–77; Charles A. Rowland to Catherine Rowland, May 27, 1864, Rowland Family Papers, Georgia Department of Archives and History, Atlanta; "A Grand Reunion," *Atlanta Constitution*, July 21, 1888.

15. Confederates during and after the war often referred to the July 22, 1864, battle of Atlanta as a victory, offering as proof the number of prisoners, cannon, and flags they captured. See Castel, *Decision in the West*, 408, 411; "The Soldier Boys"; "A Grand Reunion," *Atlanta Constitution*, July 23, 1887; "Veterans' Day"; "Reunion of Veterans," *Atlanta Constitution*, July 20, 1885; "Famous Forty-Second."

16. "Reunion of the 52nd Georgia Regiment"; "Re-union of the Fourth Georgia Regiment," *Milledgeville Union Recorder*, August 18, 1885; "Cobb and Phillips," *Atlanta Constitution*, August 25, 1893.

17. Flags were almost a prerequisite at reunions. Units without their regimental battle flags sometimes carried company flags, borrowed banners from other units, or made new flags. See "The Old Reb Vets"; "The Eighth Georgia," *Atlanta Constitution*, September 1, 1889; "The Blue and the Gray," *Atlanta Constitution*, August 1, 1889; "The Boys in Gray"; "Reunion 3d [*sic*] Ga. Regiment," *Cartersville Courant-American*, September 5, 1889; "The Soldier Boys"; Foster, *Ghosts of the Confederacy*, 139.

18. "Reunion of the 52d Georgia Regiment."

19. Foster, *Ghosts of the Confederacy*, 67; "A Big Day!"

20. "The Old Soldiers," *Atlanta Constitution*, August 2, 1887; "The Third Georgia," *Atlanta Constitution*, July 19, 1889.

21. Foster, *Ghosts of the Confederacy*, 67; "Meetings of Old Veterans"; "The

Soldier Boys". See also Edward Ayers, *The Promise of the New South* (New York: Oxford University Press, 1992), 338; and Stuart McConnell, *Glorious Contentment: The Grand Army of the Republic, 1865–1900* (Chapel Hill: University of North Carolina Press, 1992), 189–92.

22. Michael Kammen, *Mystic Chords of Memory* (New York: Alfred A. Knopf, 1991), 110; Foster, *Ghosts of the Confederacy,* 68.

23. "A Grand Reunion," July 23, 1887; Foster, *Ghosts of the Confederacy,* 140.

24. "A Big Day!"; "The Bloody Seventh," July 21, 1889; "The Seventh's Veterans"; "A Grand Reunion," July 23, 1887. See also "The Bloody Seventh," *Atlanta Constitution,* July 27, 1890.

25. "The Bloody Seventh," July 21, 1889; "Meeting of Old Veterans," *Cartersville Courant-American,* September 5, 1889.

26. "The Bloody Seventh," *Atlanta Constitution,* July 7, 1900.

27. "Tige's Brigade," *Atlanta Constitution,* July 22, 1891; "The Bloody Seventh," July 27, 1890. See also comments of J. D. Stewart in "A Big Day!"

28. "A Big Day!"; "Tige's Brigade"; "Re-union of the Fourth Georgia Regiment"; "The Men in Gray."

29. "A Grand Reunion," July 21, 1888.

30. "Meeting of Old Veterans."

31. C. Vann Woodward, *Origins of the New South, 1877–1913,* rev. ed. (Baton Rouge: Lousiana State University Press, 1971), 254–55; Ralph L. Eckert, *John Brown Gordon: Soldier, Southerner, American* (Baton Rouge: Louisiana State University Press, 1989), 294; "The Bloody Seventh," *Atlanta Constitution,* July 17, 1900.

32. "The Bloody Seventh," July 21, 1889; "The Bloody Seventh," July 27, 1890.

33. "Cobb and Phillips." See also Henry Thomas, *History of the Doles-Cook Brigade* (Atlanta: Franklin Printing Co., 1903), 613, 615.

34. "The Soldier Boys"; Leon Litwack, *Trouble in Mind: Black Southerners in the Age of Jim Crow* (New York: Alfred A. Knopf, 1998), 193–97; Foster, *Ghosts of the Confederacy,* 140.

35. "A Rare Reunion," *Atlanta Constitution,* July 28, 1889; "Meeting of Old Veterans"; "Reunion of the 52d Georgia Regiment"; "Two Reunions."

36. "The Bloody Seventh," July 17, 1900; "Old Vets Meet Again"; "The Third Georgia," July 21, 1892.

37. "It will be a Great Reunion," *Atlanta Constitution,* August 15, 1893; "The Third Georgia," July 21, 1892; "Reunion 3d [*sic*] Ga. Regiment"; "The Dinner Washed Away," *Atlanta Constitution,* July 20, 1889; "The Bloody Seventh," July 21, 1889.

38. "A Glorious Day," *Atlanta Constitution,* July 14, 1888; "Re-union of the Fourth Georgia Regiment"; "Celebrating Manassas"; "The Reunion of

the 42d," *Atlanta Constitution,* July 23, 1886; "Forty-Second Georgia," *Atlanta Constitution,* July 7, 1886.

39. Foster, *Ghosts of the Confederacy,* 140; White, *The Confederate Veteran,* 86–87; "Heroes Gather," *Atlanta Constitution,* July 23, 1894.

40. Newspaper articles offer no evidence that political debates took place at reunions, although reporters and editors may have mentioned only those politicians their newspapers supported. See "Military Reunions"; "They Meet at Roberta."

41. "A Big Day!"; "Reunion of the 52d Georgia Regiment."

42. "A Memorable Day," *Atlanta Constitution,* August 15, 1889; "The Reunion." See also "Arp's Sunday Chat," *Atlanta Constitution,* August 16, 1891.

43. White, *The Confederate Veteran,* 107–108; R. B. Rosenburg, *Living Monuments: Confederate Soldiers' Homes in the New South* (Chapel Hill: University of North Carolina Press, 1993), 47–48.

44. "The Old Soldiers"; "Indigent Veterans," *Atlanta Constitution,* August 30, 1887; Rosenburg, *Living Monuments,* 47–48.

45. Rosenburg, *Living Monuments,* 46–50. See also Eckert, *John Brown Gordon,* 292. For evidence of veterans' appreciation of Grady's efforts, see resolution in "The Lumpkin Veterans," *Atlanta Constitution,* August 10, 1889; "A Memorable Day."

46. "The Veterans' Home," *Atlanta Constitution,* August 18, 1891; "Tige's Brigade"; "Veterans Meet Again"; "Two Reunions"; "Bloody Thirtieth," *Atlanta Constitution,* August 1, 1891; Rosenburg, *Living Monuments,* 53–68.

47. Foster, *Ghosts of the Confederacy,* 194–95; Robert C. McMath, *American Populism: A Social History 1877–1898* (New York: Hill and Wang, 1993), 45, 64, 167.

48. Barton Shaw, *The Wool-Hat Boys: Georgia's Populist Party* (Baton Rouge: Louisiana State University Press, 1984), 68–72; "The Veterans Meet," *Atlanta Constitution,* July 14, 1892. For Gordon's use of race baiting in his quest for the Senate, see Eckert, *John Brown Gordon,* 303.

49. "The Forty-Fourth Georgia," *Atlanta Constitution,* August 5, 1891; Paul M. Gaston, *The New South Creed: A Study in Southern Myth Making* (New York: Alfred A. Knopf, 1970), 7, 8, 184. See also remarks of Henry L. Wilson in "Tige's Brigade."

50. "The 5th Ga. Reunion," *Griffin Weekly News,* August 28, 1885; "Reception at the Capitol," *Atlanta Constitution,* August 16, 1889; "The Bloody Seventh," July 21, 1889; "A Grand Reunion," July 23, 1887; Ayers, *The Promise of the New South,* 336. See also extracts from a speech by Walter C. Beeks in "The Forty Fourth!," *Griffin Weekly News & Sun,* August 5, 1891. Gaines Foster has noted that by the turn of the century many Southerners found the term "rebel" insulting. (Foster, *Ghosts of the Confederacy,* 118.)

51. "The Bloody Seventh," July 21, 1889; n.a., *Addresses Delivered Before the Confederate Veterans' Association of Savannah Ga* (Savannah: Braid and Hutton, 1893).

52. "The Veterans Meet," August 20, 1889; "A Rare Reunion"; "Veterans Meet," *Atlanta Constitution*, July 27, 1891; "Old Vets Meet Again"; "Tige's Brigade"; "Two Reunions."

53. Foster, *Ghosts of the Confederacy*, 136–37; Nina Silber, *The Romance of Reunion* (Chapel Hill: University of North Carolina Press, 1993), 167–69.

54. "Tige's Brigade"; "Reunion 3d [*sic*] Ga. Regiment"; Charles R. Wilson, *Baptized in Blood: The Religion of the Lost Cause, 1865–1920* (Athens: University of Georgia Press, 1980), 9–14.

55. "Reunion of the 52nd Georgia Regiment"; "The Boys in Gray."

56. "The Gallant Seventh"; "Heroes Gather"; Foster, *Ghosts of the Confederacy*, 196.

Five

New South Visionaries
Virginia's Last Generation of Slaveholders, the Gospel of Progress, and the Lost Cause

Peter S. Carmichael

During the last week of May 1890, more than a hundred thousand Southerners congregated in Richmond, Virginia, to unveil a statue of Robert E. Lee. The city had not welcomed so many dignitaries and visitors since Jefferson Davis's arrival as the Confederacy's president in 1861. Just as Davis had made the symbolic connection between the Confederacy to the revolutionary past by speaking under the equestrian statue of George Washington, the 1890 celebration also evoked a similar historical message. Pictures of Lee and Washington decorated the city's streets with hundreds of Confederate and Union flags draped from the buildings. Bands played patriotic music and other tunes that stirred memories of the war. On May 29, after an extensive parade of some four miles, the assembly gathered at the Lee monument where Archer Anderson delivered the keynote address. Anderson, a veteran of the Army of Northern Virginia who worked for his father in the famous Tredegar Iron Works, paid tribute to Lee in classic Lost Cause fashion. He defended the Southern crusade as a righteous one, supremely led but defeated by superior numbers and technology. Anderson saw in the commanding general the rare combination of Christian virtues and the bravery of old Roman manhood. But he was not content to focus on the heroic nature of Lee and the Confederacy. Like many spokesmen for the Lost Cause, Anderson moved beyond a narrow justification of the South's actions during the war. He portrayed Lee as a man of action, intelligence, and vigor who offered a model of behavior for Southerners trying to adapt to the realities of the New South.[1]

The essence of Anderson's address, with its appeal to entrepreneurial values and sectional reconciliation, clashed with the message of other prominent Lost Cause spokesmen, such as Jubal A. Early and William Nelson Pendleton. Both of these men renounced the industrial program of the New South as a reprehensible course that would turn Dixie into "Yankeedom." Anderson, on the other hand, was of a younger generation that came of age during the 1850s, when Virginia made rapid strides toward a market economy. Spending his formative years at such a time made him more receptive to economic change after the war. By endorsing the New South vision, he affirmed the message of John B. Gordon and Henry Grady. Although Anderson had a more personal stake in developing Virginia's manufacturing capacity because of his familial ties to Tredegar, he did not act solely out of selfish reasons. He upheld the "progressive" agenda advocated by young Virginians born between 1831 and 1842, who, with few exceptions, called for economic diversification, internal improvements, and industrial growth—a plea that they had made before Appomattox.[2]

Unlike many disciples of the Lost Cause who sought refuge in the "moonlight and magnolias" view of the Old South, the last generation understood the potential dangers of trying to recapture a golden age because of its stifling effects on intellectual creativity. In the 1850s they witnessed the wasted energies of their fellow Virginians who obsessed about the lost glories of the Revolutionary past. Instead of charting a course into the future, it seemed that Virginians were more worried about resurrecting a mythic past to prove that they were once a great people. Members of Anderson's age group charged that a tendency to rest on the laurels of the state's Revolutionary War heroes had paralyzed the leaders of their fathers' generation. The Old Dominion had failed to keep pace with the North and the rest of the world. As young men, members of the last generation desperately wanted their state to become a progressive land blessed by material prosperity, technological advancement, scientific inquiry, and educational opportunities. Few others in antebellum Virginia made such a determined argument for economic diversification and development of the state's resources.[3]

Reconstruction marked the ascension of the last generation to a position of authority in Virginia. They figured prominently in the development of a Lost Cause mythology that would help justify the new order in postwar Virginia. The intellectual thrust of their New South message originated in their critique of antebellum Virginia society. While warning Virginians not to repeat the sins of their fathers, they preached the social gospel of self-improvement and progress, just as they had done in the 1850s. This was the nexus between New and Old South thought in Virginia. Ironically, the war interrupted the last generation's progressive plans for the Old Dominion. The industrial might of Northern armies did not awaken the last generation to the ideas of economic innovation and development.[4] They had advocated such a course before Fort Sumter. Their campaign, however, had produced uneven results, leaving them frustrated and bitter in the 1850s. Reconstruction provided a second chance to instill in Virginians a spirit of innovation, reform, and prosperity. Although most of these young men had been unyielding Confederates during the war, they made the transition to Union with relative ease. Their antebellum mission to modernize Virginia might explain why many had minimal difficulty accepting the realities of reunion and industrial capitalism.

No single idea united members of the last generation before the Civil War. They shared instead a dilemma: How to restore Virginia to a position of leadership in the Union without sacrificing the virtues of the past or, even worse, remaining in the intellectual backwaters of the world. Exhausted lands and poor economic conditions had forced more than three hundred thousand Virginians to leave for the Deep South or the West by 1850. With an overall declining population, Virginia had fallen to fifth in national population on the eve of the Civil War. In 1810 the state sent twenty-three members to Congress, but in 1860 only eleven represented the Old Dominion in Washington. No longer did Virginia enjoy a prominent position of leadership in the country's political affairs.[5]

In comparison to the North, the scarcity of railroads, canals, and light industry in Virginia, as well as the paltry sum devoted to education, attested to the state's backwardness. Older Virginians who resisted progressive reforms and technological innovations were derisively called old fogeys by young Virginians who condemned this class of leaders in general terms. In their attacks on the fogeys, the last generation refrained from singling out an individual politician or a specific political organization. A Hampden-Sydney student captured the frustration of his contemporaries when he wrote in 1859 that "there is an amount of old fogyism amongst us that is absolutely appalling." Why it took "a generation for a canal to get to Buchanan" and another "twenty-five or thirty years to construct a railroad from one end of the State to the other" he could not understand.[6] It should be remembered that not every father of the last generation was an old fogey, but virtually every old fogey was an older Virginian. They came from Democratic and Whig ranks, residing in all parts of the state but never organizing formally or becoming a political force in the state.

The attack on old fogeyism included a plea for Virginians to embrace Protestant Christianity as a means to ensure moral and material progress. Southerners had long insisted that both needed to advance in tandem. To achieve such a goal, the last generation embarked on a religious crusade that emanated from Virginia universities. Besides the primary goal of converting souls, they wanted the message of Christianity to infuse Virginians with an entrepreneurial ethos that included the values of thrift, hard work, and the desire for social mobility. If the religious awakening succeeded, the slaveholding class and other whites would no longer admire aristocratic ease and carefree living. They would become ambitious and career-minded, inspired by innovation and reform without abandoning a sense of duty to society. To their peers, young Virginians challenged the popular stereotype of the lazy, dissipated Southern youth, vilified at home and mocked in the North. They wanted members of their age group to emulate the model of the Christian gentleman.

Ambition became the rallying cry of young Virginians. They believed a larger dose of ambition would motivate their fathers' age group to leave the comfort of their verandas. This shift in thinking among younger Virginians reflected a broader change as to what it meant to be a man. They no longer aspired to the aristocratic ease of a Southern gentleman but instead admired an aggressive, career-driven man who sought public recognition through innovation and reform. None of these young men wanted to die in obscurity, so they often turned to ambition to rescue them from the complacency of the past.[7] What accounted for literary achievements, scientific advancements, and oratory splendor but ambition? Even the founding fathers projected themselves as highly ambitious men, although they had submitted those desires to Providence's guidance and had adhered to a strict moral code. In a book written for college youth, Henry Clay Pate, a native of Bedford County who attended the University of Virginia before moving to the West, declared that "ambition is not *necessarily* a dangerous sentiment." He pointed to the "illustrious examples" of Washington, Jefferson, and "hundreds of eminent statesmen of our country" as proof of the "loftiest results of ambitious desires." "*Let the youth of our land be* ambitious," Pate contended, "and emulate the example set before them by our great men!" He rebuked as "absurd" the notion expressed by some parents that "ambition is *dangerous*." Speaking to the young men at the Hampton Academy in 1857, Walter Monteiro, a twenty-three-year-old lawyer from Goochland County, also rejected the traditional belief that ambition was "the daughter of vanity and the mother of monster." He implored his audience to pursue a purer form of ambition, free of selfishness and directed by Christian motives. "Without it," Monteiro concluded, "all our finer feelings and passions would sink into darkness of eternal night."[8]

In the eyes of the last generation, older Virginians tended to lack a controlled use of ambition or they were simply content to rest upon the heroic accomplishments of their Revolutionary War ancestors. Secondary scholarship has supported this perception of their fathers' generation. George B. Forgie points out that men who were socialized in the New Republic resigned themselves to maintaining the Union, a mundane task that could never lead to immortal fame. History, they believed, had not blessed them with an opportunity to create something lasting and influential for humankind. Their job was simply to preserve.[9]

This complacent outlook, the last generation charged, had done irredeemable harm to the Old Dominion's reputation in the Union. Northerners mocked Virginians as modern-day Don Quixotes who hallucinated about becoming chivalrous knights while economic and intellectual stagnation silenced their state's voice in the Union. Even though Alexander Pendleton considered Virginia citizenship "a passport . . . through the country," he realized that the "evils amongst us" had made "others sometimes sneer."[10] Republican spokesmen such as Frederick Law Olmsted highlighted Virginia's decline as proof that slavery degraded white people. The "peculiar institution" had extinguished innovation and intellectual curiosity in the Commonwealth, leaving the state in the hands of a decrepit aristocracy. Once the home of the greatest minds in the country, Virginia had not produced anyone of national or international fame in politics, the arts, or sciences since the Revolution (Edgar Allan Poe's scandalous personal life made it difficult for Virginians to take pride in his literary accomplishments).[11]

The last generation believed Virginia must chart a new course and enter the age of progress. These young men envied the amazing technological innovations and economic advancements that had transformed Northern society during the 1850s. An editor for *The Virginia University Magazine* wished "that some of the spirit of sister States could be infused into Virginia to lead her to develop all her resources, and become first in the march of progress and richest in material glory, as she is richest in the glowing memories and reminiscences of the past." When Henry Pate surveyed Virginia's abundant natural resources, especially in the western portion of the state, he could not think of another place "in the Union . . . so vastly favored by nature." "It is to be hoped," he added, "that the time will soon come, when the Mother of States will educate her children—then will her hills and valleys bloom with the rich product of labor."[12]

The reasons to develop Virginia's resources during the 1850s seemed more urgent to young men who visited the North and saw various modern improvements. The differences between the two regions highlighted the material backwardness of the Old Dominion. Walking along the Cumberland Valley Railroad toward Harrisburg, Pennsylvania, William Kinzer of southwest Virginia saw his first wire fence—something he had "often read of . . . but had not seen any before." He also admired the "durable houses," "substantial barns," and "finely cultivated farms." His sojourn made him wish that "the people of Va. would cultivate their farms more and better, and educate their sons and daughters, like the people of Pa."[13]

In the race for material prosperity against the North, these young Virginians found an element of their calling, a transcendent mission that they believed would rejuvenate the moral energies of Virginians. If successful, they would be immortalized as the redeemers of Virginia. To produce virtuous leaders who could return prosperity and prestige to Virginia, members of the last generation pinned their hopes on education. Once again, the Revolutionary War fathers' wise example offered a proper course for the Old Dominion to follow. Alexander Pendleton reminded his fellow Virginians that George Washington recognized the importance of higher education by donating personal stock to form Washington College. Pendleton implored the state's current leaders to make the refurbishment of Virginia's universities a priority. With the necessary funds, the last generation confidently believed the Old Dominion would again produce men of eminence and virtue. In *The Virginia University Magazine,* an editor wrote in 1860 that the seats of learning had a duty "to extend and enlarge, by every means" the Old Dominion's "material prosperity." The last generation prepared for the challenge, eager to build upon "the glowing memories and reminiscences of the past."[14]

Educational reform depended more upon additional state funds than inspiration from the past. Public enthusiasm for higher education had been waning for some time because many adults dismissed the classical training at Virginia colleges as irrelevant to the practical demands of life. In the nineteenth century, American universities faced the universal problem of underfunding because they could not show a utilitarian value to the people.[15] Not all Virginians were hostile to higher education, however. Governor Henry Wise vigorously promoted the interests of state-supported schools, campaigned against illiteracy, and even floated the idea of a public school system for the poor. After assuming office in 1856, Wise softened his stance. He abandoned his proposal for common schools, no longer called for taxing the rich to pay educational expenditures, and focused instead on trying to enlarge the patronage of the Virginia Military Institute (VMI), the University of Virginia, and other colleges. Wise persuaded the General Assembly to pass modest increases in appropriations for VMI and the university during his tenure.[16]

A number of young men believed the General Assembly had not been generous enough in its support of the state's universities, and they held the older generation responsible for the apathetic attitude toward education. Such a backward stance, they charged, accounted for the stagnant, anti-progressive thinking that had brought ruin to the Old Dominion. Governor Wise reinforced the negative perception of the state's public servants by exposing the misappropriation of $150,000 from the literary fund that served the state debt—an illegal activity that occurred between 1851 and 1857.[17] Another setback to the cause of education occurred in 1860 when the legislature decided against an endowment fund for the University of Virginia, killing an appropriations bill of $25,000.[18] The students at Charlottesville denounced this action as a consequence of party politics. An editor for *The Virginia University Magazine* explained that a "portion of the Legislature known for their hostility to the University, who look upon its prosperity with a jealous eye and are willing to see it decline, have again triumphed in their cause and succeeded in keeping the institution in a state of financial embarrassment." "When our legislators prostitute their positions and attempt to make them serve for party purposes," the young man bitterly added, "it is high time for the people to demand an examination of the matter and see if these suspicions are well founded." Most members of the last generation would have endorsed Charles S. Venable's 1858 condemnation of the General Assembly, wherein the educator declared that "the heart of every patriotic son of the Old Dominion is sad and indignant to know that, in her legislative halls the rights of her youth are disregarded."[19]

Although young Virginians lobbied for increased public funding to reduce tuition fees, to expand the library, and to increase faculty salaries, their concerns extended beyond practical matters. Education must become a priority, they affirmed, if the state were to compete with the North and maintain the University of Virginia's reputation as the finest school in the South. The last generation considered the University of Virginia the key to redeeming the Old Dominion. A superior educational institution in Virginia would show the world that intellect and creativity could flourish in a slave society.

Secession derailed the last generation's plan of turning Virginia into a progressive land. In the destructive wake of war, survivors of the last generation returned home to find their communities and homesteads in shambles. Wherever they turned, they saw despondent looks or heard discouraging words. A year after Appomattox, William Gordon McCabe of Hampton observed that "things are bad enough here, and we must tear down 'Sic Semper', and write 'Ichabod' on our shield." "There is an apathy," he concluded "beyond anything you can imagine." These feelings of hopelessness persisted for years. In 1873, Richmond's Archer Anderson encountered countless Virginians full of despair "because the land will no longer produce the old abundant fruits, or because business is stripped of its former profits."[20] The trauma of military defeat and the overthrow of the South's social system inflicted tremendous personal and emotional hardship. Members of the last generation responded in various ways. Some fell into a deep depression while others rejected reconciliation outright, but most sought reintegration into the Union by connecting with their antebellum heritage. The destruction of their social system made it difficult to reconstruct a bridge to the past. Nonetheless, they tried to recreate their identities by resurrecting their antebellum dream of transforming Virginia into a progressive land. Their agenda assumed a tone more in keeping with the challenges of a free labor society. Their mission, moreover, complemented the ideas of industrial capitalism, a force that was conquering the world and would give rise to the New South movement.

The last generation drew a compelling lesson from the conflict. The demands of war, some argued, awakened the state from its deep slumber, brought the listless to life, and invigorated the moral energies of Virginians. Veteran John Hampden Chamberlayne of Hanover County admitted that the state "was weak" before the war. Armed conflict, however, "awoke that public spirit which had seemed dead, but was only sleeping." "The slothful became energetic," he added, "the luxurious hardy, the arrogant submitted to discipline, the selfish subdued self to the common good, and the four years began of sacrifice, devotion, endurance and achievement." Another young officer from Lee's army, John Warwick Daniel, also endorsed this interpretation of the war. "The whole country was converted into an arsenal and a hospital," he observed in 1877, "and under trial and hardship which would have broken a feeble race, her genius burst forth in exploits of mechanical invention and economical skill not less splendid than her feats of arms." With an eye toward the future, Daniel, a native of Lynchburg, wanted Virginians to duplicate their wartime achievements. If Southerners could plow fields, harvest trees, build roads, and develop industries in the face of Federal armies, they should achieve even greater feats during peacetime. Daniel reminded his audience that "the first gun of Sumter broke the stagnant, dreamy langor [sic] of our Southern lotus-land."[21] Men of

Daniel's generation believed the war had extinguished any notion that Southern talents rest exclusively with agricultural pursuits. The Confederacy's successful conversion to war production demonstrated that Southerners possessed the ability and genius to make lasting achievements in the mechanical arts.

Southerners of all ages emphasized Northern industrial power as the deciding factor of the war. Edward A. Pollard, a Lost Cause historian and member of the last generation, concluded that the Confederacy lost because of "a characteristic infirmity of the South . . . the want of business talent." John Warwick Daniel also argued that "commerce was the conqueror" of the South during the Civil War.[22] But the impulse to modernize the economy did not originate solely from military defeat. Northern victory only intensified a desire for progressive reforms that the last generation had debated in the 1850s. They resumed the cry for progress after Appomattox, paying special attention to frame their campaign within the familiar jeremiad of the state's decline since the Revolution. Drawing from the generational message of the 1850s, Chamberlayne reminded his audience that with the passing of the Revolutionary War generation, Virginia spiraled into a decline. "Public spirit, in truth, was all but dead," he told a group of students at Randolph Macon College in 1875. "No museums were established, no libraries endowed, no schools founded. . . . New York debated, extended and completed her Erie Canal; Baltimore devised her road to the Lakes, while Virginia Legislators swore and sweated and scrambled over a mud pike from Poverty Hill to Scuffletown."[23] Why had railroads, canals, mines, and industries flourished in other states? Who allowed the state to fall in economic ruin and intellectual decline while the rest of the world sneered? Had the legacy of Jefferson and Washington cast a shadow over the state that would never be eclipsed by future generations?

The period of stagnation between the "Era of Good Feeling" and the Civil War in Virginia offered the last generation a useful parallel to the "dark days" of Reconstruction. By turning to history, members of the last generation wanted their fellow Virginians to confront the future without losing sight of the lessons of the past. "With the year 1825," Chamberlayne asserted, "the heroic period of Virginia may be said to end, and a decadence followed which we are apt enough to forget, but which to study is our highest duty, since the lessons it teaches are needful." Archer Anderson also reminded his audience at Randolph Macon of their gloomy past: "But let me read you one more lesson out of your own annals. Virginia has, within the memory of living men, recovered from a painful condition of ruin and bankruptcy, only to furnish an arena for the long pent up passions of sectional strife." He wanted Virginians to "compare the depression of all her material interests" following the "peace of 1815" with the energy and determination of the war years.[24] Anderson bluntly presented the options facing his fellow Virginians; they could either lead the state down the road of progress or return to the lethargic days of the old fogeys who kept the Old Dominion in the backwaters of the world.

Although members of the last generation wanted Virginians to draw inspiration from the memory of the Revolutionary War's heroes, they recognized the impossibility of surpassing the achievements of 1776. They also feared that comparisons to the founders might create unreasonable expectations, frustrating those who were trying to rebuild the Old Dominion. In the 1850s, young Virginians charged that their fathers seemed paralyzed by the legacy of the Revolutionary War generation. Instead of charting their own course, the old fogeys decided to bask in the glories of the past. Members of the last generation did not want the memory of the founders to become a burden to Virginians as it had been for their fathers before the war.[25]

In a sharp break with their antebellum past, members of the last generation did not search for a savior during Reconstruction who resembled Washington, Jefferson, or Patrick Henry. They reminded Virginians that each generation would be judged on its assigned mission, not by earlier standards. During an 1880 address to the alumni at the University of Virginia, Chamberlayne admitted that "we have no man to rival a Washington, a Jefferson or a Henry." What Virginians should remember, he concluded, was the power of "the average people of this day, [who] are head and shoulder above the average people" of earlier times. He expected ordinary Virginians to embark on a collective effort that would rejuvenate the state. John Warwick Daniel offered a similar interpretation when he argued that "young men are more like the age that they live in than they are like their fathers." In reference to the Revolutionary War generation, he instructed that "we have another and different work to do, and are not called to do theirs over again." Archer Anderson offered the most forceful opinion on this subject, saying that "each era has its own appointed work, and its own set of conditions under which that work has to be done, and when you come to look closely into these modifying conditions, if you bring away any fixed lesson from your historical studies, I think it is likely to be that men are essentially very much the same in all times and countries. What changes most is the medium in which they live."[26]

While members of the last generation distanced themselves from the heritage of the Revolutionary War generation during Reconstruction, they resurrected the antebellum message of self-improvement and social aspiration. As Beth Barton Schweiger has persuasively argued, antebellum Virginians drew values of social uplift and innovation from Protestant Christianity. These ideas gave substance and form to their Lost Cause expression while preparing them for the challenges of the New South.[27] Such a message had inspired young Virginians to emulate career-minded Christian gentlemen during the 1850s. In the postwar years, the men of the last generation did not lose their religious perspective. They emphasized the religious example of Confederate heroes to inspire social activism and progressive reform. The Revolutionary War heroes, many of whom entertained curious religious beliefs, faded into the background. No one could question the faith of Lee, "Stonewall" Jackson, and a host of other pious Confederates. They made ideal symbols for the move toward the New South. The image of the founders was not as compelling.

While the fervent Christian beliefs of Lee and Jackson appealed to traditional Southern sensibilities, their careers did not resemble the old, aristocratic elite, hopelessly mired in the past and wedded to values unfit for the age of progress. New South advocates stressed that Confederate officers were men of action, drive, and innovation who broke with the tradition of aristocratic ease without sacrificing their faith. In his famous Richmond address, Anderson paid homage to Lee as a Christian gentleman, but he was also careful to portray the general as a model for the New South. He praised Lee for his abilities as an administrator where he revealed "energy, forecast, and watchfulness . . . in the prosaic work of providing the means of subsistence for his army!" Anderson considered these "the necessary elements" of his "great character," the individual skills needed for Southerners to thrive in the emerging world of industrial capitalism.[28]

In keeping with the last generation's message in the 1850s, these Virginians pointed to ambition as the key to self-improvement and the betterment of society as a whole. The hard-driven careers of military men made Confederate generals, especially those who were aggressive on the battlefield, perfect role models for the New South campaign. In an 1868 speech at Manassas, Virginia, Daniel applauded Stonewall Jackson's overpowering ambition and ceaseless drive to improve himself for the benefit of others. "Jackson was a man of the highest ambition. He aspired to eminence in whatever he undertook," Daniel proclaimed. "He had that thirst for glory which is the almost invariable quality of elevated minds." "By severe discipline he has acquired the power of concentrating or relaxing his energies at will," Daniel added, ". . . his punctuality became a proverb. He slept, ate, studied, and did every duty by clockwork; and his associates kept the time of day by the movements of Major Jackson."[29] Daniel was careful to emphasize the aspects of Jackson's behavior that Virginians would need to imitate in order to succeed in the New South.

The example of the common soldier was also used to inspire action among Virginians. Once again Protestant Christianity and the New South crusade for economic change flowed together and reinforced compatible goals. A call to emulate the Christian bearing of Confederate soldiers did not mean a resurrection of the "moonlight and magnolias" dream shared by some Lost Cause advocates. Reverend J. William Jones, a prominent member of the last generation, spent much of the postwar period praising the religious zeal of the Southern rank and file. In his most famous book, *Christ in the Camp or Religion in the Confederate Army,* Jones recounted the story of a one-armed veteran who found his farm in a shambles after Appomattox. This soldier had been "raised in the lap of luxury" and was on the verge of graduating with honors when secession interrupted his ambitious plans. War blighted his dreams, destroyed his fortune, and wrecked his body. In the face of relentless adversity, the young man refused to give up. After the war Jones spotted the veteran "plowing in the field, guiding the plow with one hand, while an empty sleeve hung at his side." When Jones tried to express sympathy for the man, the soldier quickly replied with "a proud smile: 'Oh, Brother Jones, that is all right. *I thank God that I have one arm left and an opportunity to use it for the support of those I love.*'" Jones desperately wished the words of that maimed hero "could reach all the young men of the South." If they could hear such sentiments, Jones predicted that they would emulate "the example of our returned Confederate soldiers, who, as a rule, went to work with an energy and patient industry which have made them a real power in the land to-day."[30]

In keeping with their antebellum past, members of the last generation resurrected the platform of increased public funding for education to promote their progressive vision for postwar Virginia. However, a noticeable shift in favor of common schools occurred during Reconstruction. In 1866, Daniel told some University of Virginia students that the state must educate "the masses of the People, thus preparing them in knowledge for their high office, and elevating the moral character." In a reversal of his prewar views, Chamberlayne criticized Virginia's halfhearted commitment to public education prior to Fort Sumter: "The sectarian spirit stifled" the development of common schools, he opined, and "Virginia was left . . . to be the itinerant ignoramus." The political realities of reunion and the emergence of a new order based on nineteenth-century liberal capitalism persuaded many to embrace mass education. But Yankee bayonets and Radical Reconstruction do not fully explain the last generation's acceptance of free schools. Such an interpretation overlooks that some young Virginians desired a more expansive public education system before the war, one that resembled the North's. In an 1858 issue of *The Virginia University Magazine*, a student published an article entitled a "Plea on behalf of Popular Education." Although he denounced the social leveling of common schools, he confessed "a preference for 'some ideas of arithmetic, geography and account'" for the masses. This student reminded his audience that morality and education reinforced one another. "Yet philosophy and experience lend us their aid in proving that little religious culture is possible whilst the mind is wholly neglected," he concluded.[31]

The inevitable advance of industrial capitalism and its attendant ideology of free labor, buttressed by a powerful national government, convinced most Virginians of the necessity of public education. Conservatives like Edward Pollard, who condemned common schools before the war, welcomed universal education during Reconstruction as a means to stabilize society. The destruction of slavery, subjugation to Republican rule, and need to rebuild the South's infrastructure compelled members of Pollard's generation, like all Confederates, to adjust their thinking. While young Virginians like Pollard might have been quick to embrace aspects of New South ideology, the last generation worried about the social consequences and the leveling of traditional southern values. Those fears never left.

In the end, the last generation was able to come to grips with the revolutionary effects of the war by connecting with the past. The ideas of self-improvement, social reform, mass education, and economic development—the very basis of the entrepreneurial ethos of the New South—originated before the war. Virginia's rapid move toward a market economy in the 1850s makes the experience of the last generation unique in comparison to most Southerners.[32] As young men they witnessed the development of commercial ties between the Shenandoah Valley and the North, the rise of light industry in Richmond, the building of mines and railroads in the southwest, and a vigorous debate over public education. Spending their formative years at a time when the slave economy assumed a more capitalistic dimension might help explain why these young men reintegrated themselves into Union with amazing rapidity. Their Lost Cause message revived an antebellum dream that complemented the values of free labor, which they viewed as the way of the future. Except for their defense of slavery, the Virginians of the last generation had made peace with the ideas of the North prior to Appomattox.

Notes

1. Archer Anderson, "Robert Edward Lee: An Address Delivered at the Dedication of the Lee Monument," in *Southern Historical Society Papers*, J. William Jones et al., eds., 52 vols. and 2-vol. index (1876–1959; reprint, Millwood, N.Y.: Kraus Reprint Co., 1977–80), 17:315.

2. On the antebellum experience of the last generation, see Peter S. Carmichael, "The Last Generation: Sons of Virginia Slaveholders and the Creation of a Southern Identity, 1850–1865" (Ph.D. diss., The Pennsylvania State University, 1996).

3. Ibid.

4. Historians who argue that the Southern impulse to industrialize originated during the Civil War include Jack P. Maddex Jr., *The Virginia Conservatives, 1867–1879: A Study in Reconstruction Politics* (Chapel Hill: University of North Carolina Press, 1970); and Paul M. Gaston, *The New South Creed: A Study in Southern Myth Making* (New York: Alfred A. Knopf, 1970).

5. Virginius Dabney, *Virginia: The New Dominion* (Garden City, N.Y.: Doubleday, 1971), 275–76.

6. "The Education System of Prussia," *The Hampden-Sydney Magazine* 1 (June 1859): 227.

7. James DeWitt Hankins to Virginia Wilson Hankins, March 29, 1857, Hankins Family Papers, Virginia Historical Society, Richmond (hereafter cited as VHS). For a similar view of ambition, see Robert T. Scott to Fanny Scott (Carter) Scott, November 23, 1857, Keith Family Papers, VHS. On the potential dangers of ambition for a society dedicated to reciprocal duties, see William M. Radford, "Success in Life," *The Virginia University Magazine* 4 (November 1859): 83–84; H. H. Harris, "New Preachment From an Old Text," *The Virginia University Magazine* 4 (May 1859): 445–46.

8. Henry Clay Pate, *The American Vade Mecum: or the Companion of Youth and Guide to College* (Cincinnati: Morgan, 1852), 32–33; Walter Monteiro, *Address Delivered Before the Neotrophian Society of the Hampton Academy, On the Twenty-Eighth of July, 1857* (Richmond: H. K. Ellyson, 1857), 20–21. For other favorable appraisals of ambition, see "Ambition," *The Virginia University Magazine* 3 (November 1858): 80–83.

9. George B. Forgie, *Patricide in the House Divided: A Psychological Interpretation of Lincoln and His Age* (New York: W. W. Norton, 1979), 63–70.

10. Alexander S. Pendleton, "Cincinnati Oration," July 2, 1857, Porcher Gads-

den Papers, Washington and Lee University, Lexington, Virginia (hereafter cited as W&L).

11. Craig M. Simpson, *A Good Southerner: The Life of Henry A. Wise of Virginia* (Chapel Hill: University of North Carolina Press, 1985), 119, 136.

12. "Editor's Table," *The Virginia University Magazine* 4 (March 1860): 336; Pate, *American Vade Mecum,* 75–76.

13. William T. Kinzer diary, January 11, 1856, William T. Kinzer Papers, VHS; George W. Turner to Charles W. Turner, May 10, 1856, George W. Turner Papers, William R. Perkins Library, Manuscript Department, Duke University, Durham, N.C. (hereafter cited as DU).

14. Alexander S. Pendleton, "Cincinnati Oration," July 2, 1857, Porcher Gadsden Papers, W&L; "Editor's Table," 336. Students at Virginia universities made frequent pleas for additional state funding for their respective institutions during the 1850s. They rooted their arguments in the assumption that the state's institutions of higher learning could no longer compete with Northern schools. See "State Aid To Our College," *The Hampden Sidney Magazine* 2 (January 1860): 41–43; "Endowment of the University," *The Virginia University Magazine* 4 (March 1860): 330–34; "The University and Its Politics," ibid., 4 (May 1860): 461–64.

15. Oscar Handlin and Mary F. Handlin, *The American College and American Culture: Socialization as a Function of Higher Education* (New York: McGraw-Hill, 1970), 2; Frederick Rudolph, *The American College and University* (New York: Alfred A. Knopf, 1965), 110.

16. Simpson, *A Good Southerner,* 151–53; Berkeley Minor and James F. Minor, comps., *Legislative History of The University of Virginia as set forth in the Acts of The General Assembly of Virginia, 1802–1927* (n.p.: The Rector and Visitors, 1928), 30–34.

17. Simpson, *A Good Southerner,* 152.

18. "Editor's Table," 333.

19. Ibid., 461–62; Charles S. Venable, *An Address Delivered Before the Society of Alumni, of the University of Virginia, at its annual meeting held in the Public Hall, July 26, 1858* (Richmond: MacFarlane and Fergusson, 1859), 30.

20. Armistead Churchill Gordon, *Memories and Memorials of William Gordon McCabe,* 2 vols. (Richmond: Old Dominion Press, 1925), 1:325; Archer Anderson, *An Address Delivered Before the Washington Literary Society of Randolph Macon College* (Richmond: Washington Literary Society, 1873), 4.

21. John Hampden Chamberlayne, *Public Spirit: An Address Delivered at Randolph Macon College before the Washington Literary Society, June 23, 1875* (Norfolk: Virginian Book and Job Print, 1875), 12; John Warwick Daniel, "Conquered Nations," in *Speeches and Orations of John Warwick Daniel,* compiled by Edward M. Daniel (Lynchburg: J. P. Bell, 1911), 146.

22. Quoted from Maddex, *The Virginia Conservatives,* 33; John Warwick Daniel, "Speech delivered before the Annual Reunion of Confederate Veterans at

New Orleans, April 9, 1892," in *Speeches and Orations*, 393. For a similar interpretation of Confederate defeat, see Archer Anderson, "Robert Edward Lee: An Address Delivered at the Dedication of the Lee Monument," *Southern Historical Society Papers*, 17:323.

23. Chamberlayne, "Public Spirit," 10.

24. Ibid., 6; Anderson, "Address Delivered Before the Washington Literary Society," 7.

25. Carmichael, "The Last Generation," 30–32.

26. John Hampden Chamberlayne, *Why Despair: An Address Delivered Before the Society of the Alumni of a University of Virginia, July 1, 1880* (Richmond: Society of the Alumni, 1880), 12; Daniel, "Conquered Nations," 156; Anderson, "Address Delivered Before the Washington Literary Society," 9.

27. See Beth Barton Schweiger, *The Gospel Working Up: Progress and the Pulpit in Nineteenth-Century Virginia* (New York: Oxford University Press, 2000).

28. Anderson, "Robert Edward Lee," 17:315. For a discussion of how Lost Cause mythology was used to advance the goals of the New South, see Gaines M. Foster, *Ghosts of the Confederacy: Defeat, the Lost Cause, and the Emergence of the New South, 1865 to 1913* (New York: Oxford University Press, 1987), 79–85.

29. John Warwick Daniel, "Character of Stonewall Jackson," in *Speeches and Orations*, 45–46, 47.

30. J. William Jones, *Christ in the Camp or Religion in the Confederate Army* (1887; reprint, Harrisonburg, Va.: Sprinkle Publications, 1986), 463, 464.

31. John Warwick Daniel, "The People: An Address Delivered Before the Jefferson Literary Society of the University of Virginia," in *Speeches and Orations*, 26; Chamberlayne, "Public Spirit," 11; "Plea on Behalf of Popular Education," *The Virginia University Magazine* 2 (March 1858): 100, 101.

32. On Virginia's move toward a market economy in the 1850s, see Henry T. Shanks, *The Secession Movement in Virginia, 1847–1861* (Richmond: Garrett and Massie, 1934), 1–17; William A. Blair, "Virginia's Private War: The Contours of Dissent and Loyalty in the Confederacy" (Ph.D. diss., The Pennsylvania State University, 1995), 5–6; Avery Craven, *Soil Exhaustion as a Factor in the Agricultural History of Virginia and Maryland, 1606–1860* (1926; reprint, Gloucester, Mass.: Peter Smith, 1965), 122–62; Kenneth W. Noe, *Southwest Virginia's Railroad: Modernization and the Sectional Crisis* (Urbana: University of Illinois Press, 1994), 4–9; Steven Elliott Tripp, *Yankee Town, Southern City: Race and Class Relations in Civil War Lynchburg* (New York: New York University Press, 1997), 6–12.

Six

James Longstreet and the Lost Cause

Jeffry D. Wert

Richmond, Virginia, resonated with the sights and sounds of the past during the final week of May 1890. The thousands of spectators and participants who thronged into the city received a warm welcome and encountered buildings festooned with the symbols of Richmond's days as capital of the Confederacy. A "frenzy of Southern feeling," in the words of a newspaperman, gripped the residents and visitors.

The decorations, the crowds, and this rekindled "frenzy of Southern feeling" resulted from the planned unveiling of a monument to Robert E. Lee, sculpted by J. A. C. Mercie. A committee of distinguished Southerners, including a number of Lee's former lieutenants, had commissioned the sculptor, extended invitations to veterans of the Confederate armies, and prepared a program of speeches and a parade. To the organizers, the ceremonies would be an affirmation of the justness of the Lost Cause and the greatness of Lee's genius as a military chieftain. The sacrifices of the Southern people during four years of civil war would be praised in flowery words and carved stone.

The ceremonies began at noon on May 29 with a parade on Broad Street. Bands, young men in uniform, and veterans of such terrible clashes as Malvern Hill, Sharpsburg, Chancellorsville, Gettysburg, and Chickamauga passed before thousands of spectators. In carriages and on horseback rode former generals, men such as Jubal A. Early, John B. Gordon, Fitzhugh Lee, Joseph E. Johnston, E. Porter Alexander, and Joseph B. Kershaw. These renowned officers had returned to the capital at the invitation of the committee.

Another of Lee's lieutenants, invited by members of an artillery bat-

127

tery as their escort, rode in a carriage in the parade. He looked "old, feeble, indeed badly broken up," his presence most unwelcome to committee members. For much of the past two decades, James Longstreet, former commander of the Army of Northern Virginia's First Corps and Lee's senior subordinate, had been an apostate in his own native region, the man held responsible for the Confederate defeat at Gettysburg and thus of the cause itself.

Longstreet's attendance elicited cheers from the men who had stood in the ranks of the First Corps. Despite the vilification of Longstreet and the falsification of his war record in print, his former soldiers remembered him as a leader who had attended to their welfare and had proved his skill and courage on the battlefield. But their voices had already been muted by others who had fashioned a history of the conflict that would outlast all of those in attendance.[1]

When James Longstreet rode away from Appomattox in April 1865, few, if any, would have predicted that in time he would become the scapegoat for the Confederate defeat. He had been with the army from the beginning at First Manassas to its surrender at Appomattox. He had risen to the rank of lieutenant general, corps command, and been Lee's senior subordinate. Like other high-ranking generals in the army, he had had his failings, but his performance ranked him with "Stonewall" Jackson as Lee's finest officers. His organizational abilities and tactical skill made him one of the war's best corps commanders. He had received a crippling wound at the Wilderness on May 6, 1864, and suffered from its effects for the remainder of his life.[2]

His personal sacrifices and devotion to duty seemingly assured Longstreet's place in the forefront of Lee's lieutenants. The initial histories of the conflict, written within the first two years of the war's end, reflected the common judgment about Longstreet. James Dabney McCabe Jr.'s *Life and Campaigns of General Robert E. Lee* (1866), William Parker Snow's *Southern Generals: Their Lives and Campaigns* (1866), and Edward A. Pollard's *Lee and His Lieutenants* (1867) all offered favorable assessments of Longstreet's generalship.[3]

William Swinton's *Campaigns of the Army of the Potomac* also appeared in 1866. A popular history, heavily researched, and written by a skillful author, the book was praised in both sections as fair and balanced. Swinton blamed Lee, Early, and Richard S. Ewell for the defeat at Gettysburg. The Confederate victory on July 1, according to Swinton, gave Lee "the taste of blood." The Confederate commander believed his army could achieve anything and lost "the equipoise in which his faculties commonly moved."[4]

Longstreet had provided Swinton with material and information for the book, and in it, the author attributed to the former general that Lee had promised to fight a defensive battle in Pennsylvania once the armies met. Longstreet, however, never made such a claim, although he had implied it, and once the book appeared he did not publicly discount Swinton's assertion. With its research and wide readership, Swinton's account became regarded as an authoritative study.[5]

Longstreet, meanwhile, had settled with his family in New Orleans and become a partner in a cotton brokerage. A realist, he had accepted the Confederate defeat and endeavored to fashion a livelihood in the postwar nation. When Congress passed the Reconstruction Acts in 1867, which imposed military rule upon the region, he cautioned his fellow Southerners "to accept the terms that are now offered by the conquerors." Other former Confederate officers and politicians echoed Longstreet's views. But the Georgian went further by arguing for cooperation with the Republican Party to preserve the South and to control the vote of newly enfranchised freedmen. Warned by friends and family that a public avowal of such views would result in a firestorm of protest, Longstreet nevertheless had a letter that presented these points published in a New Orleans newspaper.[6]

Southerners reacted with fury and indignation, some of them branding him a traitor and others sending him death threats. He was surprised and confused by the fierce reaction to his letter and probably never understood the portent of his words about race relations in the South. Longstreet worsened his public image when, in March 1869, he accepted the position of surveyor of customs for the Port of New Orleans from Republican president Ulysses S. Grant, his closest friend in the antebellum army. To many Southerners, the former general had committed an unpardonable sin, becoming a member of the hated Black Republicans.[7]

Robert E. Lee died in Lexington, Virginia, on October 12, 1870. His death brought an outpouring of grief from Southerners. He and "Stonewall" Jackson, who died as a martyr to the cause during the war, were the foremost Confederate heroes. Lee's character, religious devotion, adherence to duty, and wartime brilliance as a general had come to embody the Southern ideal of manhood. His passage also soon brought a concerted effort to enhance further Lee's reputation and the creation of a Southern interpretation of the terrible conflict that had cost the region so much in blood and property.

Lee's death crystallized the efforts of individuals who would fashion the "Lost Cause" interpretation. Jubal Early, William Nelson Pendleton, and Rev. John William Jones led the refashioning of history, and along with others, mostly fellow Virginians, would dominate the forthcoming histories of the war. In 1873, Early and his followers seized control of the fledgling Southern Historical Society and used the organization as the central organ for the espousal of their views. Three years later, with Jones as editor, the Society began publishing the *Southern Historical Society Papers.* The Lost Cause interpretation prevailed in its pages, which ultimately totaled fifty-two volumes. Jones and other contributors were committed to the defense of secession and the Confederate conduct of the war.[8]

The Lost Cause interpretation offered Southerners a comforting explanation for their sacrifices and the reality of defeat. They had stood shoulder to shoulder in battle ranks for a righteous cause blessed by God, had given undying devotion to it, and had endured unparalleled sacrifices during the conflict. In the end, Confederate soldiers had not been defeated in battle, they were instead overwhelmed by the Union's materiel superiority and armed might. They had waged an honorable struggle, a four-year war for independence and the perpetuation of a superior society. The conflict's cost and ultimate defeat demanded justification, and the creators of the Lost Cause provided "the perpetuation of the Confederate ideal."[9]

Central to the arguments fashioned by Early, Pendleton, Jones, and others was Lee's reputation. In their hands, Lee surpassed Jackson in stature, the flawless general who single-handedly almost achieved Southern independence. Lee's generalship rose above criticism, and any individual who found fault with the Confederate commander committed heresy. The Virginian became encased in a historical image few, if any, dared to challenge.[10]

However, Lee's defeat at Gettysburg, in the words of two modern historians, "threatened the entire rationale" of the Lost Cause argument. Lee's performance and responsibility for the battle's outcome required explanation and a defense. Early and his fellow adherents felt compelled to demonstrate that Lee was blameless at Gettysburg, a battle that would become the great "if" of Confederate history. They needed a scapegoat, a subordinate officer whose conduct had been so egregious as to bring defeat to the great Lee and the Confederate cause. That officer was James Longstreet, a turncoat Southerner who had evidently criticized Lee in Swinton's pages and had joined the Republican Party. The result was, according to Thomas L. Connelly and Barbara L. Bellows, "a historiographical puzzle, involving a total 'rewriting' of the Gettysburg saga by former Confederates."[11]

Like Longstreet, Jubal Early had been a lieutenant general and corps commander in Lee's army. The Virginian, however, had been subjected to criticism during the war and in its immediate aftermath for his performances at Gettysburg and in the 1864 Shenandoah Valley campaign in which he had commanded Confederate forces and had suffered three battlefield defeats. He was irascible, contentious, and an unreconstructed rebel who had fled the country for a time after Appomattox. Early could be a formidable, even relentless, opponent when it came to his reputation and Lee's.

In a January 1872 speech, Early framed the primary charge against Longstreet at Gettysburg, asserting that the First Corps commander had been slow to act on July 2. Early claimed Lee expected Longstreet to attack the Federal line at dawn on the battle's second day. Instead, Longstreet did not begin the assault until four o'clock in the afternoon, resulting in defeat on that critical day. Early's contention, although historically false, became the accepted explanation for the Confederate defeat in Pennsylvania.[12]

A year later, Lee's former artillery chief, William Nelson Pendleton, reiterated Early's allegations, claiming that Lee had issued an order to Longstreet to attack the Yankees at sunrise. This so-called "sunrise order" was "completely fabricated" by the inept former artillerist, who went even further than Early, accusing Longstreet of "culpable disobedience" and "treachery." Both Early's and Pendleton's speeches were either printed or repeated by them throughout the South.[13]

When Early, Pendleton, and Jones assumed control of the Southern Historical Society they had an organ to spread their views. The Society commenced publication of its *Papers* in 1876, and beginning with volume three in 1877, undertook a so-called Gettysburg Series. The charges against Longstreet initiated by Early and Pendleton soon became entrenched as the central factor that led to the Confederate defeat at Gettysburg. A number of former Confederates weighed in with articles indicting the former First Corps commander. Their indictment of Longstreet exonerated Lee and further bolstered the Lost Cause interpretation.[14]

At first, Longstreet reacted to the charges with silence. He knew that his critics were wrong, and, as he confided to a friend, he preferred "that I should bear the responsibility than to put it upon our chief." But former comrades urged him to answer the allegations. Finally, in the spring of 1875, he wrote to Pendleton, demanding evidence of a "sunrise order." He also corresponded with former members of Lee's staff— Walter Taylor, Charles Marshall, Charles Venable, and Armistead L. Long—for assistance. Each one replied in writing, stating that he knew nothing of the existence of such an order.[15]

Longstreet would have been better served had he heeded his own words and not responded publicly to the allegations. But to stand accused as the man who had cost the Confederacy its independence merited a response to Early, Pendleton, and the others. Unfortunately for Longstreet, he was neither a skillful nor a careful writer, and he replied in articles and a memoir that contained misstatements of fact and unfair criticisms of Lee and his fellow officers in the army. His writings only fueled the acrimony and increased the number of critics.[16]

During the next two decades Longstreet contributed articles to the *Philadelphia Weekly Times,* which were bound with other veterans' writings into *The Annals of the War* (1879), and to *Century Magazine*'s *Battles and Leaders of the Civil War* series. His memoir, *From Manassas to Appomattox,* appeared in 1896. He had decided to answer his critics in print, as he explained in his "Lee In Pennsylvania" piece for the *Weekly Times,* because "I have been so repeatedly and so rancorously assailed by those whose intimacy with the commanding general in that battle gave an apparent importance to their assaults." His purpose, he added, was to present "a plain and logical recital of the facts both timely and important."[17]

But the old warrior offered more than a "recital of the facts," crediting himself with more than was historically accurate, blaming others for his mistakes, denying his own culpability, and, worst of all to his opponents, criticizing Lee in a manner that was uncharitable and unfair. In his memoir, Longstreet stated that at Gettysburg the fact that Lee "was excited and off his balance was evident on the afternoon of the 1st, and he labored under that oppression until enough blood was shed to appease him."[18]

These latter words in particular infuriated Southerners and further alienated Longstreet from them. Even the former officers and men of the First Corps, who still regarded him with affection and respect, could not defend their commander. Earlier, when Longstreet had attributed to himself the plan to strike George B. McClellan's right flank at Mechanicsville in the Seven Days' campaign, Lee's staff officers joined the opposition, and their accounts reflected the central elements of the Lost Cause argument. By the turn of the century, Longstreet's critics were, according to one historian, "able to destroy much of his reputation."[19]

Longstreet died at his daughter's home in Gainesville, Georgia, on January 2, 1904. Hundreds of people, including First Corps veterans, attended his funeral. Notably, however, numerous camps of the United Confederate Veterans refused either to send a delegation or to offer resolutions of condolences. Helen Dortch Longstreet, who had married the widowed general in 1897, prepared a defense of her husband's Civil War career that was published in 1904. *Lee and Longstreet at High Tide: Get-*

tysburg in the Light of the Official Records recounted his life as a soldier, focusing on his role at Gettysburg, and reproduced 133 pages worth of letters and tributes that she had received upon his death.[20]

Within three years, two important books written by wartime intimates of Longstreet appeared. G. Moxley Sorrel's *Recollections of a Confederate Staff Officer* was published in 1905, and was followed two years later by E. Porter Alexander's *Military Memoirs of a Confederate*. Both authors—Sorrel was Longstreet's chief of staff and Alexander his artillery chief—were fair but not uncritical in their assessments of their former commander. To the present, both works are highly regarded by historians, with Alexander's book standing as the finest account of Lee's army written by a participant. But Sorrell's, Alexander's, and Helen Longstreet's books were not able to salvage the general's reputation after three decades of printed attacks by his critics.[21]

By the first decade of the twentieth century, the basic elements of the Lost Cause argument had become entrenched in interpretations of the war. It was as if the South had achieved ultimate victory in the war by winning the recounting of its history. However, the Lost Cause's shadow would only lengthen and darken historical studies as historians replaced Civil War veterans as chroniclers of the country's greatest tragedy. In the hands of historians, would Longstreet still stand arraigned, as he once said, "as the person and only one responsible for the loss of the cause"?[22]

During the 1930s and 1940s, Charles Scribner's Sons published *R. E. Lee: A Biography* and *Lee's Lieutenants: A Study in Command*, multivolume studies written by Douglas Southall Freeman, the most important historian of the Army of Northern Virginia. In magnificent prose, Freeman, a Virginian and the son of one of Lee's veterans, painted portraits of Lee and his subordinate officers that remain unmatched by any succeeding historians. Freeman's magisterial works confirmed both Lee's qualities as a man and his greatness as a general and Stonewall Jackson's brilliance as a subordinate and his rank as Lee's finest lieutenant. Freeman's analyses and judgments would have a profound, even unparalleled, impact upon future studies of the army.[23]

Arguably, no officer in Lee's army suffered more in Freeman's volumes than did Longstreet. His description and assessment of the First Corps commander seemingly gave a stamp of authenticity to a number of elements of the Lost Cause argument. Although Freeman refined the criticisms leveled at Longstreet during the postwar decades, the author accused the Georgian of slowness, sulkiness, and even "insubordination" at Gettysburg. He condemned Longstreet for his ambition, his jealousies, and, in telling words, charged that Lee's senior subordinate was "beguiled by circumstances into thinking himself a strategist as well as an executive officer. His failure at Gettysburg is one result of his mistake concerning his aptitudes."[24]

Freeman's harsh treatment of Longstreet in his Pulitzer Prize–winning biography of Lee was moderated in his study of the army's senior lieutenants. In the Lee biography, for instance, Freeman stated that on August 29, 1862, at Second Manassas, when Lee agreed to postpone an attack on Longstreet's advice, "the seeds of much of the disaster at Gettysburg were sown in that instant—when Lee yielded to Longstreet and Longstreet discovered that he would." Less than a year later at Gettysburg, Longstreet, according to Freeman, "desired to delay the action indefinitely" on July 2, was "listless and despairing" on the third, and acted throughout the battle "in sullen resentment that Lee rejected his long-cherished plan of a strategic offensive and a tactical defensive."[25]

A decade later, in *Lee's Lieutenants*, Freeman offered a fairer, more historically accurate assessment of Longstreet. The Virginian praised Lee's senior subordinate for his performance during the Seven Days' campaign, asserting that he "stood pre-eminent" among the division commanders. As for Second Manassas, Freeman now left open to question whether Longstreet thought that he could impose his will upon Lee. The author noted, however, that Jackson's troops bore the brunt of the combat and ignored Jackson's failure to advance in support of Longstreet's counterattack on the afternoon of August 30. Finally, Freeman dismissed the allegation that Longstreet was slow in his march to the Wilderness battlefield in May 1864, arguing that the charges "rest on no sure foundation."[26]

Most significantly, however, Freeman wrote of Longstreet at Gettysburg: "it does not warrant the traditional accusation that he was the villain of the piece. The mistakes of Lee, and of Ewell and the long absence of Stuart were personal factors of failure as serious as Longstreet's." Furthermore, the author contended that the corps commander's "instinct was correct" in opposing the July 2 assault and that "the orders should not have been given" by Lee for an attack. To Freeman, the allegation that Longstreet was slow to act on July 2 had no merit. His research indicated that the Federals occupied Cemetery Ridge in strength by 7 A.M., and "in that fact, which is historically verifiable," he concluded, "much of the criticism of Longstreet evaporates."[27]

Freeman believed, however, that Longstreet's disagreement with Lee over the resumption of the offensive on the second affected the subordinate's conduct. Freeman quoted Moxley Sorrel, who in his recollections stated that "there was apparent apathy in his [Longstreet's] movements. They lacked the fire and point of his usual bearing on the battlefield." After 11 A.M., when Lee issued the order to attack, Longstreet's "every important act for the next few hours showed that he had resolved to put on Lee the entire responsibility for what happened. In plain, ugly words, he sulked." In other words, "the dissent of Longstreet's mind was a brake on his energies."[28]

In the end, according to Freeman, "lacking Jackson, Lee could not win. The price of victory at Chancellorsville was defeat at Gettysburg." Although Freeman's conclusion was impossible to prove, his view reflected the general tenor of his study of command in Lee's army. Jackson dominated the pages, emerging as Lee's unrivaled chief lieutenant. When his death at Chancellorsville dissolved the partnership between the two men, the army was doomed to ultimate defeat. Consequently, Jackson's preeminence in Freeman's pages relegated the rest of Lee's lieutenants, and most notably Longstreet, to a diminished stature. It harked back to Jubal Early's portrayal of Lee and Jackson together leading the army to a string of victories until fate interceded in the dark woods around Chancellorsville.[29]

More than a half century after the publication of Freeman's multivolume works, the face of Civil War history and scholarship has been transformed. During the intervening years, public interest in the conflict has increased, luring more historians into the field, and the demands of research and scholarship have expanded knowledge in all areas related to the four-year struggle and reshaped interpretations. The vast array of books and articles has left unexamined few, if any, aspects of the war. The treatment accorded James Longstreet during these decades reflects the deep imprint of the Lost Cause argument and the new conclusions fashioned from the scholarly use of more manuscript material.

Two Virginians, H. J. Eckenrode and Bryan Conrad, a historian and a retired army officer respectively, produced the first in-depth biography of Longstreet in 1936. Eckenrode and Conrad were highly critical of Lee's "Old War Horse," finding fault with the general's performance on nearly every major battlefield. The authors concluded that Longstreet was "not a great commander" and "not much more really than an average corps general." His "sin" was "overwhelming ambition." They added that Longstreet "was beside himself with the thirst and hunger for fame and high position." Unlike Jackson, they asserted, "Longstreet always thought first of himself, secondarily of the cause."[30]

In 1952, Donald Bridgman Sanger and Thomas Robson Hay followed with another, more complete, biography of Longstreet. Sanger and Hay were sympathetic biographers, arguing that the Confederate general was "far above the average" as a combat officer and a "dogged fighter and brilliant tactician." At Gettysburg, Longstreet had, in their view, committed the "sin of omission." They believed that "Longstreet erred—but not to the extent that most writers have asserted."[31]

During the late 1950s and the 1960s, four books penned by two gifted writers appeared that revealed the strident controversy still associated with Longstreet's performance in the war. Clifford Dowdey, a Virginian, seemed to embrace the major tenets of the Lost Cause interpretation as it pertained to Longstreet. In his *Death of a Nation: The Story of Lee and His Men at Gettysburg* (1958) and *Lee* (1965), Dowdey described Longstreet as "methodical and slow-moving," "deluded" by a desire for independent command, jealous of Jackson, insubordinate at Gettysburg and late at the Wilderness, and "a limited soldier." The general's postwar writings, in Dowdey's view, revealed a man who "invented things that never happened, distorted recorded incidents, told outright lies apparently without realizing it, and contributed himself in his various accounts." Curiously, Dowdey utilized accounts that contained the same faults he attributed to Longstreet as the basis for his research.[32]

At Gettysburg, according to Dowdey, "Longstreet's behavior revealed the resentful, intransigent humor of a rejected collaborator." When Lee rejected Longstreet's proposal for a flank movement, the subordinate "lost control of himself" and acted "like a sulky child." On July 3, Longstreet committed "insubordination" when he did not obey orders to attack at an early hour and became "unfit to direct" the afternoon assault because of his "frame of mind."[33]

In contrast to Dowdey, Glenn Tucker offered a more favorable evaluation of Longstreet in *High Tide at Gettysburg: The Campaign in Pennsylvania* (1958) and *Lee and Longstreet at Gettysburg* (1968). Tucker avowed that there was no evidence of the "sunrise order" allegedly issued by Lee on July 2. "Both from time and from lack of substance," he wrote, the historical claim that Longstreet was responsible for the Confederate defeat falls apart on a reexamination of the sources. To Tucker, Lee's senior subordinate "liked to win. He was not a man to gamble much in battle," and this caution explains much of his dispute with Lee on the Pennsylvania battlefield.[34]

The same year in which Tucker's *Lee and Longstreet at Gettysburg* appeared, Edwin B. Coddington's *The Gettysburg Campaign: A Study in Command* was published. Regarded as the finest single-volume study of the operation, Coddington's book rendered a judicious, even-handed interpretation of Longstreet's performance. The general's "mistake," in Coddington's judgment, "was to take a pragmatic observation [the superiority of the tactical defensive over the tactical offensive] and mold it into a dogma." He claims Longstreet deserves censure for failing to begin shifting his troops to the right, toward the Federal left flank, between nine and eleven o'clock on the morning of July 2. He describes the subsequent march as "a comedy of errors," but adds that the soundness of Lee's attack plan was "debatable." On July 3, according to Coddington, when Longstreet did not assail the Union position soon after daylight, he "stretched his orders out of shape by interpreting them too liberally." Like other ranking officers in the army, including Lee, Longstreet contributed to the outcome.[35]

But more recent studies reveal how tenacious the Lost Cause interpretation remains in Civil War historiography. Steven E. Woodworth has asserted that at Gettysburg Longstreet "had come as close as anyone could to losing single-handedly what passed for the great battle of the war." In another book, Woodworth, while admitting that Longstreet could handle a large body of troops better than other generals "of far greater intellect and genius for the art of war," said the corps commander's actions showed that he "required guidance in the application of his skills."[36]

Emory Thomas in his biography of Lee echoes some of Woodworth's views, arguing that "Longstreet seemed incapable of initiative or action when left to his own devices." Lee, according to Thomas, often shared a march or a campsite with Longstreet "in order to advise his 'Old War Horse' and when necessary to prod him into action."[37]

In his retelling of events at Gettysburg, Thomas relied upon the works of Lee's staff officers and Freeman's biography of the army commander, not Freeman's more favorable portrait in *Lee's Lieutenants*. Thomas repeats the charge that Lee had ordered Longstreet to attack "as soon as possible" on July 2, before he left his subordinate to confer with Richard S. Ewell. "Longstreet acted out of petulance on July 2," according to Thomas. He adds that the Georgian "seemed determined to do everything in his power within the letter of military law to render his dire prophecy [that the Federals welcomed an attack] self-fulfilling. No one can know what would have happened had Longstreet attacked earlier in the day. But as it happened, the officers and men of Longstreet's corps paid a high price for attacking when they did." Nevertheless, Thomas attributes the defeat to Lee because the commander preferred to suggest rather than to order.[38]

However, no other present-day historian has attacked Longstreet's performance at Gettysburg more than Robert K. Krick. In a volume of essays by various scholars on the second day's battle, Krick describes Longstreet as "small minded and mean spirited," with a "tincture of the dullard." The author quotes Armistead Long of Lee's staff—"what *can* detain Longstreet," Lee said to Long—but places the comment out of the proper chronological sequence on that day. Krick further colors his characterization of Longstreet by using the words "sullen" and "sulking" to indicate Longstreet's temperament. His portrait of Longstreet is harsh, unleavened by countervailing evidence.[39]

Two other books, neither of which deals with Gettysburg, typify how the standard, if not tired, condemnations of Longstreet have persisted. James I. Robertson Jr. states in a biography of Stonewall Jackson that Longstreet demonstrated "a slowness that would breed generations of postwar controversy." Additionally, Joseph L. Harsh has used the phrases "stubborn subordinate" and "unenthusiastic subordinate" to describe Longstreet at Second Manassas. Harsh contends that on August 29 there was "undue influence seemingly exerted by Longstreet over Lee." He further states that during the Confederate attack on the thirtieth "effective coordination between Longstreet and Jackson was never established"—without noting that Jackson, despite orders from Lee, did not advance until two hours after Longstreet's troops moved to the assault.[40]

During the past several years a number of books have offered a counterbalance to history's traditional judgment of Longstreet. In a fine study of the Second Manassas campaign, for instance, John J. Hennessy has destroyed the allegation of Longstreet's recalcitrance and imposition of his will upon Lee on August 29. Longstreet's concerns on that day were "valid," in Hennessy's view. He adds that "Longstreet did not overbear or dominate R. E. Lee." In fact, his "timely, powerful, and swift" counterattack the next day "would come as close to destroying a Union army as any ever could." That it did not, Hennessy indicates, perhaps resulted from Jackson's failure to "advance promptly," which "stands as one of the mysteries of the battle." In the end, Hennessy concludes, "Second Manassas represented James Longstreet's most important contribution to any of Lee's victories."[41]

Moreover, three recent books have focused on Longstreet as a soldier and on his place in Southern history. William Garrett Piston has examined the general's wartime career and the Lost Cause authors' efforts to shape that record during the postwar years. Similarly, I have written a biography of the soldier, the bulk of which covers the Civil War years. Finally, several scholars have contributed essays on Longstreet as a modern soldier, his antebellum career, at Gettysburg, at Chickamauga, on his staff, and in Southern history in a recently published study. Combined, these works provide a nontraditional, anti–Lost Cause examination of Longstreet's life and military career.[42]

To be sure, James Longstreet had failings as a general. He evidently misunderstood his orders at Seven Pines on May 31, 1862, and bungled the attack while blaming other officers after the action for the outcome. He merits censure for not attending to duties between nine and eleven o'clock on the morning of July 2, 1863, at Gettysburg, which required him to prepare for an offensive attack that he opposed. He became embroiled in a plot among ranking officers in the Army of Tennessee to remove its commander, Braxton Bragg, during the autumn of 1863. Finally, he mishandled operations against Knoxville, Tennessee, later that year, then preferred charges against subordinates in its aftermath.[43]

Despite these failures, Longstreet ranks as one of the conflict's finest combat officers and corps commanders. He demonstrated a talent for handling large numbers of troops on the march and in battle. He was not slow at Second Manassas, late at the Wilderness, or insubordinate at Gettysburg. His troops' counterattacks in size and power at Second Manassas and at the Wilderness remain unmatched by any other Confederate general. He saw war starkly and understood that the Confederacy could not continue to allow its lifeblood to flow away in attacks and expect to win against a numerically superior North. He advocated the strategic offensive and the tactical defensive. At Gettysburg, his belief clashed with Lee's desire to assail the enemy, resulting in what would become, arguably, the most heated controversy in the military history of the war.[44]

It was this disagreement with Lee and Longstreet's reaction to it that has formed the cornerstone of criticism about his generalship at Gettysburg and on other battlefields. Early and Pendleton fabricated the initial charge that Longstreet disobeyed a "sunrise order." It persisted in historical writing for nearly a century and helped to create the image of a stubborn and opinionated—if not insubordinate—general who was slow to act in battle. Their portrayal of Longstreet as a sulking, delaying, and disobedient subordinate resulted in his being tarred with the responsibility for the defeat at Gettysburg, the "High Tide of the Confederacy."

The reality is that Longstreet did not reach the southern Pennsylvania crossroads town until about 5 P.M. on July 1 because he remained behind to expedite the movement of troops and wagons on the Chambersburg Pike when Lee spurred ahead upon hearing cannon fire about midday. Upon his arrival, he found Lee near the Lutheran seminary buildings. Lee was busy, so Longstreet studied the terrain beyond the town—Culp's Hill and Cemetery Ridge. He saw the ground's natural strength and did not like what he saw.[45]

When Lee finished his work, Longstreet turned to his commander and friend, and said: "We could not call the enemy to position better suited to our plans. All that we have to do is file around his left and secure good ground between him and his capital."

Lee's reaction to the suggestion indicated disapproval. He pointed toward the Federals, and exclaimed, "If the enemy is there tomorrow, we must attack him."

"If he is there," replied Longstreet, "it will be because he is anxious that we should attack him—a good reason, in my judgment for not doing so."[46]

In their meetings at Fredericksburg before the campaign began and during the march north into Pennsylvania, Lee and Longstreet, in the words of the latter, had concurred on "the ruling idea of the campaign." As Longstreet explained to Lafayette McLaws in a postwar letter: "Under no circumstances were we to give battle, but exhaust our skill in trying to force the enemy to do so in a position of our own choosing. The 1st Corps to receive the attack and fight the battle. The other corps to then fall upon and try to destroy the Army of the Potomac."[47]

The letter is significant, giving credence to Longstreet's postwar writings on the campaign and an explanation of the two generals' thinking in the weeks before the battle. Other senior officers and Lee's staff members believed similarly that, if circumstances permitted, the army would offer battle from a defensive position. But on the afternoon of July 1, Lee reacted to what he had just witnessed—the rout of two Union corps. He had not wanted a battle that day. However, because Jeb Stuart and his cavalry were missing, Lee could not find the flank of George Meade's army nor screen the movement of his own. He correctly rejected Longstreet's plan. The battle was at hand, and Lee decided to wage it.[48]

Longstreet believed that Lee was wrong. Early on the morning of July 2 he repeated his proposal, and Lee again rejected it. Although Longstreet's strategic flanking movement had too many uncertainties for Lee to adopt it, the corps commander's belief in waging a defensive fight was, from history's perspective, right. E. Porter Alexander asserted later that the Yankees held at Gettysburg a "wonderfully strong position" that "could never have been successfully assaulted." Moreover, Meade had the advantage of interior lines to hasten the movement of troops and a position anchored on both flanks by high ground. Conversely, Alexander described the five-mile-long Confederate line as an "*utter absurdity*," adding that "it was simply preposterous to *hope* to win a battle when so strung out & separated that cooperation between the three corps was impossible except by a miracle. And comparatively little pains was exercised to bring it about either."[49]

Longstreet, however, allowed his disagreement with Lee to affect his conduct on July 2 and 3. In Moxley Sorrel's words, his commander "failed to conceal some anger." Longstreet knew by 9 A.M. on the second that Lee had settled upon an assault against the Union left flank. Duty required that he attend to the details of the march, reconnoiter the route and terrain, and probably begin to move in that direction. He did none of those things. Instead, he waited for Lee to return from a meeting with Ewell. When Lee finally appeared, he issued the attack order.[50]

Although the subsequent march required a countermarch when the column came in sight of a Union signal station on Little Round Top, it was not "a comedy of errors," as described by Coddington. Longstreet moved fourteen thousand troops several miles and brought them into position in a little more than three hours. In turn, Longstreet has been criticized for rejecting John Bell Hood's proposal for a tactical flanking movement around Big Round Top. But time had run out on the Confederates, and the evidence indicates that Lee was nearby and might have concurred with Longstreet. The argument that Hood's plan offered success is predicated upon the assumption that the Federals would not have reacted to a movement which would have been visible to them.[51]

At 4 P.M., Longstreet's troops launched their attack. The Confederates struck the Union Third Corps, commanded by Daniel Sickles, who had moved off of Cemetery Ridge into the valley at the Peach Orchard and Devil's Den. Sickles's action created a salient that the rebels crushed, after which they threatened to wrest Little Round Top from the Federals. Had Sickles not abandoned the heights, Longstreet's units would not have had a target. Lee's offensive plans did not make tactical sense if the Northerners held Cemetery Ridge. He had fashioned them from an erroneous report given to him by a reconnaissance party. Yet for most of the morning and early afternoon neither Lee nor Longstreet, or any other officer, conducted another reconnaissance. They were undoubtedly surprised to find the enemy in force along the Emmitsburg Road. Their failure to reconnoiter the Federal position before the attack was indicative of the breakdown of the Confederate command system at Gettysburg.[52]

That night, Lee issued instructions for a renewal of the offensive against both flanks of Meade's army at daylight. In his memoir, Longstreet denied that he received the order, but that was not true; in fact, he began to implement it. However, neither he nor Lee had informed George E. Pickett, whose division was bivouacked a few miles to the west, to be on the field at daylight. Consequently, when Lee joined Longstreet early on the morning of July 3, the latter was not beginning the attack. Instead, Longstreet proposed another flanking movement, which Lee rejected with an apparent show of some anger. On the opposite flank, Ewell's troops had engaged in a struggle for Culp's Hill.[53]

Once again, Lee had to adapt his plans. The result was the doomed attack on the Union center that afternoon. Although Longstreet strongly objected to it, Lee placed him in command of the assault. How well the Georgian performed his duties on that day remains open to dispute. What is certain is that he could barely issue the order for Pickett to advance: "Never was I so depressed as upon that day. I felt that my men were to be sacrificed and that I should have to order them to make a hopeless charge."[54]

Reasons for the Confederate defeat at Gettysburg are numerous, not the least of which was the performance of Meade and his army. Lee, along with others, believed that his troops could accomplish almost anything, and he asked them to do it at Gettysburg. Longstreet, of course, must share responsibility for the outcome. But, as Porter Alexander noted afterward, his superior's performance could be vindicated. "It is true," wrote Alexander of Longstreet, "that he obeyed *reluctantly* at Gettysburg, on the 2nd & on the 3rd, but it must be admitted that his judgment in both matters was sound & he owed it to Lee *to be reluctant*, for failure was *inevitable* do it soon, or do it late, either day." Lee, Longstreet, and the army had fought the wrong battle on the wrong field.[55]

When Longstreet rode away from Appomattox he was deservedly proud of his record as a Confederate soldier. He bore the scars of a wound that would maim him for life. He possessed the affection and respect of his men, who had appreciated his reluctance to send them forward in a doomed assault. He had demonstrated executive ability as a corps commander, created the finest staff in the army, and enjoyed Lee's friendship and respect.[56]

With the war's end, he belonged to history, and it would not be kind. When the attacks came from former comrades, he answered, contributing to history's verdict with his own writings. He overstated his own accomplishments, misstated facts, and appeared to be arrogant. His postwar career in the Republican Party made him a vulnerable target, denying him the sympathy and support that he needed. By the time of his death, his opponents had created a history of the conflict that continues to this day. Undoubtedly, James Longstreet was the greatest victim of the Lost Cause interpretation.[57]

Longstreet confided privately in 1876 that "it has been my feeling and opinion, that it would have been better to leave to the historian, and the student of future days, the records of our struggle from which the history should be made; that those of us who bore prominent parts in the struggle should recognize its failure, and should submit to the responsibilities of that failure, as belonging to us all in proportion to our positions and opportunities." Had he known what his share of history's judgment would be, he might have thought otherwise.[58]

Notes

1. Jeffry D. Wert, *General James Longstreet: The Confederacy's Most Controversial Soldier—A Biography* (New York: Simon and Schuster, 1993), 17–19.

2. Ibid.

3. William Garrett Piston, *Lee's Tarnished Lieutenant: James Longstreet and His Place in Southern History* (Athens: University of Georgia Press, 1987), 98.

4. Quoted in Thomas L. Connelly, *The Marble Man: Robert E. Lee and His Image in American Society* (New York: Alfred A. Knopf, 1977), 56–57.

5. Ibid., 56; Piston, *Lee's Tarnished Lieutenant*, 96.

6. Wert, *General James Longstreet*, 407–12.

7. Ibid., 412–13.

8. Piston, *Lee's Tarnished Lieutenant*, 118, 119, 133; Connelly, *Marble Man*, 72, 73.

9. Piston, *Lee's Tarnished Lieutenant*, 109–13; Thomas L. Connelly and Barbara L. Bellows, *God and General Longstreet: The Lost Cause and the Southern Mind* (Baton Rouge: Louisiana State University Press, 1982), 2, 10, 22.

10. Connelly, *Marble Man*, chaps. 1–3.

11. Connelly and Bellows, *God and General Longstreet*, 31, 32.

12. Ibid., 34; Piston, *Lee's Tarnished Lieutenant*, 119, 121; Connelly, *Marble Man*, 56.

13. Piston, *Lee's Tarnished Lieutenant*, 121, 122.

14. Ibid., x, 133; Connelly, *Marble Man*, 87; *Southern Historical Society Papers* (reprint, Millwood, N.Y.: Kraus Reprint Co., 1977), see particularly vols. 3–6.

15. Wert, *General James Longstreet*, 422–23; Piston, *Lee's Tarnished Lieutenant*, 124; Walter H. Taylor, *Four Years with General Lee* (reprint, Bloomington: Indiana University Press, 1962), 98; *The Annals of the War, Written by Leading Participants North and South* (reprint, Dayton, Ohio: Morningside House, 1988), 437–38.

16. Wert, *General James Longstreet*, 423; Piston, *Lee's Tarnished Lieutenant*, 124, 125.

17. *Annals*, 414–46 (quote on 415), 619–33; Robert Underwood Johnson and Clarence Clough Buel, eds., *Battles and Leaders of the Civil War* (reprint, New York: Thomas Yoseloff, 1956), 2:396–405, 512–26, 663–74; 3:70–85,

244–50, 339–53. See also James Longstreet, *From Manassas to Appomattox: Memoirs of the Civil War in America* (Philadelphia: J. B. Lippincott, 1896).

18. *Annals*, 421, 422, 433; Longstreet, *From Manassas to Appomattox*, 384, 385, 388.

19. Wert, *General James Longstreet*, 295–97; Piston, *Lee's Tarnished Lieutenant*, 127, 128; Connelly, *Marble Man*, 64. For examples of former Confederates critical of Longstreet, see Taylor, *Four Years;* Walter H. Taylor, *General Lee: His Campaigns In Virginia, 1861–1865, With Personal Reminiscences* (reprint, Dayton, Ohio: Morningside, 1975); Frederick Maurice, ed., *An Aide-De-Camp Of Lee: Being The Papers Of Colonel Marshall Sometime Aide-De-Camp, Military Secretary, And Assistant Adjutant General On The Staff Of Robert E. Lee 1862–1865* (Boston: Little, Brown, 1927); and Armistead L. Long, *Memoirs Of Robert E. Lee: His Military And Personal History* (New York and Philadelphia: J. M. Stoddart, 1886).

20. Wert, *General James Longstreet*, 425–27; Helen D. Longstreet, *Lee And Longstreet at High Tide: Gettysburg in the Light of the Official Records* (reprint, Wilmington, N.C.: Broadfoot, 1989).

21. G. Moxley Sorrel, *Recollections of a Confederate Staff Officer* (New York and Washington: Neale, 1905); E. P. Alexander, *Military Memoirs Of A Confederate: A Critical Narrative* (New York: Charles Scribner's Sons, 1907).

22. Quoted in Wert, *General James Longstreet*, 13.

23. Douglas Southall Freeman, *R. E. Lee: A Biography*, 4 vols. (New York: Charles Scribner's Sons, 1934–35); and *Lee's Lieutenants: A Study in Command*, 3 vols. (New York: Charles Scribner's Sons, 1942–44).

24. Freeman, *R. E. Lee*, 3:87, 89, 94; *Lee's Lieutenants*, 1:169; 3:xxix.

25. Freeman, *R. E. Lee*, 2:325; 3:85, 87, 89, 90, 94, 109, 147–52.

26. Freeman, *Lee's Lieutenants*, 1:663, 2:136–38, 3:441.

27. Ibid., 3:xii, 170, 173, 174, 175, 189.

28. Ibid., 3:115, 170, 173; Sorrel, *Recollections*, 157.

29. Freeman, *Lee's Lieutenants*, 3:xiii. See particularly vol. 2 for Jackson's dominance in the work.

30. H. J. Eckenrode and Bryan Conrad, *James Longstreet: Lee's War Horse* (Chapel Hill: University of North Carolina Press, 1936), 189, 190, 361, 362, 367, 368.

31. Donald Bridgman Sanger and Thomas Robson Hay, *James Longstreet: I. Soldier, II. Politician, Officeholder, and Writer* (Baton Rouge: Louisiana State University Press, 1952), 188, 446, 447. A very sympathetic biography is Wilbur Thomas, *General James "Pete" Longstreet, Lee's "Old War Horse": Scapegoat For Gettysburg* (Parsons, W.Va.: McClain, 1979).

32. Clifford Dowdey, *Lee* (Boston: Little, Brown, 1965) 291, 373, 376, 377, 383; and *Death of a Nation: The Story of Lee and His Men at Gettysburg*

(New York: Alfred A. Knopf, 1958), 117, 167, 169, 171, 173, 253; Connelly, *Marble Man*, 160.

33. Dowdey, *Lee*, 373–77, 383; *Death of a Nation*, 169–73, 185, 253, 257.

34. Glenn Tucker, *Lee and Longstreet at Gettysburg* (Indianapolis: Bobbs-Merrill, 1968), 167, 172 (a careful analysis of the "sunrise order" can be found in chaps. 1–3); and *High Tide at Gettysburg: The Campaign in Pennsylvania* (Indianapolis: Bobbs-Merrill, 1958), 7, 217–19.

35. Edwin B. Coddington, *The Gettysburg Campaign: A Study in Command* (New York: Charles Scribner's Sons, 1968), 361, 378, 384, 455, 456, 457.

36. Steven E. Woodworth, *Jefferson Davis and His Generals: The Failure of Confederate Command in the West* (Lawrence: University Press of Kansas, 1990), 235; and *Davis and Lee at War* (Lawrence: University Press of Kansas, 1995), 144, 245.

37. Emory M. Thomas, *Robert E. Lee: A Biography* (New York: W. W. Norton, 1995), 280, 290.

38. Ibid., 297, 302, 444 n 31, 32.

39. Robert K. Krick, "'If Longstreet . . . Says So, It Is Most Likely Not True': James Longstreet and the Second Day at Gettysburg," in *The Second Day At Gettysburg: Essays on Confederate and Union Leadership*, ed. Gary W. Gallagher (Kent, Ohio: Kent State University Press, 1993), 57, 58, 60–62, 68, 70 72, 74, 75, 77, 78.

40. James I. Robertson Jr., *Stonewall Jackson: The Man, The Soldier, The Legend* (New York: Macmillan, 1997), 463, 496, 574, 575; Joseph L. Harsh, *Confederate Tide Rising: Robert E. Lee and the Making of Southern Strategy, 1861–1862* (Kent, Ohio: Kent State University Press, 1998), 157, 158, 162.

41. John J. Hennessy, *Return to Bull Run: The Campaign and Battle of Second Manassas* (New York: Simon and Schuster, 1993), 459–61.

42. In *Lee's Tarnished Lieutenant*, 36, Piston concludes that "when it came to directing troops once the fighting had begun, he probably had no superior on either side during the war." See also Wert, *General James Longstreet;* and R. L. DiNardo and Albert A. Nofi, eds., *James Longstreet: The Man, The Soldier, The Controversy* (Conshohocken, Pa.: Combined Publishing, 1998).

43. See descriptions and analyses in Wert, *General James Longstreet*, chaps. 6, 13, 16, 17.

44. Ibid., chaps. 13, 14, and pp. 404–406.

45. Described in ibid., 256–57.

46. Longstreet's versions of this conversation varied. See *Battles and Leaders*, 3:339; *Annals*, 421; Longstreet, *From Manassas to Appomattox*, 358–59; Taylor, *Four Years*, 77.

47. James Longstreet to Lafayette McLaws, July 25, 1873, quoted in Wert, *General James Longstreet*, 266.

48. Ibid., 266–68.

49. E. P. Alexander to Frederick Colston, July 22, 1903, quoted in ibid., 266–67.

50. Ibid., 268–69; Sorrel, *Recollections*, 157.

51. Wert, *General James Longstreet*, 268–71.

52. Ibid., 274–78.

53. Ibid., 281–83; Longstreet, *From Manassas to Appomattox*, 385.

54. Wert, *General James Longstreet*, 283–92; *Annals*, 430.

55. E. P. Alexander to Mr. Bancroft, October 30, 1904, quoted in Wert, *General James Longstreet*, 295–96.

56. Ibid., 404–406, 407–408.

57. Ibid., chap. 20; Piston, *Lee's Tarnished Lieutenant*, chaps. 6–11.

58. James Longstreet to Henry B. Dawson, March 27, 1876, quoted in Wert, *General James Longstreet*, 13.

Seven

Continuous Hammering and Mere Attrition
Lost Cause Critics and the Military Reputation of Ulysses S. Grant

Brooks D. Simpson

On April 10, 1865, less than twenty-four hours after he had surrendered the Army of Northern Virginia to Ulysses S. Grant at Appomattox Courthouse, Robert E. Lee commenced a new conflict, one featuring rival explanations for defeat. To Lee it was all quite simple: although his men had displayed "unsurpassed courage and fortitude," they had been "compelled to yield to overwhelming numbers and resources."[1] Perhaps he could not have said anything else. He refrained from mentioning his concern about popular support for the Confederate war effort or errors committed by the Confederate civil and military hierarchy; it was not the time to say anything about the performance of the generals and armies that had prevailed. It was a time to commiserate and console; later generations might take a more dispassionate view. Yet that is not quite what happened: the Lee paradigm remains vibrant and robust as an explanation for the outcome of the American Civil War.

It did not take long for Southern chroniclers of the military history of the Confederacy to build upon the premises embodied in General Order No. 9 to explain what happened between 1861 and 1865. However, from the beginning the premises of these efforts contained potentially irksome contradictions. If Yankee victory was inevitable, a product of vastly superior resources that simply overwhelmed a valiant foe, then why speculate on critical moments when the Confederates glimpsed triumph? Why the intensive infighting and finger-pointing to determine who fell short at various junctures? If Appomattox represented the verdict of fate or God's will, why struggle to resist an outcome that in any case appeared preordained or fashioned by destiny? Yet such "what ifs" continued to haunt those white Southerners who wanted to refight every engagement, celebrate the valor of Johnny Reb, and praise the generalship of Lee and his trustworthy lieutenants. If the Confederacy had indeed been doomed to defeat, the futility of such an enterprise should have been self-evident. If the quest for Southern independence could have succeeded, then one had to account for why it fell short—and that in turn meant either making a begrudging admission about the quality of the foe or searching for scapegoats or other answers.

Lost Cause propagandists, scholars, and veterans did not always acknowledge these tensions and contradictions in their writings; to some extent they persist to this day, complicating the efforts of those people who held that the ending was inescapable. And yet one measure of the success of the Lost Cause version of Confederate defeat is the image a good number of Americans still have of the quality of generalship displayed by the Union commander most responsible for crushing secession: Ulysses S. Grant. At first glance one might think that Grant's story would inspire Americans, showing how ordinary people can accomplish extraordinary things, and how a seemingly common person has within him ability and character that emerges in times of crisis. But that would not do for Lost Cause explicators. What was most troubling to them about Grant was that he had prevailed over Robert E. Lee. If one could no longer defeat Grant, at least one might take solace in denigrating him. And that is what these scribes and speakers set out to do. Why and how they succeeded makes for an interesting tale in the crafting of American memory.

Perhaps the first book that set forth the Confederate case against the generalship of Ulysses S. Grant was Edward A. Pollard's *The Lost Cause.* A member of the editorial board of the *Richmond Examiner,* Pollard, like his Northern counterpart, the *New York Tribune*'s Horace Greeley, had issued several wartime histories; but *The Lost Cause* represented a chance to pull everything together in light of the war's outcome. Appearing first in 1866, then in a revised edition the following year, Pollard's book set forth a powerful and widely circulated analysis of the conflict through Confederate eyes. One of his prime targets was the Union's general-in-chief.[2]

Pollard repeatedly and diligently denigrated Grant's military record and attributed his success on the battlefield to factors other than his skilled generalship. At Fort Donelson, he explained, the Confederates failed to exploit their breakout attack in order to make good their escape. At Shiloh, P. G. T. Beauregard's decision not to press forward on the evening of April 6 proved fatal (he dismissed assertions made by advocates of Don Carlos Buell's army that it arrived in time to save the day). The Confederates lost Vicksburg because of the incompetence of John C. Pemberton (Pollard was quick to remind readers that Pemberton was the choice of Jefferson Davis, "who was constantly startling the public by the most unexpected and grotesque selections for the most important posts of military service"). Pollard also indicted Davis for the defeat at Chattanooga, for Davis had ordered James Longstreet to leave Braxton Bragg's Army of Tennessee to strike at Knoxville, evidence of his "singular fondness for erratic campaigns."[3]

None of these triumphs was due to any skill on Grant's part. That the Union commander had gained "a great reputation for persistency" meant little, for he had "at his disposal abundant means, and at his back a government so generous and rich as never to call its officers into account for the loss of life and of treasure in any case of ultimate success." That such claims did not reflect Grant's actual experience in the West was of little matter to Pollard. Grant, he asserted, "was one of the most remarkable accidents of the war . . . a man without any marked ability, certainly without genius, without fortune, without influence." His fame was a matter of some astonishment: "It is some consolation to reflect that the verdict of history is neither the sensation of a mob nor the fiat of a political faction." Although the general undoubtedly possessed "many good qualities of heart and great propriety of behavior," he "contained no spark of military genius; his idea of war was to the last degree rude—no strategy, no mere application of the *vis inertiae;* he had none of that quick perception on the field of action which decides it by sudden strokes; he had no conception of battle beyond the momentum of numbers." Now he would gather all his vast resources "to conquer the little army and overcome the consummate skill of General Lee"; lacking "appreciation of the higher aims and intellectual exercises of war . . . he proposed to decide it by a mere competition in the sacrifice of human life." After all, did not Grant admit in his final report that he had planned to prevail "by mere attrition, if in no other way"?[4]

Given Pollard's perspective, it comes as no surprise to readers of *The Lost Cause* to discover that he denigrates even Grant's most decided victories. Thus the fall of Petersburg was nothing more than "the consummation of the disgrace of this commander," for it had taken Grant eleven months to capture a position held by a force one-third the size of his own, having lost in the process two men for every one he faced. "As long as the intelligent of this world are persuaded of the opinion that a great general is he who accomplishes his purposes with small, but admirably drilled armies; who defeats large armies with small ones; who accomplishes great military results by strategy, more than by fighting; who makes of war an intellectual exercise rather than a match of brute force, that title will be given to Robert E. Lee above all men in America, and the Confederate commander will be declared to have been much greater in defeat than Grant in his boasted victory."[5]

To a remarkable extent, Pollard's narrative prefigured the traditional critique of Grant's generalship. Detractors claimed that his triumphs in the West were fortuitous, the result of fate or inferior performances by his counterpart, and that Grant prevailed in the East only because he possessed vast (and unlimited) resources. Some of these explanations ran athwart of one another. Having held that Beauregard's hesitation to press his advantage at Shiloh was fatal, Pollard insisted that Don Carlos Buell's Army of the Ohio had "rescued" him at Shiloh (and at Perryville, a remarkable feat in light of the fact that Grant was not present). Others depended upon a rather curious calculation of the comparative sizes and losses of rival armies. At the outset of the Wilderness campaign Pollard estimated Grant's force at 141,166; Lee could barely muster fifty thousand men of all arms, and opposed Grant with "*less than forty thousand muskets!*" Nevertheless, in the Wilderness (May 5–6, 1864), Union losses totaled 27,310, while Lee lost less than 7,000 men (and "the wounds were comparatively slight"). At Spotsylvania, on May 12 alone Grant lost another 18,000 men (versus Confederate losses that were somewhat less than half of that). To expend life at such a prodigious rate to reach a position along the James River that could have been seized at the onset of operations "without loss or opposition" was "simply and at once, absurd, disastrous, shocking, and contemptible." Lucky in the West and a blundering butcher in the East, Grant was certainly not a great captain.[6]

Several assessments offered by Confederate memorialists in the 1870s reinforced this impression. Richard Taylor's narrative recapitulated Pollard's analysis, attributing the outcome at Shiloh to the death of Albert Sidney Johnston. Taylor further concluded that "one has but to study the Virginia campaign of 1864, and imagine an exchange of resources by Grant and Lee, to find the true place of the former among the world's commanders." So, too, did Dabney H. Maury, who tried after the war to build the reputation denied him during the conflict by using his pen to rehabilitate himself through reflected fame by dropping names whenever he could. His analysis was novel chiefly because he grudgingly admitted that Grant's triumph at Donelson was "masterly" and credited him not only with the victory at Vicksburg but also with all of William T. Sherman's successes in 1864 and 1865. Nevertheless, Grant embraced attrition as a strategy. "Humanity revolts at it and history will arraign Grant for the recklessness with which he dashed his men to death," Maury announced. To persist in it was "criminal" (this from a man who in his writings did all he could to get Nathan Bedford Forrest off the hook for Fort Pillow). Maury arraigned Grant for the cessation of prisoner exchanges and claimed that he "was never stinted in material nor in men." These charges overshadowed Maury's admission that Grant was courageous, possessed good judgment, skillfully managed both his generals and his army, and was generous in victory. Still, "a fair review of Grant's career will not rank him high amongst the generals of history, and will not furnish such illustrations of the art of war as will cause military men to study his campaigns."[7]

A comparison of these evaluations of Grant's overall performance reveals the difficulties involved in Pollard's initial assessment of Grant's generalship in the West. It was one thing for a sharp-tongued newspaper editor often at odds with the Davis administration to highlight the incompetent performance of his appointees as instrumental in their Union counterpart's rise to prominence, but it behooved generals who served in the West—like Maury and Taylor—to come up with alternative explanations. That Joseph E. Johnston, Jefferson Davis, and John Pemberton expended much energy in affixing blame for the fall of Vicksburg did not flatter any of the participants. There were other dangers inherent in such an approach. If one attributed Grant's success to incompetent Confederate leadership in the West, could not a critic claim that Robert E. Lee built his reputation by foiling the awkward efforts of fumbling Federal generals in the East, depriving him of any true claim to greatness? Surely the superior resources and manpower argument invoked to explain the outcome in Virginia in 1864–65 was problematic in explaining what happened at Shiloh on April 6 (where the Confederates on the field outnumbered Grant's command at Pittsburg Landing), Vicksburg, or Chattanooga (where it was Longstreets's detachment that left Grant with a meaningful edge over Bragg).

Thus, aside from the repeated claim that only the death of Albert Sidney Johnston deprived the Confederacy of victory at Shiloh, Confederate military historians did not examine Grant's generalship in the West with care. It would be left to Grant's rivals in blue, notably those who swore allegiance to the Army of the Cumberland, to raise questions about what happened at Shiloh and Chattanooga; less important were debates over who conceived of the Forts Henry and Donelson offensive and the Vicksburg campaign. Instead, Confederate critics concentrated on taking apart Grant's performance against Robert E. Lee, determined to prove that what had happened in no way reflected any sort of superior generalship on Grant's part over the man so many had come to worship.

Although Pollard provided the outlines of a template to use in assailing Grant, it was left to former Confederate general Jubal Early to press the offensive. Just over a month after Lee's death on October 12, 1870, Early—incensed by a piece in the *London Standard* that argued that the numerical disparity between Lee's and Grant's forces in 1864 was nowhere near the estimates offered by Pollard and others—offered an extensive rebuttal based upon Secretary of War Edwin M. Stanton's annual report for 1865. In that report, Stanton offered an estimate of 141,160 officers and men available for duty in the Army of the Potomac and Ambrose Burnside's Ninth Corps on May 1, 1864. If one added to this number the forces present elsewhere in Virginia, Maryland, and the Washington defenses, the total skyrocketed to 278,832. What Grant proposed to accomplish with this force, Early argued, was to be found in the Union commander's report, in which he outlined his intention to mobilize the largest force possible, employ it in simultaneous movements against the Confederate defenders, and "to hammer continuously against the armed force of the enemy and his resources, until by mere attrition, if in no other way," the Union would prevail. Early then cited William Swinton's *Campaigns of the Army of the Potomac* in support of the claim that Grant lost some 60,000 men during the first forty days of battle against Lee. These numbers meant little without an assessment of Confederate strength, which Early, once again drawing upon estimates presumably composed by Swinton, concluded was in the neighborhood of 50,000 men. The following year, Lee biographer John Esten Cooke offered a similar assessment based upon the same evidence—although he added that Grant lost 13,000 men within the space of an hour on June 3 at Cold Harbor—a rather blatant distortion of the actual data, but one which helped clinch the case for Grant as a butcher.[8]

In 1872 Early fired another volley. Speaking before a friendly audience at Washington and Lee University, he again set forth some of the major premises of the anti-Grant school. Repeating his estimates of relative strengths and once more reciting the wording of Grant's report, Early then offered eloquent testimony to the skill and valor of Lee and his men, who dealt Grant's force blow after blow, leaving it "crippled and bleeding" after forty days of combat, even though it had received a steady stream of reinforcements. Following this onslaught, Grant was finally "compelled to take refuge on the South side of the James River." It was Confederate generalship at its finest: "When we consider the disparity of the forces engaged in this campaign, the advantages of the enemy for reinforcing his army, and the time consumed in actual battle, it must rank as the most remarkable campaign of ancient or modern times. . . . [W]here shall we find the history of such a prolonged struggle, in which such enormous advantages of numbers, equipped, resources and supplies, were on the side of the defeated party [?]" Had Grant not been able to draw on his waterborne supply lines and "constant accessions of troops," Lee would have destroyed his foe.

Maintaining his novel interpretation that Grant's decision to cross the James represented a defensive move, Early nevertheless acknowledged that its implications were serious. "We must destroy this army of Grant's before he gets to [the] James River," he quoted Lee as saying. "If he gets there, it will become a siege, and then it will be a mere question of time." Once perched opposite Petersburg, Grant's force "could be reinforced indefinitely, until by the process of attrition, the exhaustion of our resources, and the employment of mechanism and the improved engines of war against them, the brave defenders of our cause would gradually melt away." Eventually, "the unlimited resources of our enemies must finally prevail over all the genius and chivalric daring, which had so long baffled their mighty efforts in the field." Nevertheless, for nine more months "the unequal contest [was] protracted by the genius of one man" and "the valor of his little force." Only the modern weapons made possible by industrialized warfare "finally produced that exhaustion of our army and resources, and that accumulation of numbers on the other side, which wrought the final disaster." In such a contest, it was as inane to compare Lee to Grant as it was to "compare the great pyramid which rears its majestic proportions in the valley of the Nile, to a pigmy perched on Mount Atlas."[9]

Francis Lawley repeated Early's arguments in a March 1872 piece in *Blackwood's Edinburgh Magazine,* complete with the Pollard/Early estimates of strengths and losses and Swinton's analysis. Surely, he argued, if it had been left to Grant and Lee alone to determine the outcome of the conflict, the Confederacy would have prevailed. In 1876 W. Gordon McCabe, who served under artillerist William R. J. Pegram during the last year of the war, prefaced an examination of the siege of Petersburg with a review of the Overland campaign. He also invoked the Pollard/Early estimates; quoted Grant's July 1865 report to support the claim that this was a campaign of attrition; claimed that Lee had forced Grant to change his line of operations four times inside of five weeks while wrecking his army through repeated assaults; and emphasized that when it came to strategy Grant simply relied upon "sheer weight of numbers."[10]

The following year, one of Lee's staff officers, Walter H. Taylor, echoed Early in *Four Years with General Lee.* After carefully setting forth the strength of the two field armies at the commencement of the campaign (he credited Lee with just under 64,000 men, including slightly more than 50,000 infantry, and repeated the now-traditional estimate of 141,160 for Grant), Taylor argued that Lee's "brilliant genius made amend for paucity of numbers, and proved more than a match for brute force, as illustrated in the hammering policy of General Grant." Taylor presented extracts from "notes" (actually letters home) written in the aftermath of Spotsylvania to show that it was his opinion at the time that Grant was being "completely outgeneraled," "entirely reckless with the lives of his men," and could have reached the outskirts of Richmond without a single casualty. Nevertheless, he also admitted that Grant's "remarkable pertinacity" distinguished him from his predecessors. The loyal staff officer also chose to include an 1876 speech given by Capt. John H. Chamberlayne on the anniversary of Lee's birth. Chamberlayne made the remarkable claim that Grant and Sherman together, with "Europe for their recruiting-ground, and a boundless credit for their military chest," unable to defeat Lee "by skill or daring," prevailed due to "weight of numbers and brutal exchange of many lives for one." Lee's defeat, Chamberlayne concluded, was due to the success of Union arms elsewhere.[11]

Such commentaries set the tone for subsequent Confederate characterizations of Grant's generalship in 1864–65. In 1878 Cadmus M. Wilcox, who had been one of Grant's groomsmen at his wedding in 1848, recited the now-traditional strength estimates (although he claimed Lee commenced the campaign with only about forty-two thousand infantrymen), quoted Grant's comment about hammering continuously and "mere attrition," and presented the Union commander as someone who underestimated a foe who outfoxed him at every turn in the Wilderness and inflicted over forty thousand casualties—about as wild an estimate as could be made. Finally, in *The Rise and Fall of the Confederate Government*, Jefferson Davis noted that Grant "had sacrificed a hecatomb of men," and added that such attrition "can hardly be regarded as generalship, or be offered to military students as an example worthy of imitation."[12]

In the tendency to reduce discussions of the 1864 military campaigning in Virginia to an exercise in the calculation of raw numbers, one should remember that Lee himself helped set the terms of the discussion. At the end of July 1865 he revealed his plans to collect materials for a history of the campaigns of the Army of Northern Virginia to Walter Taylor. "I am particularly anxious that its actual strength in the different battles it has fought be correctly stated," he added. Lee recognized that the destruction of headquarters records made that an especially difficult task, and Taylor, eager to assist his former chief in this task, called upon Thomas White, the chief clerk for the army's adjutant general, to comb his memory for estimates. What White provided proved to be underestimates (sometimes badly so) of the army's strength at various junctures, in part because the numbers were reported as estimates of "effective" strength. Nevertheless, Lee was insistent on gathering such data. "It will be difficult to get the world to understand the odds against which we fought," he declared in 1866.[13]

Concentrating on the disparity of numbers of soldiers available and the casualties suffered might appear to be a shrewd way to erode Grant's reputation by sheer repetition if nothing else, but it also raised troubling questions. Had the South and the North possessed equal resources in the first place, it is doubtful that there would have been a secession crisis, for white Southerners would have possessed the political and economic clout to hold their own in the Union. It was the very inequality of numbers and resources—and the evidence that the disparity would continue to grow—which caused many white Southerners to contemplate secession in the first place. Thus the disparity in population and resources was assumed at the outset of the struggle (and helped to explain why there was a conflict). In turn, Union war aims and the means of carrying them out required superior numbers. The burden of offensive operations, including the need to occupy territory and protect supply lines, eroded a great deal of the advantage superior numbers gave Union forces. Reciting numbers also led to a continuous reassessment of the evidence on which such estimates were based, an exercise that continues to this day. Although advocates of the numbers approach to military analysis assumed that the figures would speak for themselves, they clearly did not. Nor did the tendency to evaluate victory and defeat by reference to a body count advance understanding of military operations. Of course, understanding was never the goal of that exercise.

An explanation of the 1864 campaign in Virginia that rested in the end on brute numbers brutally applied came close to conceding that Confederate defeat had become inevitable by that time. Why, then, did Lee persist? It was a puzzling question, but one that demanded an answer that went beyond the usual professions of honor and duty. And why, if Grant was such an inferior general, was Lee unable to defeat him as he had Grant's predecessors? Surely Joseph Hooker had enjoyed a like margin of manpower superiority, as did George McClellan at critical moments. Finally, if Grant's success in Virginia was due primarily to superior numbers and resources, how did one explain his rise in the West, where neither prerequisite applied as it did in Virginia? Confederate military critics usually chose to pass over these issues in silence, preferring instead to continue contrasting Grant and Lee much to the latter's advantage.

In constructing their case against Grant, Confederate military historians, following Pollard's lead, exploited three resources: Edwin M. Stanton's 1865 report to Congress, Grant's own report of the final year of operations, and William Swinton's *Campaigns of the Army of the Potomac*. In an effort to demonstrate how well he had supplied Grant with men, Stanton used rather generous estimates of army strength. In turn, comparisons of Union and Confederate figures often blurred or overlooked altogether the different ways in which the two armies assessed strength and counted casualties (a Confederate soldier had to be declared unfit for duty to be counted as wounded, a far more stringent requirement than applied to the Union forces). Moreover, Stanton's estimates did not take into account either the expiring enlistments that would sap the Union army of strength in the spring and summer of 1864 or the degree of desertion among conscripts and substitutes. By taking the most optimistic estimates of Union strength and comparing them to pessimistic estimates of Confederate manpower, critics exaggerated the disparity in the strength of the contending armies. By minimizing rebel losses and accepting at face value some wild estimate of how many Yankees fell in battle, the accounting of casualties reinforced the conclusion that Grant bled his army white.[14]

More unfortunate in some ways was the wording of Grant's own report. Pollard, Early, and their successors omitted Grant's discussion of how the need to garrison occupied territory and shield lines of communication and supply offset the Union's superior resources and manpower. They also ignored his plan to conduct coordinated and simultaneous offensives to give the Confederates no rest. Rather, they cited again and again his statement that his plan called on Union forces "to hammer continuously against the armed force of the enemy and his resources, until by mere attrition, if in no other way," the Confederacy would collapse. That, of course, did not make attrition through repeated assaults Grant's preferred approach. His plan of operations for Virginia called for a far different campaign than that which unfolded in May and June 1864. That he called for wearing away Confederate armies *and* resources also eluded their notice. What Grant had outlined was a plan whereby he would keep the pressure on, as opposed to the sporadic go-and-stop uncoordinated campaigning that had characterized earlier offensives. Instead, by twisting Grant's words, Confederate critics made it sound as if all the Union commander intended to do was to bludgeon away regardless of the human cost, sacrificing men in a bloodbath. "My idea, from the start, had been to beat Lee's army north of Richmond, if possible," Grant observed. "Then, after destroying his lines of communication north of the James River, to transfer the army to the south side, and besiege Lee in Richmond, or follow him south if he should retreat. . . . Without a greater sacrifice of life than I was willing to make, all could not be accomplished that I had designed north of Richmond." For some reason, this explanation did not draw comment from the Confederate critics.[15]

Perhaps most frustrating, however, was the use these Confederate defenders made of Swinton's *Campaigns of the Army of the Potomac*. Published in 1866, this book, prepared by a *New York Times* correspondent who had been twice ejected from Grant's army during the Overland campaign, was replete with premature judgments based upon incomplete evidence that bore signs of previous friction with many of the principal commanders in the Union army. That was of little consequence to the Southerners, who waxed eloquent about Swinton, calling him "a shrewd observer and candid historian" (McCabe) who was "in general quite accurate" (Wilcox) and the campaign's "best historian" (Lawley). Early and Taylor also made use of Swinton to bolster their indictments.[16]

Several of Swinton's statements proved especially useful to constructing a case against Grant. Having identified Grant and Lee as the best generals on each side, he asserted that Grant had relied "exclusively on the application of brute masses, in rapid and remorseless blows, or, as he has himself phrased it, in 'hammering continuously.'" In support of this claim, Swinton recalled a conversation between Grant and George G. Meade in which Grant interrupted a discourse by Meade about maneuvering by exclaiming, "Oh! I never maneuver." In the weeks that followed, Grant hammered away until he had cost his army over sixty thousand casualties. Swinton's review of the campaign suggested that Grant was not much of a general (especially when he could have reached the James without the loss of a single man). At Cold Harbor Grant's own men offered the most pointed rebuke of his tactics when they refused to renew the assault on June 3. Some of Swinton's other conclusions were passed over by his Confederate readers because they did not comport with the case they were constructing. They obviously believed it best to borrow only that which affirmed their argument, and then celebrate the source as authoritative and unbiased (although the same would not be said when Swinton relied on James Longstreet to present an account of Gettysburg that was critical of Lee).[17]

It did not take long for Grant to respond to Swinton's book. In May 1866 he told a newspaper reporter that Swinton's evaluation of the wisdom of the Overland campaign rested upon the erroneous assumption that one could win a war without fighting a battle. "Fighting, hard knocks, only could accomplish the work. . . . The problem given was to destroy the fighting material of the Confederacy, and that could only be done by a sacrifice of life on our side." Some of the general's own assertions, especially that Lee lost more men than did Grant at the Wilderness and Spotsylvania, were dubious; they tended to obscure his larger point about the need to engage and defeat Lee's army. But that Swinton had inflicted damage became clear when Charles A. Dana and James H. Wilson took the occasion of preparing a Grant campaign biography in 1868 to counter the correspondent's claims point by point, complete with page references to the offending material.[18]

In years to come evidence would appear that would challenge Stanton's numbers, set Grant's comments in his final report about hammering and mere attrition in context, and revise Swinton's early account. Little of that would make its way into the Confederate historiographical offensive, however. Moreover, Grant's generalship soon came under attack from other quarters. The general's entrance into politics gave birth to a new series of military critics who sought to discredit his military record in order to damage his electoral prospects. Equally eager to make their own cases were other Union generals who resented the awarding of plaudits to the hero of Appomattox. Especially active in this latter pursuit were members of the Army of the Cumberland. Had not Don Carlos Buell (who commanded the army's forerunner, the Army of the Ohio) saved Grant at Shiloh? Was it not true that George H. Thomas's men took Missionary Ridge on their own, resulting in victory at Chattanooga?

By the time Adam Badeau went to work on his account of Grant's tenure as general-in-chief, he had to fend off many critics, North and South. He expended much energy in countering the estimates of numbers and losses that had been cited by Pollard, Early, and others to present Grant's operations in a negative light. In 1870 he asked Secretary of War William W. Belknap to furnish him with information to challenge Pollard's estimates. Later that year he advanced the claim that when the campaign opened, Grant had some 98,019 men available, whereas Lee had confronted him with 72,278 soldiers—the estimate that sparked Early's reply. Although Badeau later adjusted his own numbers, he held fast to his effort to call the figures cited by Pollard and Early into question. Conceding that Stanton's report showed some 662,345 men comprised "the aggregate available force present for duty" on May 1, 1864, Badeau added that an examination of field returns of those "present for duty equipped" showed only 533,447. In short, Stanton's numbers were of dubious worth in determining the number of officers and men ready to fight. Field returns suggested that on May 4, 1864, Grant had just under 120,000 men of all arms ready to move and that Lee could muster some 75,000 men to oppose him.[19]

What at first was supposed to appear a year or two after the publication of Badeau's initial volume in 1868 (covering Grant's career in the West) took the erstwhile court historian and minor diplomatic functionary far longer—the two volumes covering the period 1864–65 did not appear until 1881. Part of the reason was that Badeau had busied himself countering the attacks of Early, Taylor, and others—proving relentless in his pursuit of criticisms of Grant's generalship during the spring of 1864. At times, when he quoted specific documents, he proved persuasive; other arguments were not always as clearly presented. Moreover, whatever he said was sure to rouse opposition from Grant's rivals in blue as well as from his opponents in gray. One critic in the *Philadelphia Times* declared that Badeau was simply Grant's official biographer, and his account "revives doubts as to Grant's achievements and confirms convictions as to their fortuitous nature."[20]

One of the most controversial topics on which Badeau had to weigh in was a continuing debate on whether Grant initially preferred to move upon Richmond by the James River. According to several commentators— including Swinton, Taylor, Maury, and McCabe—Grant had pressed for such a campaign, only to be overruled by Lincoln and Stanton. There was something to this story, for on the eve of his appointment as general-in-chief, Grant, responding to a request from Halleck, outlined a plan for operations in the East that featured a major offensive thrust from the mouth of the James through North Carolina. Halleck in turn set forth his objections, adding that the administration would not favor anything resembling McClellan's 1862 Peninsula campaign.[21]

Although Swinton had brought up this notion as early as 1866, its revival in the 1870s—especially in the nationally circulated comments of Richard Taylor and Gideon Welles—sparked a response from Grant, who directed Badeau, then with him in Italy, to deny the story. Grant then did the same in an interview with newspaperman John Russell Young, who accompanied him on his global travels. He was exacerbated by such charges. Left to themselves, he asserted, "Welles, Taylor & co. would soon have it pass into history that we had a 100,000 men killed in getting to the James river, when we could have gone by boat, without loss, and ignoring the fact that Lee sustained any loss whatever." In fact, Welles was no longer a threat, having died earlier that year. Taylor, however, persisted in his charge, citing additional testimony.[22]

What was puzzling about the whole affair was that Maury, Taylor, and

McCabe were actually offering Grant a way out from assuming full responsibility for what happened in 1864. Moreover, whatever the merits of the specifics of their assertion that Grant had been overruled by his superiors, the general had indeed explored other ways to solve the strategic dilemmas presented by Virginia, Richmond, Robert E. Lee, and the Army of Northern Virginia. Remnants of Grant's January 1864 proposal found their way into his plan framed in March and April of that year. His confrontation with Lee was part of a larger plan of campaign, designed to strike at Lee's links to the rest of the South and to endanger his rear. What happened between the Wilderness and Cold Harbor was attributable at least in part to the failure of other generals to carry out their parts of this plan. Most notable were Franz Sigel's collapse in the Shenandoah Valley (which preserved Lee's supply lines and freed up reinforcements) and Benjamin F. Butler's sputtering effort to threaten Richmond. Furthermore, Henry W. Halleck *had* raised objections to Grant's decision to cross the James River and threaten Richmond from the south. Yet Grant remained silent on these issues.[23]

Part of the answer may be that Grant did not want to expose any schism between Abraham Lincoln and himself. He never mentioned Lincoln's reservations about him in 1862, and he shied away from connecting the activities of John A. McClernand to supplant him as the commander of the expedition against Vicksburg by highlighting the president's role in that controversy. Instead, both in his postwar interviews and his later writings, Grant endeavored to present the picture of a united front in which he enjoyed the president's full support and was not pressured to do anything in response to political necessity (although no one could avoid the political implications of military operations in the presidential election year of 1864). He valued preserving that impression more than he did an open discussion of his strategic preferences and the ways in which his January 1864 campaign reflected assumptions imperfectly fitted into his final plan of operations in Virginia. As early as 1868, Dana and Wilson in their campaign biography had done what they could to stifle this argument (which had been raised by Swinton). In turn, this debate has helped to warp scholarly discussion of what Grant intended to do in 1864 as opposed to the campaign that unfolded.[24]

As one might expect, Badeau's account of Grant's service as general-in-chief drew fire when it appeared. Although he was already a target of Confederate advocates, some of the harshest criticism came from other Union writers. In *The Virginia Campaign of '64 and '65* (1883), a contribution to the "Campaigns of the Civil War" series, Andrew A. Humphreys, former chief of staff of the Army of the Potomac and commander of the Second Corps, seemed more interested in discrediting Badeau than in presenting a full account of the 1864 campaign. Humphreys's account was praised by those critics who were quick to disparage Grant's generalship, betraying a clear sense of resentment that it had been left to someone from the West (and not one of the Army of the Potomac's own favorites) to bring Lee to bay. John C. Ropes, who gained some renown as a military historian in the 1880s, echoed the now-familiar criticisms of Grant's Overland campaign in an 1884 address before the Military Historical Society of Massachusetts, offering comparisons between George B. McClellan and Grant that redounded in favor of the former. However, Ropes never could come to grips with the question that stalked Little Mac's advocates: If McClellan was so skilled, why did he fail? But what truly plagued Badeau's account was that it had been too much shaped by a desire to defend Grant's record. Furthermore, in countering wild claims the author advanced a few of his own, which continued the battle along the same lines set forth by Grant's critics and made but minimal impact on the arguments he rejected.[25]

During his presidency Ulysses S. Grant rarely commented on his military career. Not until he left the White House and embarked on what eventually evolved into a tour around the world did he reflect on the Civil War in conversations intended for publication. Accompanying him on his journeys was *New York Herald* correspondent John Russell Young. In a series of interviews with the former president Young set down his comments on his military and political careers; in turn, when these interviews appeared in the *Herald,* they elicited much response and criticism.

When it came to discussing the Civil War, Grant was determined to puncture the accounts of his critics, both North and South, and to counter the emerging celebrations of Confederate leadership. "The cry was in the air that the North had only won by brute force; that the generalship and valor were with the South. This has gone into history, with so many other illusions that are historical." Grant questioned the military genius of Thomas J. "Stonewall" Jackson, suggesting that Jackson's exploits came at the expense of untrained opponents and left it an open question as to whether he would have risen to the challenge posed by an able general. He also noted that both Braxton Bragg and Albert Sidney Johnston fell short of the high expectations he had for them at the beginning of the conflict—and took pains to deny that Johnston's death cost the Confederates victory at Shiloh. Time after time, however, he held up Joseph E. Johnston as his most formidable opponent. "I have had nearly all of the Southern generals in high command in front of me," he said, "and Joe Johnston gave me more anxiety than any of the others." He then added, quite pointedly, "I was never half so anxious about Lee." After reviewing Johnston's role in the Vicksburg campaign, Grant observed, "Take it all in all, the South, in my opinion, had no better soldier than Joe Johnston—none at least that gave me more trouble."[26]

Grant openly questioned Lee's skills as a general. "I never ranked Lee as high as have some others of the army," he remarked, "that is to say, I never had as much anxiety when he was in my front as when Joe Johnston was in front. Lee was a good man, a fair commander, who had everything in his favor. He was a man who needed sunshine. He was supported by the unanimous voice of the South; he was supported by a large party in the North; he had the support and sympathy of the outside world. All of this is of an immense advantage to a general. Lee had this in a remarkable degree. Everything he did was right. He was treated like a demigod. Our generals had a hostile press, lukewarm friends, and a public opinion outside." These advantages concealed Lee's shortcomings, as far as Grant was concerned: "Lee was of a slow, conservative, cautious nature, without imagination or humor, always the same, with grave dignity. I never could see in his achievements what justifies his reputation. The illusion that nothing but heavy odds beat him will not stand the ultimate light of history. I know it is not true."[27]

Such comments did not go unchallenged. As expected, the *Southern Historical Society Papers* rushed to the defense of the Confederate chieftain. After declaring that Grant's opinion about his antagonist was "a matter of small moment," an editorial betrayed that it was of sufficient importance to merit a detailed response. Other Union commanders ranked Lee as the Confederacy's most able general, this editorial writer opined, as did several European military critics. In light of such praise, Lee's supporters "may well afford to pass by in silence the sneers of a man whom he outgeneraled at every point and whipped, until at last [and here Grant's words came back to haunt him once more] 'by mere attrition,' his thin lines were worn away, and he was 'compelled to yield to overwhelming numbers and resources.'" But the editorial's author did not heed his own advice, as he once more repeated Jubal Early's strength estimates, which were beginning to assume the power of a Lost Cause mantra. Once more Stanton's report and Swinton's assessment were paraded across the editorial page. Once more readers learned that during the Overland campaign "Lee foiled Grant in every move he made, defeated him in every battle they fought, and so completely crushed him in that last trial of strength at Cold Harbor, that his men refused to attack again." The editorial writer added that a close inspection of the records suggested Grant had lost a hundred thousand men during that campaign. Apparently the same calculating spirit that had once claimed that one Confederate was equal to ten Yankees was still at work; that it was not aimed at someone who had once aspired to be a mathematics professor rendered the routine all the more satisfying. "It will take a large amount of 'table-talk' to get over the logic of these facts and figures."[28]

Grant returned to defending his performance, first in a series of articles for *Century Magazine,* then in his *Memoirs* (which incorporated his pieces on Shiloh, Chattanooga, Vicksburg, the Wilderness, and Appomattox). He had heard enough of the wonderful performance of Confederate arms. Some twenty years after the war's end, supposedly loyal writers still endeavored "to prove that the Union forces were not victorious; practically, they say, we were slashed around from Donelson to Vicksburg and to Chattanooga; and in the East from Gettysburg to Appomattox, when the physical rebellion gave out from sheer exhaustion." To read such accounts disappointed him. While he did not want to gloat over Confederate defeat, "I would like to see truthful history written."[29]

For Grant, "truthful history" meant, among other things, disabusing readers of certain favorite notions. In arguing that the personal acquaintances he made during the Mexican-American War provided him with insight into the character, personality, and preferences of his counterparts in gray, he specifically cited Lee. "The natural disposition of most people is to clothe a commander of a large army with almost superhuman abilities." A large part of the National army, for instance, and most of the press of the country, clothed General Lee with just such qualities, but I had known him personally, and knew that he was mortal; and it was just as well that I felt this." Nor, upon reflection, did he think much of Albert Sidney Johnston's generalship, and he quickly dismissed the argument that Johnston's death prevented a Confederate victory. "*Ifs* defeated the Confederates at Shiloh," he sarcastically remarked. "There is little doubt that we would have been disgracefully beaten *if* all the shells and bullets fired by us had passed harmlessly over the enemy and *if* all of theirs had taken effect." Certainly Confederate generals, officers, and soldiers deserved credit for what they did accomplish; certainly some Confederate authors exaggerated what they did; yet "the Confederate claimants for superiority in strategy, superiority in generalship and superiority in dash and prowess are not so unjust to the Union troops engaged at Shiloh as are many Northern writers."[30]

Throughout the *Memoirs* Grant took on his critics, although sometimes he did so in such an understated manner that it was difficult to see what he was doing. He singled out Swinton for special treatment, reminding readers that he had spied on confidential meetings and had been ejected from the army in June (Grant added that Ambrose Burnside had proposed to execute him; perhaps in retrospect Grant should have declined to interfere). Once more he defended his 1864 campaign plan (although he offered no information on his January 1864 proposal). Only sustained, bloody, determined combat could decide the issue, he claimed; the previous years had produced a strategic stalemate. In that struggle, Lee could take advantage of the terrain, which provided defenders with cover and hampered offensive operations. At times the Confederates escaped disaster due to confusion about the ground or simple good fortune. Had one of Lee's division commanders not pressed on during the night of May 7–8, for example, Lee would never have secured Spotsylvania Court House. It was just another reminder that "accident often decides the fate of battle."[31]

Grant did admit making mistakes, and sought to explain his reasoning. The most famous involved his decision to assault on June 3 at Cold Harbor. Even then, however, Grant reminded readers that Lee's army no longer launched significant attacks as it had in 1862 and 1863—evidence that his approach was not without positive effect. Moreover, in explaining his thinking behind each movement and attack, he quietly countered notions of him as bullheaded, unimaginative, and wedded to frontal assaults whatever the cost. Here and there he highlighted flaws in Lee's performance to challenge portrayals of Lee as all-knowing and uncommonly prescient, once remarking that the Confederate commander "seemed really to be misled as to my designs." He also addressed the matter of numbers, going so far as to present figures that showed his total losses between May 5 and June 12 as under forty thousand, and arguing that Lee's strength approached eighty thousand at the outset of the campaign. He further claimed that both armies received equal reinforcements once one deducted the number of Union soldiers whose terms of enlistment were expiring. "All circumstances considered we did not have any advantage in numbers," he concluded.[32]

If Grant understood the nature of the contest in 1864, he also grasped what was at stake after the war. Just as Confederate scribes had blasted his military skill as a way to exalt Lee, so he had to question Lee's generalship to preserve his own claims to greatness. In doing so, he recognized the extent to which the image of Lee's superiority was not confined to the South. "General Lee . . . was a very highly estimated man in the Confederate army and States, and filled also a very high place in the estimation of the people and press of the Northern States," he wrote. "His praise was sounded throughout the entire North after every action he was engaged in: the number of his forces was always lowered and that of the National forces exaggerated." Northern as well as Southern authors fell into the same trap in their postwar narratives. No wonder some people came to believe that the Army of Northern Virginia was, man for man, superior to its counterpart, the Army of the Potomac.[33]

Grant returned to the numbers game once more near the end of the second volume of his narrative. "There has always been a great conflict of opinion as to the number of troops engaged in every battle," he observed, adding that in such discussions Southerners were often seen "magnifying the number of Union troops engaged and belittling their own." Indeed, he claimed, "there were no large engagements where the National numbers compensated for the advantage of position and intrenchment occupied by the enemy." In his own assessment, however, Grant shifted some three million from the Union to Confederate column (confusing free versus slave state populations with Union versus Confederate populations). However, his own argument rested not so much upon numbers as upon drawing attention to the Confederacy's compensating advantages in mobilizing for war and in defending one's homeland (as opposed to detaching troops for occupation duty). He also reiterated his claim that disloyalty in the North hampered the successful prosecution of the war effort—revealing his awareness that many of his critics hailed from north of the Mason-Dixon line. In composing his account, he was as cognizant of what they had said as he was of the charges hurled against him by his Southern assailants.[34]

In setting forth these arguments, Grant fell into a trap that he had so often avoided on the battlefield—that of letting his protagonists choose the terms of the debate. Yet superior numbers did not guarantee military victory, as he had argued elsewhere—especially when the definition of Union victory required the complete capitulation of the Confederacy. Nor would raw numbers explain why Grant succeeded where others had failed. Finally, it seemed absurd to blame Grant for exploiting his advantages. A much sounder debate would have concerned whether he did so to the utmost, and what other concerns shaped his plan and execution of military operations. Had Grant failed to take advantage of his situation, he would have been culpable indeed.

To understand how Grant waged war in 1864 and 1865 requires remembering that Grant's vision was not limited to Virginia alone. In some respects, his greatest accomplishment was in preventing Lee from nullifying the impact of Union triumphs in the West. Grant did not have to defeat Lee to win the war. The pressure was on Lee to beat Grant, and the Confederate leader could not do it. Even more unfortunate was how the debate over Grant's generalship during the final year of the war came to overshadow his performance in the West, where the superior resources and manpower argument simply lacked persuasiveness because of its shaky foundation of evidence. Just as some Confederates (and future historians) protested equating the Confederate war effort with the progress of arms in the East, so too could Grant argue that an obsession with the eastern theater obscured the real achievements of Union generalship in the West.

As masterful as Grant's *Memoirs* may have been, they did not put an end to the debate over his generalship. Some criticism was spurred by reaction to the *Memoirs*. While Lost Cause advocates and Confederate veterans had their complaints, the objections were not confined to the South. As expected, Buell contested Grant's account of Shiloh; William S. Rosecrans was nettled by his account of Chattanooga; William F. Smith protested what Grant had to say about Petersburg as well as Chattanooga. Carswell McClellan, a staff officer with the Army of the Potomac, lumped Grant and Badeau together in *The Personal Memoirs and Military History of U. S. Grant Versus the Record of the Army of the Potomac* (1887), relying on Humphreys (his old boss) to counter the claims advanced in those works. Equally quarrelsome was the account of the Virginia campaign of 1864–65 offered in Francis A. Walker's account of the history of the Union Second Corps, an animus sharpened by Walker's postwar foray into the ranks of the anti-Grant Liberal Republican movement. Most harsh was the assessment set forth by Augustus W. Alexander in his 1887 book *Grant as a Soldier*. Alexander, whose preference for Grant foe John A. McClernand was evident, sounded once more the same themes—including Grant's preference for "brute force" over "intellect," his mindless and fortunate triumphs in the West, the marvels of Swinton's account, and the series of bloody blunders that characterized his generalship in Virginia where he ordered "thousands of men to useless slaughter. Can this wanton and terrible and ghastly crime be paralleled in history?" Even Joshua Chamberlain contributed to the denigration of Grant, concluding that the Union general-in-chief "seemed to rely on sheer force, rather than skillful maneuver." Furthermore, wrote Chamberlain, since Grant did not study his counterparts with care, "he was sometimes outgeneraled—we do not like to say outwitted—by them."[35]

Lost Cause apologists, notably Edward Pollard and Jubal Early, played a pivotal role in shaping the debate over the generalship of Ulysses S. Grant. To some extent the template they helped frame persists to this day, especially in the hearts of neo-Confederates and others who do not think the cause quite lost. By skillful manipulation of material hastily presented by Union authorities (including Grant himself) immediately after the war, and assisted by William Swinton's slanted account, men like Early and Dabney Maury sought to achieve in print what they could never accomplish on the battlefield: the defeat of the Union's foremost commander. However, their efforts at denigrating Grant's performance and warping the historical record could not have succeeded without assistance from other quarters. Their criticisms dovetailed with the efforts of Northerners—especially military rivals and political opponents—who had their own reasons to disparage Grant's military achievements. Moreover, they were assisted in setting the terms of the debate by Grant's defenders, including Grant himself, who met the general's critics on a field of the critics' choosing, and who sometimes engaged in argument that proved to be as dubious as the assessments those arguments were designed to counter. It is one thing to fight it out on the same line if it takes all summer; it is quite another to continue to fight along that line for another century and a half.

Notes

1. General Order No. 9, Army of Northern Virginia, April 10, 1865, in Clifford Dowdey and Louis H. Manarin, eds., *The Wartime Papers of Robert E. Lee* (1961; reprint, New York: Da Capo, 1987), 934–35.

2. Edward A. Pollard, *The Lost Cause*, rev. ed. (New York: E. B. Treat, 1867). See also Jack P. Maddex Jr., *The Reconstruction of Edward A. Pollard: A Rebel's Conversion to Postbellum Unionism* (Chapel Hill: University of North Carolina Press, 1974). William A. Blair overlooks Pollard's pride of place over Jubal Early in presenting the case against Grant in "Grant's Second Civil War: The Battle for Historical Memory," in *The Spotsylvania Campaign*, ed. Gary W. Gallagher (Chapel Hill: University of North Carolina Press, 1998), 223–53.

3. Pollard, *The Lost Cause*, 206–207, 240–41, 386–87, 455–56.

4. Ibid., 386, 509–10.

5. Ibid., 698–99.

6. Ibid., 509, 511, 516, 520, 525.

7. Richard Taylor, *Destruction and Reconstruction* (1879; reprint, Waltham, Mass.: Blaisdell, 1968), 146; Dabney H. Maury, "Grant as a Soldier and Civilian," *Southern Historical Society Papers* 5 (May 1878): 227–39.

8. Jubal A. Early, "The Relative Strengths of the Armies of Generals Lee and Grant," *Southern Historical Society Papers* 2 (July 1876): 6–21 (reprinting

a letter from Early to the *London Standard*, November 19, 1870); Cooke quoted in Francis Lawley, "General Lee," in *Lee the Soldier*, ed. Gary W. Gallaher (Lincoln: University of Nebraska Press, 1996), 90.

9. Jubal Early, "The Campaigns of Robert E. Lee," in *Lee the Soldier*, ed. Gallagher, 63–71.

10. Lawley, "General Lee," 89–90; W. Gordon McCabe, "Defence of Petersburg," *Southern Historical Society Papers* 2 (December 1876): 257–306.

11. Walter H. Taylor, *Four Years with General Lee* (1877; reprint, Bloomington: Indiana University Press, 1962), 125, 132–33, 190–91, 198.

12. C. M. Wilcox, "Lee and Grant in the Wilderness," in *The Annals of the War*, ed. Alexander K. McClure (Philadelphia: Times, 1878), 485–501; Jefferson Davis, *The Rise and Fall of the Confederate Government* (1881; reprint, New York: D. Appleton, 1912), 2:526.

13. Robert E. Lee to Walter H. Taylor, July 31, 1865, in Taylor, *Four Years with General Lee*, 156–57; Lee to Jubal Early, March 15, 1866, in Early, "The Relative Strength of the Armies of Generals Lee and Grant," 16.

14. Edwin B. Coddington, *The Gettysburg Campaign: A Study in Command* (New York: Scribners, 1968), 808 n 8.

15. Grant's report is reproduced as an appendix to Ulysses S. Grant, *Personal Memoirs of U. S. Grant* (New York: Charles Webster, 1885–86), 2:555–632. The quotations appear on 555–56 and 570.

16. McCabe, "Defense of Petersburg," 263; Wilcox, "Lee and Grant," 496; Lawley, "General Lee," Gallagher, ed., *Lee the Soldier*, 89.

17. William Swinton, *Campaigns of the Army of the Potomac* (1866; reprint, Secaucus, N.J.: Blue and Grey, 1988), 406, 440, 487, 491, 494.

18. *Missouri Democrat*, May 31, 1866; Charles A. Dana and James H. Wilson, *Life of General U.S. Grant* (Springfield, Mass: Gordon Bill, 1868).

19. Badeau to William W. Belknap, March 26, 1870, Huntington Library, San Marino, Calif.; *Historical Magazine*, February 1871, 102–11; Adam Badeau, *Military History of Ulysses S. Grant*, 3 vols. (New York: D. Appleton, 1868–81), 3:32, 94–95.

20. *Philadelphia Times*, August 5, 1881.

21. Swinton, *Campaigns of the Army of the Potomac*, 491; Taylor, *Destruction and Reconstruction*, 25–26; Maury, "Grant as a Soldier and Civilian," 235; McCabe, "Defence of Petersburg," 264–65. For the discussion about strategy, see Brooks D. Simpson, *Ulysses S. Grant: Triumph over Adversity, 1822–1865* (Boston: Houghton Mifflin, 2000), 250–53.

22. Gideon Welles, "Administration of Abraham Lincoln," *Galaxy* 24 (December 1877): 744; Grant to Badeau, May 19, 1878, and August 22, 1878, in Adam Badeau, *Grant in Peace: From Appomattox to Mt. McGregor* (Hartford, Conn.: S. S. Scranton, 1887), 499–500, 504–505; Taylor, *Destruction and Reconstruction*, 26–27.

23. Simpson, *Ulysses S. Grant*, 269–73, 332–33.

24. Dana and Wilson, *Life of Ulysses S. Grant,* 178–79.

25. Andrew A. Humphreys, *The Virginia Campaign of '64 and '65* (New York: Scribners, 1883); John Watts DePeyster, *From the Rapidan to Appomattox Court-House* (Philadelphia: n.p., 1883); John C. Ropes, "Grant's Campaign in Virginia in 1864," *Papers of the Military Historical Society of Massachusetts* (reprint, Wilmington, N.C.: Broadfoot, 1989), 4:363–406.

26. J. Russell Young, *Around the World with General Grant* (New York: American News, 1879), 2:210–13, 459, 472–73.

27. Ibid., 2:458–59.

28. "Editorial Paragraphs," *Southern Historical Society Papers* 6 (September 1878): 142–44.

29. Grant, *Memoirs,* 1:169–70.

30. Ibid., 2:192, 360, 363, 365.

31. Ibid., 2:142–45, 177–78, 211–12.

32. Ibid., 2:244, 258, 289–91.

33. Ibid., 2:291–92.

34. Ibid., 2:500–505. Blair, "Grant's Second Civil War," 241, highlights Grant's flawed estimate, but the same estimates were offered in *Southern Historical Society Papers* 6 (September 1878): 143.

35. Don Carlos Buell, "Shiloh Reviewed," in *Battles and Leaders of the Civil War,* ed. Robert Underwood Johnson and Clarence Clough Buel (Century, 1887), 1:487–536; William F. Smith and Henry M. Cist, "Comments on General Grant's 'Chattanooga,'" in *Battles and Leaders,* ed. Johnson and Buel, 3:714–18; William S. Rosecrans, "The Mistakes of Grant," *North American Review* 140 (December 1885): 580–99; William F. Smith, *From Chattanooga to Petersburg under Grant and Butler* (Boston: Houghton Mifflin, 1893); Carswell McClellan, *The Personal Memoirs and Military History of U.S. Grant Versus the Record of the Army of the Potomac* (Boston: n.p., 1887); Augustus W. Alexander, *Grant as a Soldier* (St. Louis: privately published, 1887), 5, 68, 76, 201–203, 204, 216; Joshua L. Chamberlain, *The Passing of the Armies* (New York: G. P. Putnam's Sons, 1915), 380–81.

Eight

"Let the People See the Old Life as It Was"

LaSalle Corbell Pickett and the Myth of the Lost Cause

Lesley J. Gordon

In her 1916 book *Across My Path,* LaSalle Corbell Pickett recounted meeting Julia Ward Howe, the noted abolitionist, suffragist, and author of the decidedly Northern song "The Battle Hymn of the Republic." Pickett remarked to Howe how much she admired the wartime tune. Howe was taken aback. "I should not think that you would like the Battle Hymn," she said.

"Why not?" Pickett responded. "Do not you like 'Maryland, my Maryland'?"

"No; I do not," Howe answered, adding that she thought the pro-Confederate song was flat and lacked expression.

Later during the interview Pickett praised Howe for her refusal to dwell on the past. "She treasured the lessons of the past," Pickett wrote, "but never for a moment of her long life did she live in the past."[1]

The irony of this exchange is striking. LaSalle Corbell Pickett was the widow of famed Confederate general George E. Pickett. She outlived him by fifty years and spent most of that time publicly fostering an idealized and romanticized image of him, herself, and the Old South. Her short stories, fiction, poems, lectures, "official histories," and interviews with famous contemporaries all promoted the basic tenets of the Lost Cause myth. Her published writings and lectures repeatedly stressed the South's right of secession, the righteousness of the "cause," the valor of Confederate soldiers, the devotion of Southern women, and the loyalty of the childlike slaves. She participated in veterans' reunions, monument dedications, parades, and other rituals important to the Lost Cause faithful. In 1900 she wrote: "The oft repeated phrase 'Before the war' brings back pictures far brighter, than any which the newer time has ever hung upon the walls of memory. The reminiscence of the faraway life lingers with us like the fragrance of the snowy magnolias."[2] Unlike Julia Ward Howe, LaSalle Pickett seemed to dwell exclusively in the past, although admittedly not always in the actual one she lived. She consciously devoted most of her postwar years promoting the Lost Cause not only as the official history of the Confederate South, but as part of her own personal life story.[3]

Sallie Ann Corbell was born May 16, 1843, the eldest child of John David and Elizabeth Phillips Corbell. She grew up in modest wealth on her family's plantation near Suffolk, Virginia, and attended a woman's college in Lynchburg. She married George E. Pickett September 15, 1863, in St. Paul's Church in Petersburg, Virginia. Her groom was eighteen years her senior, a native Virginian, and a professional soldier. George was a man vexed by poor health, an explosive temper, and an increasingly bitter outlook on the war itself. He had just witnessed his division shatter itself in a futile frontal charge at the battle of Gettysburg. His unit was in shambles and he was temporarily without field command. For the next two years, and into the postwar period, the Picketts endured separation, exile, illness, death, and poverty. George's sudden death in 1875 left his wife alone and destitute, struggling to support herself and their young son, George Jr. Sallie left Virginia and moved to Washington, D.C., where she worked in the federal pension office. She never remarried and never returned permanently to her native South. Bad health and financial difficulties plagued her until her death. However, sometime in the late 1880s, Sallie Pickett, calling herself LaSalle Corbell Pickett, decided to write about the past.[4] She would not recount the painful, distressing past she had endured as the wife of a troubled, controversial general. Instead, she would tell of a fairytale marriage, a heroic soldier, and a lost golden age. Remembering this past transported her "across the years to a time when life's water was wine, tinted golden with the sunlight of morning, sparkling with the jewels of youth and love. It made me a child again."[5]

Indeed, LaSalle Corbell Pickett generally wrote stories from the perspective of a child. She subtracted five years from her real age so that she could bear the title "Child-bride of the Confederacy." Assuming the identity of a child enhanced the simplicity and sentimentality of her portraits. And it enabled her to play down the independence she achieved as a single mother and professional writer.[6]

She even traced her relationship to George Pickett to her childhood. Pickett alleged that she first met her "Soldier" years before the war when she was an innocent little girl wandering the beaches of Old Point

Comfort near Fort Monroe, Virginia. One day, suffering from a bout with whooping cough, she spotted a lonely officer sitting under an umbrella, staring into space. She interrupted his ruminations, demanding to know if his isolation was due to his having the same ailment. The young officer smiled sadly and responded that he had something much worse than a cough—he had a broken heart. The dashing soldier confided that he was mourning the loss of his wife and baby. "In return for his confidence I promised to comfort him for his losses and to be his little girl now and his wife just as soon as I was grown up to be a lady." That day on the beach became Sallie Pickett's "point of beginning—a period back of which life, to present consciousness, was not."[7]

Pickett's descriptions of her husband fit the model of the courageous Southern gentleman and duty-bound Confederate officer. Gone were his bitterness, anger, and seething resentments. Instead, her idealized "Soldier" was noble, peace loving, and unselfish.[8] He fought valiantly for a "just cause," but he would have preferred peace.[9] He was a "man of culture, of countless interests, of warm sympathy, of unshakable faith."[10] Her Soldier wiped the tears of a Jewish boy whose shoes were too tight and carried him home in his arm; freely shared food with a starving private; and gave money to an old black woman so she could buy a coffin for her dead baby.[11] His was not an easy life, she admitted, but despite the disappointments and tragedies he "was always grave and dignified," "fond of jokes," gentle and kind.[12] His men loved him almost as much as his "child-bride" did, she wrote.[13] In her short novel *Bugles of Gettysburg,* the fictional Jasper Garnett tells his lover Kate that "the soldier who thrills me as no other is the Commander of our Division, General Pickett. It is an inspiration to see him ride along our lines, his wavy dark hair floating out on the wind, the boys cheering as if they would never stop."[14] "The General possessed," Pickett wrote, "the greatest capacity for happiness, and such dauntless courage and self-control that, to all appearances, he could as cheerfully and buoyantly steer his way over the angry, menacing, tumultuous surges of life as over the waves that glide in tranquil smoothness and sparkle in the sunlight of a calm, clear sky."[15]

LaSalle Pickett's idealized portrait of her husband made him a Confederate hero. He never reached the status of Robert E. Lee or "Stonewall" Jackson, but his association with the famed but futile charge at Gettysburg helped. Virginia veterans and newspapers began romanticizing Pickett's all-Virginia division's role soon after the battle; it was almost by association that George too would share in the idolization. This transformation began in earnest with his death in the summer of 1875. Eulogies celebrated Pickett as the "hero of Gettysburg" and one of

"Virginia's great generals." Sallie must have taken comfort in these words, but they also may have inspired her to take an active role in spreading the myth. By the late 1880s, Mrs. Pickett was a common sight at veteran reunions and monument dedications. She was the toast of the twenty-fourth anniversary reunion at Gettysburg, shaking hands, signing autographs, and handing out flowers. In February 1889, Pickett informed a family member that she was running low on autographs and pictures of her late husband. "I have had to grant so many like favors to those who loved his memory and honored his name that I have no letters I could spare and but a few names left," she wrote.[16]

LaSalle Pickett did offer the public a collection of her husband's wartime letters, but today these missives are generally accepted as more her writing than his. Unsuspecting readers, hungry for fables of the Old South and eager to know more about the personal side of Confederate heroes, perused the letters with great interest. "They are brought to the light of to-day," Pickett stated, "not alone for their bearing upon historic events, but yet more for the story they tell of a man's heart and life in the fiery storm of the greatest war our country has ever known."[17] These letters contained "the flavor of the past, romantic, glamorous, sad, gay, tender, sweetly sentimental, imbued with unquestioning faith in Almighty God, in Virginia, in honor, in the brave young 'war-bride' of his love."[18]

LaSalle Pickett always insisted on the authenticity of all of her published works. She set her books and short stories in her home state of Virginia before or during the war. Confederate luminaries like Robert E. Lee, Stonewall Jackson, and Jefferson Davis often made guest appearances. Faithful slaves were also prominently featured—complete with what Pickett claimed was "phonetically genuine" black dialect recorded carefully by the author.[19]

Her literary identity was deeply rooted in the plantation South. It was a mythical place of deference, paternalism, stability, and peace. Her grandfather, Thomas Corbell, "believed in God, woman and blood." She described her father as stately and erect, "always courteous and gallant, always solicitous of and interested in his people, and always thoughtful and considerate of every one."[20] Her mother was a beautiful and fair plantation mistress, and she equally idealized her father-in-law, Robert Pickett. An elderly ex-slave fondly confides in Pickett's book *Jinny* that the general's father was "de bes' man Gord-er-Moughy ebber meked." He provided for his slaves and was kind. "En der nebber would er been no wah en deforces," the former slave concluded, "ef he had libed."[21]

Pickett's writings portrayed plantation life as idyllic. Slaves were content and cared for, masters were kind, and yeomen were nonexistent. White Southerners were proud, honorable people, quietly minding their own business until a handful of mischief-making Northerners interfered. When an old slave asked whether hanging John Brown "wuz a li'l abrup," Southern whites laughingly agreed—with scant acknowledgement of the shock and horror Brown's raid caused in the region.[22] When a Northern gentleman overheard Pickett discussing "romances of the olden times," he exclaimed: "If I had known what an interesting and fascinating life we were breaking up down there I might have been an anti-Abolitionist."[23]

According to Pickett, her family's slaves were obedient and respectfully submissive to whites. "There was no word held in more reverential love and fear by the faithful Southern slave," she told readers in *Kunnoo Sperits*, "than the one word 'Master.'"[24] Repeatedly, slaves in Pickett's writings refer to "dem good ole times" on the plantation "'fo' de wah."[25] Her book *The Bugles of Gettysburg* featured a slave named "Ole Pete" who was so stubbornly devoted to his master that he refused to leave him wounded on the field of battle.[26] Her racist characterization of slaves depicted blacks as uniformly superstitious and crude, childish and comical, and happily ignorant and simple-hearted. They refused freedom even when offered it, Pickett affirmed, preferring to stay with their beloved white masters.[27]

Although Pickett devoted a good deal of her writings to slaves and what she deemed slave culture, she, like other Lost Cause writers, argued that Southern secession had nothing to do with slavery. In her 1899 book *Pickett and His Men*, she explained to readers that "the commercial greed of England" introduced African slavery to the United States against colonists' wishes. The North, however, quickly rid itself of this "wicked" and "revolting" traffic and cast the "blight of slavery" on the South.[28] Nevertheless, Pickett admitted that the South had developed into an economically subsistent region and that slavery became a "component part of the life of the South." "To separate it from that life," she asserted, "was like taking a vital part from a highly evolved organism and expecting its functions to continue." The Republican Party platform vowing to stop slavery from spreading into the western territories "made [Southerners] to feel that they no longer had any part in a government for which, when treated with justice and fairness, they would gladly have died." She further contended that the slave was not prepared for political, economic, or moral freedom "because his nature and training had not fitted him for liberty."[29] In 1913 she added that "Many of our greatest warriors were not slave-holders, and as a matter of principle were strongly opposed to the holding of human beings as property."[30] Yet she also labeled slavery a "curse" and a "black stain" that destroyed the Union.[31] LaSalle Pickett's convoluted views on slavery were consistent with other Lost Cause promoters, especially after 1890, who sought to diminish the importance of slavery in causing the war.[32]

Secession was legal and logical to Lost Cause writers, and LaSalle Pickett agreed. "From near the beginning of our constitutional history," she stated, "secession has been regarded as the remedy for all grievances, real or fancied."[33] New England Federalists had considered secession, and so too did John C. Calhoun. Pickett declared: "The right of secession, as shown in the historical facts . . . has at different periods been claimed by every section in this country." "Thus all the history of the United States, North and South, since the adoption of the Constitution, pointed toward secession as the remedy for all sectional wrongs and misfortunes." West Point cadets learned, along with their lessons on war, the "doctrine of states' rights."[34] Southern states had freely consented to join the Union, Pickett reasoned, and their decision to withdraw that consent was not rebellion.[35] "Under the Southern flag," she concluded, there "were *no traitors, no rebels.* To state the reverse of this proposition is to falsify history; to charge it is a crime."[36]

Pickett's descriptions of the war itself mixed again what she claimed to be personal experience with an almost formulaic Lost Cause view of the conflict. Confederate soldiers were consistently brave, white Southern women were unquestioningly loyal, and "the cause" was indisputably noble. Southern warriors wearing dingy and worn-out uniforms were still beautiful, their death in battle grand and glorious.[37] Pickett described once standing beside Varina Davis at a veterans' reception as the two greeted men grateful to have known their famous husbands. Varina, Pickett claimed, spoke fondly of the Southern soldiers' loyalty and remarked that President Davis and General Pickett "could inspire the hearts of so many, from the laborer with his rough toil-worn hand to the great professional man with soft white hand and strong brain."[38] The South was unified, its women and men—young and old, yeoman and planter—joined for a righteous cause. Pickett even extolled wartime poets like Henry Timrod, Paul Hamilton Hayne, and Father Abram Ryan for devoting their talents and lives "to their country as truly as if their blood had crimsoned the sod of hard fought fields. They gave their best to our cause."[39]

The Battle of Gettysburg was central to Pickett's idealized portrait of both her husband and the war. She usually mentioned the famed charge with which her husband's name has been forever linked, and, as Carol Reardon has recently demonstrated, she played an active role in creating the mythology of the charge itself. Mrs. Pickett stole the show at the 1887 Gettysburg reunion, shaking hands, signing autographs, and thrilling veterans with her charm and vivaciousness. In 1913, on the fiftieth anniversary of the battle, Pickett wrote: "Time has not lessened the fame of Pickett's charge at Gettysburg, and it never will; for the changes that have taken place in the science of war leave no possibility that future history will produce its counterpart." "With its imperishable glory—overshadowing all other events in martial history, notwithstanding its appalling disaster—is linked forever the name of my soldier."[40] The "greatest battle of the western continent" instilled greatness in her husband.[41] Even the enemy was awed by the spectacle. Pickett portrayed the general as standing erect and motionless in the midst of the withering Union fire. A stunned Union soldier announced: "We can't kill a man as brave as that."[42]

But despite Pickett's repeated defense of secession and the Confederacy's "dream nation," she also welcomed peace and reunion.[43] Her husband, she claimed, easily and willingly resumed his old allegiance to the Union after the war ended. She said he had fought under the star-spangled banner and felt no qualms about returning to that flag. "I of course," he allegedly told her in the Pickett letters, "have always strenuously opposed disunion, not as doubting the right of secession, which was taught in our text-book at West Point, but as gravely questioning its expediency."[44] She gave readers many examples of his respect for the enemy, even as the war raged. At Fredericksburg, for example, as Union soldiers made their suicidal charges on Marye's Heights, her literary General Pickett claimed that he and his men forgot themselves and wildly cheered on the enemy.[45] In another of LaSalle's favorite episodes, George encountered a defiant young Pennsylvania girl waving a Union flag at him and his troops. LaSalle's gallant husband was so impressed by the girl's courage that he stopped and saluted her and each of his soldiers followed suit. The girl was so taken by the act that she exclaimed, "Oh, I wish I had a rebel flag—I'd wave that, too!"[46] In one of the published Pickett letters, he admitted that he truly believed that "American greatness" could only occur "under one flag."[47]

It was she, Pickett told her readers, who became the embittered rebel, hurt and surprised at her husband's willingness to forgive and forget the war's bitterness. She initially refused to welcome her husband's Yankee friends into their home immediately after the war. She was a "caged-tigress," defiantly instructing her baby son that when he grew up he must "fight and fight, and never surrender, and never forgive the Yankees."[48] Although in reality it was probably George who was bitter, and his wife who had to cheer him with positive thoughts of the future, her books switched their identities: He was the patient and forgiving one; she was emotional and combative. "When the great Civil War closed," she explained, "it left me, as it did other Southern women, with a bitterness of heart which could conceive of nothing good in those whom I regarded as enemies."[49]

Of course these rebellious sentiments did not last—at least not in LaSalle Corbell Pickett's public persona. Her published writings and public appearances celebrated the South and the unified nation. By the turn of the century she had outlived many of her contemporaries, and her new identity as "Mother Pickett," a living and nurturing link to the mythical past, was popular in both North and South.[50]

Pickett increasingly sought Northern audiences and acquaintances. She claimed to have met not only Julia Ward Howe, but also Clara Barton and Louisa May Alcott.[51] She befriended Joshua L. Chamberlain and sent him a copy of *Pickett and His Men* hoping that the memory of the past war would not make him too sad.[52] She even contributed a chapter to a book about the Fourth Massachusetts Cavalry, complimenting the men in the regiment for their courtesy toward Southern citizens when they raised the United States flag over the fallen Confederate capitol.[53]

Pickett's efforts increased her popularity and earned her national praise. The *Boston Transcript* endorsed her *Bugles of Gettysburg* "because it is not written with the partisan spirit, but in loyal remembrance to the whole nation."[54] The *Chicago Record* recommended *Pickett and His Men* because "She writes without bitterness, and her sympathy with the Southern cause and its leaders does not lead her into one-sided estimates of the war as a whole."[55] Her lectures were equally successful nationally. She traveled to Philadelphia; Xenia, Ohio; Portland, Maine; and Richmond, Indiana, thrilling audiences with her lectures on "The Battle of Gettysburg," "The Friends of Yesterday," and "Negro Folk-Lore—Stories of the Old South." Bostonian B. F. Keith affirmed that "Enthusiasm over Mrs. Pickett's lecture on Gettysburg surpasses anything ever known here." It was the "First time in history," Keith maintained, "[that] more than 2,000 Bostonians ever stood up when the band played 'Dixie.'"[56] Former Northern general and head of the Freedman's Bureau Oliver O. Howard applauded her "marvelous compilation of the truth." Dan Sickles acclaimed her lecture for its "frankness, simplicity and truth and the modest way in which you tell it all."[57] The biographical entry in *A Woman of the Century* described her as the "messenger of peace, trying to reconcile the two factions and bridge over the chasm once so broad and deep. No woman to-day is more widely known and honored than Mrs. Pickett."[58]

It was not just on the printed page or in the lecture hall that LaSalle Pickett promoted her idealized version of the past. Her personal correspondence echoed the same tone, phrases, and themes. In 1911, for example, when her son's illness prevented her from visiting her husband's former home in Quincy, Illinois, she wrote a Quincy resident: "I can only ask your prayers for the son who has so often said to me, 'Dear Mother, give the lecture that tells of "Pickett's Charge," to the people of Quincy that they may see that they had in him a soldier to be proud of, though that which seemed right to him was not right in their eyes'."[59] In 1926, Pickett wrote Henry Huntington on the occasion of his returning some of her husband's original papers. The very sight of his handwriting, she confided, "was wont to thrill my soul as it came to me from the field, from camp, written with the thunders of battle in his ears and the note of love in his heart, the record of the past unfolded and I read them with the old time thrill as in the days when love and hope and courage were mine."[60]

But LaSalle Pickett did not entirely dwell on the past. She openly welcomed the New South. To be sure, Pickett continued writing mainly about the old order of the plantation South and noble Confederate cause, and she frequently complained of the fast pace of the modern world. In *Literary Hearthstones of Dixie,* for example, she worried that "the electric flash of the present day" would overshadow her favorite Southern writers from view.[61] And in *Across My Path* she referred to the present as "the era of futurist nightmares."[62] But Pickett was optimistic about the future. In fact, she argued that the sufferings of war and defeat made the South stronger and ensured its future greatness. After the war Pickett portrayed ex-Confederates turning swords into plowshares and quietly working their farms to battle "hostile forces of poverty."[63] She contended that defeat and the loss of slavery scarred the South but did not destroy it. Instead, "the blow which struck the South to earth severed her shackles and set her free." "From its ruins," she predicted, "arose a new South to give the world impressive lessons in the eternal persistence of vital force."[64] In 1899, Pickett published a piece in the *Confederate Veteran* that stated that the South wanted no special rewards or help for its veterans despite all it had suffered in the war. She "does not pause in her onward march to reflect mournfully" but instead "looks bravely forward to the grand future which is hers."[65]

In *Across My Path,* Pickett recorded a supposed conversation between herself and author Margaret Sangster. After reminiscing about the Old

South, Sangster pauses to sum up the real and fictional LaSalle Corbell Pickett's life:

> You have had a wonderfully rich life and you are but a child. You have had the black mammy and the little colored playmates. The old atmosphere of the romantic South, and the plantation life that is all over now. You have had the romance of war, the excitement of the battlefield, the love of the soldiers, the nursing of the wounded hospital. You have known a new country, new president and cabinet and all the great changes of South and North alike. You have been the wife of a hero, the mother of children, the mother of an angel and now the greatest of all sorrows has come to chasten you, widowhood, and last, the highest boon that could come with all these things, the necessity for work. It is only through pain and loss that we can gain the joy of effort and the triumph of winning.

"I have had all and lost all," Pickett responded.

"You cannot lose what you have had," Sangster answered, "it is yours always and the joy of reliving it in memory and expression will be the greatest happiness of your life. Pass it on to the world before you forget, and let the people see the old life as it was."[66]

These were probably Pickett's own words and thoughts, for she did, in fact, spread her romanticized memory of the past "to the world." She publicly reconstructed her past, not only to venerate the slaveholding South and the Confederacy, but like other scarred and disconcerted white Southerners, to find meaning, comfort, and hope in her own troubled life.[67]

Historians debate whether the Lost Cause mythology had any lasting effect after 1915. Some contend that its cultural power lessened after World War I as the forces of modernization spread across the South.[68]

Yet there is recent evidence that LaSalle Corbell Pickett's influence continues.[69] In March 1998 the Virginia Division of the United Daughters of the Confederacy (UDC) and the Virginia Society of the Military Order of the Stars and Bars moved Pickett's ashes from a dilapidated mausoleum to rest beside her husband's remains in Richmond's Hollywood Cemetery. Organizers explained that this was a "unique opportunity" to "honor a woman whose postwar appearances at Gettysburg reunions led Confederate and Union veterans alike to hail her as a symbol of national reunification and healing."[70] A fife and drum corps played traditional music and men dressed in Confederate gray escorted the horse-drawn carriage that carried her remains. The ceremony was well attended and reported in newspapers across the country. There was even a Web site devoted to the event. Descendants of James Longstreet and John Bell Hood as well as Pickett relatives showed up, and the UDC awarded its "highest military honor, the Order of the Military Cross" to George and LaSalle's great-grandson. Nancy Gum, president of the UDC's Virginia Division, explained: "She is part of our heritage." "The motto of the Virginia Division is 'Love Makes Memory eternal'," noted Gum; "For us to be able to bring Mrs. Pickett back is a very inspiring thing."[71]

Notes

1. LaSalle Corbell Pickett, *Across My Path: Memories of People I Have Known* (1916; reprint, Freeport, N.Y.: Books for Libraries Press, 1970), 1–2, 6.

2. LaSalle Corbell Pickett, *Yule-Log and Others* (Washington, D.C.: Neale, 1900), 9.

3. Standard references for Lost Cause mythology include Charles Reagan Wilson, *Baptized In Blood: The Religion of the Lost Cause, 1865–1920* (Athens: University of Georgia Press, 1980); Gaines M. Foster, *Ghosts of the Confederacy: Defeat, the Lost Cause, and the Emergence of the New South, 1865 to 1913* (New York: Oxford University Press, 1987); Rollin G. Osterweis, *The Myth of the Lost Cause, 1865–1900* (Hamden, Conn.: Archon Books, 1973). See also Daniel Aaron, *The Unwritten War: American Writers and the Civil War* (1973; reprint, Madison: University of Wisconsin Press, 1987), 285–309; and Rod Andrew Jr., "Soldiers, Christians, and Patriots: The Lost Cause and Southern Military Schools, 1865–1915," *Journal of Southern History* 64 (November 1998): 677–710.

4. A page from the Corbell family Bible, census records, and a contemporary newspaper announcing her marriage all call her "Sallie"; but her postwar correspondence and published works after 1899 use the name "LaSalle." *A Woman of the Century* describes Pickett as "gifted with intellect and known as an author, though only by her pen-name." See Corbell family Bible Page, original in possession of Edwin C. Cotten, Hampton, Va.; U.S. Census Office, Eighth Census of the United States, 1860: Population Schedule, Nansemond County, Va.; *Richmond Daily Dispatch*, September 22, 1863; Frances E. Willard and Mary A. Livermore, eds., *A Woman of the Century: Fourteen Hundred-Seventy Biographical Sketches Accompanied By Portraits of Leading American Women in All Walks of Life* (Buffalo, N.Y.: Charles Wells Moulton, 1893), 571.

5. LaSalle Corbell Pickett, *Kunnoo Sperits and Others* (Washington, D.C.: Neale, 1900), 21–22. Biographical details on both Picketts from Corbell Bible Page; Lesley J. Gordon, *General George E. Pickett in Life and Legend* (Chapel Hill: University of North Carolina Press, 1998).

6. Gordon, *General George E. Pickett*, 121–23.

7. LaSalle Corbell Pickett, *What Happened to Me* (New York: Brentano, 1917), 30, 36–38.

8. For examples of these idealized traits, see Pickett, *What Happened to Me*, 113, 277–78; and "General George Pickett: His Appointment to West Point—A Letter from His Widow," *Southern Historical Society Papers* 24 (January–December 1896): 151–54.

9. Pickett, *What Happened to Me*, 134.

10. LaSalle Corbell Pickett, "Introductory Note," Arthur Crew Inman Papers, Brown University Library, Providence, R.I. (Hereafter cited as Inman Papers.)

11. LaSalle Corbell Pickett, "My Soldier," *McClure's Magazine*, March 1908, 566; ed., *The Heart of a Soldier: As Revealed in the Intimate Letters of General George E. Pickett, C.S.A.* (New York: Seth Moyle, 1913), 13; and *Jinny* (Washington, D.C.: Neale, 1901), 133.

12. Pickett, ed., *Heart of a Soldier*, 23.

13. Pickett, "Introductory Note"; ed., *Heart of a Soldier*, 59. According to LaSalle, everyone loved George. See, for example, *What Happened to Me*, 278.

14. LaSalle Corbell Pickett, *The Bugles of Gettysburg* (Chicago: F. G. Browne, 1913), 101, 162.

15. LaSalle Corbell Pickett, *Pickett and His Men* (Atlanta: Foote and Davies, 1899), 29–30.

16. LaSalle Corbell Pickett to Lida Perry, February 28, 1889, Perkins Library, Duke University, Durham, North Carolina; description of Pickett at the twenty-fourth anniversary of Gettysburg is from "Mrs. Pickett's Reception," *New York Times*, July 5, 1887; references to George Pickett's death from *Atlanta Constitution*, August 3, 1875. For a general discussion of the Picketts and the mythology of Pickett's Charge, see Carol Reardon, *Pickett's Charge in History and Memory* (Chapel Hill: University of North Carolina Press, 1997), 80–83.

17. LaSalle Corbell Pickett, "Introductory Note."

18. Ibid. The best discussion of the Pickett Letters and their suspect nature is in Gary W. Gallagher, "A Widow and Her Soldier: LaSalle Corbell Pickett as Author of the George E. Pickett Letters," *Virginia Magazine of History and Biography* 94 (July 1986): 329–44. See also Gordon, *General George E. Pickett*, 2, 5, 100–101, 174, 177. Arthur Crew Inman republished the letters in 1928 as *Soldier of the South: General Pickett's War Letters to His Wife* (Boston: Houghton Mifflin, 1928).

19. Examples of her insistence on her writing's veracity include *Pickett and His Men*, 151, 153. Pickett claimed a special knowledge of black dialect learned from childhood. See *Kunnoo Sperits*, xi–xiii; quote from xiii. *The Library of Southern Literature*, whose co-chief editor was Joel Chandler

Harris, noted: "In dialect work she is at her best." See Edwin Anderson Alderman and Joel Chandler Harris, editors in chief, *Library of Southern Literature*, 16 vols. (New Orleans: Martin and Hoyt, 1908–13), 15:343.

20. LaSalle Corbell Pickett, "An Old-Time Virginia Christmas," *Harper's Bazaar*, January 1907, 50–51, 53; and *Ebil Eye* (Washington, D.C.: Neale, 1901), 145. See also *What Happened to Me*, 74.

21. Pickett, *What Happened to Me*, 74; "An Old-Time Virginia Christmas," 53; and *Jinny*, 134.

22. Pickett, *Jinny*, 70; repeated in "The Wartime Story of General Pickett," *Cosmopolitan*, December 1913, 34.

23. Pickett, *Across My Path*, 125.

24. Pickett, *Kunnoo Sperits*, 22–23.

25. Pickett, *Ebil Eye*, 18; and *Jinny*, 59.

26. Pickett, *Bugles*, 135–38. Pickett's depiction of blacks mimicked "Plantation Tradition" authors such as Joel Chandler Harris and Thomas Nelson Page. See Osterweis, *Myth of the Lost Cause*, 42–43, 50, 53, 55; and Foster, *Ghosts of the Confederacy*, 194.

27. Examples include Pickett, *Bugles*, 68–79, 141–44, 147; *Kunnoo Sperits*, 21; *Ebil Eye*, 9, 13, 98, 148; *Pickett and His Men*, 135; and *Yule Log*, 11, 75–77.

28. Pickett, *Pickett and His Men*, 130, 132–33.

29. Ibid., 134, 153.

30. Pickett, "Wartime Story," 38.

31. Ibid., 758.

32. Wilson, *Baptized in Blood*, 100–101; Aaron, *Unwritten War*, 332–33.

33. Pickett, "Wartime Story," 757.

34. Pickett, *Pickett and His Men*, 148, 151.

35. Pickett *Across My Path*, 127–28.

36. Pickett, *Pickett and His Men*, 152, emphasis in original.

37. Pickett, *Bugles*, 92–93; "In Memory of Judge Farrar," *Confederate Veteran* 7 (March 1899): 115; and "Patriotic Southern Womanhood," *Confederate Veteran* 7 (March 1899): 114–15.

38. Pickett, *Across My Path*, 7.

39. LaSalle Corbell Pickett, *Literary Hearthstones of Dixie* (Philadelphia: J. B. Lippincott, 1912), 3. For a general discussion of these Lost Cause themes see Osterweis, *Myth of the Lost Cause*, ix; Andrew, "Soldiers, Christians and Patriots," 678–79, 696; see also Gallagher, "A Widow and Her Soldier," 344.

40. Pickett, ed., *Heart of a Soldier*, 8.

41. Ibid., 68; *Pickett and His Men*, 408.

42. Pickett, *Bugles*, 120, 126. For a description of Pickett at the twenty-fourth anniversary of Gettysburg see "Mrs. Pickett's Reception."

43. Pickett, *Pickett and His Men*, viii.

44. Pickett, ed., *Heart of a Soldier*, 34.

45. Ibid., 65–66.

46. Inman, ed., *Soldier of the South*, 44. See also Pickett, *Pickett and His Men*, 408–409.

47. Inman, ed., *Soldier of the South*, 2.

48. Pickett, *What Happened to Me*, 192, 194. See also 187–88.

49. Pickett, *Pickett and His Men*, 417; see also 24–28; *What Happened to Me*, 194–95.

50. The name "Mother Pickett" is found in LaSalle Pickett's obituary in an undated newspaper clipping, UDC-Virginia Division, Boydton, Mecklenburg County Chapter, Scrapbook, 1913–1957, Virginia Historical Society, Richmond. She is referred to as "the last link connected with the tragedy at Gettysburg" in "Mrs. Pickett and Her Books," *Confederate Veteran* 25, no. 5 (May 1917): 237. For a discussion of the popularity of Lost Cause literature in the North see Aaron, *Unwritten War*, 286.

51. Pickett describes meeting these Northern women in *Across My Path*.

52. LaSalle Corbell Pickett to Joshua L. Chamberlain, April 25, 1910, Chamberlain Papers, Bowdoin College Library, Brunswick, Me.

53. LaSalle Corbell Pickett, "The First United States Flag Raised in Richmond After the War," in *The Fourth Massachusetts Cavalry in the Closing Scenes of the War for the Maintenance of the Union*, ed. William B. Arnold (Boston: n.p., n.d.), 19–22.

54. *Boston Transcript*, May 31, 1913, p. 4.

55. *The Chicago Record*, quoted in advertisement for *Pickett and His Men*, in back pages of Pickett, *Yule-Log*.

56. B. F. Keith, March 29, 1910, printed in "Something about Entertainment," undated newspaper clipping, Howard E. Buswell Collection, Center for Pacific Northwest Studies, Western Washington University, Bellingham.

57 The National Chautauqua Bureau promotional brochure, Inman Papers.

58. Willard and Livermore, eds., *A Woman of the Century*, 571. Pickett's celebration of reconciliation mirrored other Lost Cause promoters after 1890. See Wilson, *Baptized in Blood*, 161–64.

59. LaSalle Corbell Pickett to Edward J. Parker, March 31, 1911, Ms. 269, George Pickett Papers, Historical Society of Quincy and Adams County, Quincy, Ill.

60. LaSalle Corbell Pickett to Henry E. Huntington, January 1926, LaSalle Pickett Papers, Henry E. Huntington Library, San Marino, Calif.

61. Pickett, *Literary Hearthstones*, 2. See also p. 300, where she referred to falling "upon commercial times now."

62. Pickett, *Across My Path*, 148.

63. Pickett, *Ebil Eye*, 99–100.

64. Pickett, *Pickett and His Men*, 137.

65. LaSalle Corbell Pickett, "Patriotic Southern Womanhood," *Confederate Veteran* 7 (March 1899): 114–15. Pickett's promotion of the New South, the Old South, and national reconciliation was not unusual. Rod Andrew Jr. notes: "Southerners used celebrations of the Confederacy and its heroes for various and sometimes conflicting purposes." See Andrew, "Soldiers, Christians, and Patriots," 709. See also Foster, *Ghosts of the Confederacy*, 7–8; Osterweis, *Myth of the Lost Cause*, 144.

66. Pickett, *Across My Path*, 125–26.

67. Andrew, "Soldiers, Christians and Patriots," 695; Osterweis, *Myth of the Lost Cause*, x; Wilson, *Baptized in Blood*, 16, 38.

68. Andrew, "Soldiers, Christians and Patriots," 708 n 80; Foster, *Ghosts of the Confederacy*, 8; Osterweis, *Myth of the Lost Cause*, 29.

69. In 1973, Rollin Osterweis asked what it was that most Americans remember about Gettysburg: "Meade, Hunt and the withering artillery fire, Hancock?" "Or is it the gallant Pickett leading the flower of the Southern chivalric tradition to certain destruction and what proved to be certain glory? Who really triumphed in American collective memory?" See Osterweis, *Myth of the Lost Cause*, 83. Carol Reardon has explored this phenomenon in her *Pickett's Charge*.

70. "LaSalle Corbell Pickett to Be Reunited With Husband in Richmond's Hollywood Cemetery," <www.erols.com/va-udc/lasalle.html>.

71. LaSalle Pickett is the first woman allowed in the venerated Confederate section of the cemetery. Quotes from Martha M. Boltz, "LaSalle Pickett's battle to buff husband's image," *Washington Times*, March 14, 1998, B3; and Deborah Fitts, "Pickett's Wife to Be Reburied and His Grave Rededicated in March," *Civil War News*, February/March 1998, 1. See also *Richmond Times-Dispatch*, March 23, 1998.

Nine

The Immortal Confederacy
Another Look at Lost Cause Religion

Lloyd A. Hunter

In September 1906, Lawrence M. Griffith of Bates County, Missouri, addressed the tenth annual reunion of the state division of the United Confederate Veterans (UCV) at the Club Theater in Joplin. As a representative of the Sons of Confederate Veterans (SCV), he delivered a routine speech—a denial that Confederate soldiers were traitors and, of course, a roll call of the great heroes of the gray. But there was one paragraph that contained more truth than even Griffith may have realized:

> And when the ragged remains of an army of six hundred thousand Confederate patriots returned from a four years' fight with two million seven hundred thousand invaders, to find their homes despoiled, their families hungry, and their estates dissipated, there was born in the South a new religion. They did not think it wrong to worship those ragged idols, and with almost religious zeal they have given from their scanty stores to raise monuments to their defenders; striving by word, pen and printing press to make the world listen to the truths and learn both sides of that conflict.[1]

Griffith's phrase "a new religion" was a profound one, for it spoke of a vital force in the lives of postwar Confederates, a faith centered on the late Confederacy and, in the process, creating an image of their beloved South as a sacred land. For erstwhile soldiers in gray, and for their sons and daughters, the Confederacy became, as Robert Penn Warren later put it, a "City of the Soul"—an eternal city. "We may say," Warren wrote, "that only at the moment when Lee handed Grant his sword was

185

the Confederacy born; or to state it another way, in the moment of defeat the Confederacy entered upon its immortality."[2]

This new religion of which Griffith spoke, this worship of the Immortal Confederacy, had its foundation in the myth of the Lost Cause. Conceived in the ashes of a defeated and broken Dixie, this powerful, pervasive idea claimed the devotion of countless Confederates and their female counterparts. When it reached fruition in the 1880s its votaries not only pledged their allegiance to the Lost Cause, but they also elevated it above the realm of common, patriotic impulse, making it perform a clearly religious function. At annual meetings and other gatherings of veterans' groups and their women's auxiliaries, Southerners gave sacred status to the symbols of their Confederate past, dramatized them in formalized ritual, and expressed their meaning in mythic terms. They not only mythologized, but they also made sacred the Southern way of life, laying the foundation for a Southern culture religion, a regional faith based upon Dixie's wartime experience. An amalgam of Protestant evangelicalism and Southern romanticism, this cultural faith found embodiment in the historical, memorial, and educational activities of numerous Confederate organizations, most notably the UCV and the United Daughters of the Confederacy (UDC).

The components of the culture religion, like those of America's civil religion, provided Southerners with genuine vehicles of religious self-understanding.[3] Postwar Confederates, for example, chose to elevate their wartime symbols to sacred status, thus beginning the process of sacralization. The Stars and Bars, "Dixie," and the army's gray jacket became religious emblems, symbolic of the holy cause and of the sacrifices made on its behalf. Confederate heroes also functioned as sacred symbols: Lee and Davis emerged as Christ figures, the common soldier attained sainthood, and Southern women became Marys who guarded the tomb of the Confederacy and heralded its resurrection. In addition, ex-Confederates periodically gathered to uplift and enact these symbols in ritualistic activities. Memorial Days, veterans' reunions, and monument dedications enabled Lost Cause devotees to dramatize and interpret the cultural meaning of their sacred heritage. On such occasions, and in countless literary and historical endeavors, Confederates spoke of that heritage and sought to vindicate it in the language and structure of myth. Transforming the Civil War into a moment of transcendental value, they reiterated its sacred doctrines: that the South fought for the precious right of self-government and not for slavery; that its warriors, neither traitors nor rebels, conducted an honorable war against a corrupt North; and that the cause, never lost, would know resurrection. Emerging spiritually from the ashes of defeat, the Confederacy thus became a Sacred South, an Immortal Confederacy.

That Dixie's former soldiers should transform their wartime experience into something holy should come as no surprise, for to do so is a distinctly Southern act. During the greater portion of their dramatic and sometimes bitterly tragic history, Southerners have been endlessly haunted by their past—appropriating it with a romantic, sentimental, even reverential spirit. As James McBride Dabbs has written, "The Southerner has always been inclined to regard the past with piety." He is historically minded, endowed with "a certain respect for the sources of his being," and capable of carrying his region's past into the future like some weighty piece of luggage—a burden he has never been free to lay down. After Appomattox, Dabbs notes, "this healthy respect for the past was enormously intensified and became a religious force in the South. The postwar South deified its past, and compensated for the weakness it saw by the power and splendor of its god."[4]

As Southerners sanctified their past, with its tales of valor and martyrdom, they also imparted holiness to the region in which their past had occurred. Dixie was, they believed, the Sacred South—made inviolable by those who loved it, baptized in the blood of those who died for it, and ordained to permanent changelessness by the God who guided it. No wonder, then, that some students of Southern religious life have viewed the region as a virtual model of what sociologist Howard Becker has described as a "sacred society." Such a society, in Becker's words, "incorporates and sustains an impermeable value-system," derived from its heritage and maintained as a hallowed tradition. The "new" thus receives opposition because its acceptance denotes a departure, even a betrayal, from the tenets of the sacred past. Clearly, the South's response to historical forces exhibited such a stance; indeed, as John B. Boles has noted, Dixie's resistance to change is "a central theme of southern history."[5] Lost Cause myth and ritual may be seen, then, as the Southerner's normative response to the trauma of culture shock and its related suffering.

That the South's image of itself as a sacred entity intensified during the devastating decades of cultural disruption following Appomattox is a significant fact, for, as Richard W. Comstock has indicated, it is precisely at such critical moments that human beings confront the question of meaning in both its societal and individual forms. The struggle to make sense out of meaningless suffering is, at its core, a religious, existential problem. Through myth, symbol, and their ritualistic expressions—the chief components of religion—the human being is "able to correlate the inexplicable and unacceptable elements of his life from the threat of . . . final incoherence."[6] One way to do this is to engage in the process of sacralization. To sacralize is to elevate commonplace elements of a culture to some sort of sacred, inviolable standing. In this sense, sacralization is similar to the Christian concept of sanctification—to make holy, to impart sacredness, to set apart as consecrated. The major difference between these two acts is that, in the process of sacralization, the whole culture or land takes on religious import; in the eyes of the sacralizers, the society itself becomes sacred—or at least an instrument in God's hands for carving out humanity's ultimate destiny.[7]

The key elements in the formulation of such a holy image of society are symbols, for the very process of sacralization begins with the elevation of cultural symbols to sacred status. Susanne Langer observes that symbol producing is "the fundamental process of [the human] mind."[8] Creating symbols is one of humanity's basic activities, and they constitute both the material of human thought and its major mode of expression. For the community that employs them as rallying points, symbols perform two functions: they clarify the feeling a society has for itself and, at the same time, create this sentiment. To use just one illustration: a nation's flag serves as the embodiment of the group, as a mode of self-identification, and, as such, evokes a sense of loyalty to the principles of the state. To a soldier fighting for his country, the flag itself takes first place in his consciousness, not his own physical welfare. As Emile Durkheim points out, "he loses sight of the fact that the flag is only a sign, and that it has no value in itself, but only brings to mind the reality it represents; it is treated *as if it were this reality itself.*" Obviously, the soldier who defends his flag in battle does not believe that he risks his life for a mere piece of cloth. For him, the idea transferred to the flag—loyalty to country, love of homeland—is the reality for which he is willing to die.[9]

Here we see four basic factors associated with the use of symbols which are helpful in analyzing the symbol system of the Lost Cause religion: (1) a specific material object—in this case, the flag—is taken as representative of a general, perhaps abstract object—the country and all it means; (2) the sentiment attached to the general object is transferred to the symbol, so that the symbol becomes the focal point for the feelings of the community; (3) the symbol not only evokes intellectual or emotional responses from its followers, but it also prompts them into action; and (4) in its fullest dimension, the symbol represents the society that creates it.[10]

When symbols come together in some sort of configuration, they give rise to both myth and ritual. As anthropologist Clyde Kluckhohn has defined them, "The myth is a system of word symbols, whereas ritual is a system of object and act symbols."[11] In examining myth first, it is important to establish at the outset that *myth* is not synonymous with *falsehood*. Paul Gaston, in his insightful study of the New South creed, underscores this fact as cogently as anyone when he explains that myths "are not polite euphemisms for falsehoods, but are combinations of images and symbols that reflect a people's way of perceiving truth." And Robert Bellah asserts that myth seeks "to transfigure reality so that it provides moral and spiritual meaning to individuals and societies." Myth, in other words, is a vehicle for meaning. As a carrier of meaning, myth constitutes, according to Thomas J. J. Altizer, "the deepest and most authentic means for the expressions of religious understanding and belief."[12] It is important to note that, in the context of the present study, vital, living myths develop with special cogency among people who have experienced situations of critical or tragic proportions. As Ernst Cassirer has indicated, myth "reaches its full force when man has to face an unusual or dangerous situation." It is then that people turn to myth in a desire to become "at ease" with the world around them once again, in an attempt to comprehend a social or political scene that is mysterious or threatening—in short, in a search for meaning. The Lost Cause myth thus helped Confederates deal with defeat and its attendant anxieties.[13]

So did their Lost Cause rituals. For ritual—the configuration of act symbols—dramatizes the myth, the sacred story, and thus transforms the word spoken into the word enacted. In ritual, the participants are able to act out the ideals precious to them, keep those ideals alive, and reinforce them by their own actions. Like myths, rituals are carriers of meaning. Regularly repeated, they adhere to formal patterns and serve to bind people together through the ceremonial restatement of their heritage. Some rituals, in fact, actually enable their participants to transcend time by attaching the present to the past, either through the recollection of historical events and heroes or by basing the rites upon long-established teaching—an insight especially applicable to the study of the Lost Cause religion.[14]

Not surprisingly, the least reconstructed Southerners—the women—took the initial steps in laying the foundation of the region's cultural faith. Known during the war and Reconstruction for their bitterness toward Yankees and noncombatants, Dixie's ladies balanced their uncompromising behavior by lifting their hearts and voices in homage to the sacred cause. Their devotion began during the dark days of the conflict itself. Banding themselves together in local Soldiers' Relief Societies, mothers and daughters established canteens, secured hospital supplies, ministered in the sick rooms, and even, in some cases, buried the dead. After the war these groups became memorial associations, collecting the bodies of shallowly interred Confederates and transferring them to more suitable burying grounds. Furthermore, as Charles Colcock Jones Jr. said of them, "they dignified the land with soldiers' monuments, gathered the sacred dust, guarded unmarked graves, and canonized those who suffered martyrdom during this eventful epoch."[15]

Their most lasting mark, however, was the founding of Memorial Day. The origin of this most solemn event is obscure, but probably the safest claim rests with the women of Columbus, Georgia. On April 16, 1865, one of the last battles of the war ended on the Alabama heights overlooking Columbus, and on April 26, Gen. Joseph E. Johnston surrendered the final major Confederate field army to General Sherman. At a cemetery near the battleground, the women of Columbus began to care for the soldiers' graves. One of them wrote thirty years later: "When the smoke of war cleared away, where do we find these devoted women? Where were Mary Magdalene and the other Mary after the crucifixion? At the sepulcher with sweet spices. So these women came to the soldiers' graves with choice plants and bright flowers."[16] Early in 1866, after several women had been busily caring for the cemetery, Elizabeth "Lizzie" Rutherford recommended an annual observance for the decoration of the soldiers' resting places. The idea received spontaneous approval, and the Columbus Memorial Association adopted April 26—the date of Johnston's surrender—as the most appropriate time for a universal observance. By 1900 the task of memorializing had become so weighty and ambitious that a region-wide common observance seemed desirable. On May 30 of that year delegates from memorial groups throughout the South met in Louisville, Kentucky, to form the Confederated Southern Memorial Association (CSMA), which soon established June 3, Jefferson Davis's birthday, as Confederate Memorial Day.[17]

While Southern women nurtured Memorial Day through its infancy, Confederate veterans began forming embryonic groups of their own. Most characteristic of these early bodies were those designed to perform memorial or charitable deeds, such as aiding destitute widows and orphans, assisting the disabled, erecting monuments, and writing regimental histories. In addition to these groups, numerous local and state veterans' societies emerged throughout the South in the first two decades after the war. All major cities in the region boasted of at least one active unit, such as New Orleans's Washington Light Artillery, the Confederate Survivors' Association of Augusta, Georgia, and the R. E.

Lee Camp No. 1 in Richmond. By the end of the 1880s, with veterans' groups rapidly sprouting up everywhere, the time seemed ripe for unity among ex-Confederates.[18]

Two facts about those years produced an atmosphere conducive to the growth of South-wide Confederate organizations: Reconciliation was proceeding resolutely and with much speed, and the Lost Cause had gained an important foothold in the mind of the South. The celebration of America's centennial in 1876 elevated reconciliation to a prime theme in the national arena, and in the next decade significant events helped to weld the nation together. These included the rise of Rutherford B. Hayes to the presidency and his subsequent removal of federal troops from Southern soil; Hayes's tour of Dixie during which he participated in Southern Memorial Day exercises; the universal grief over the assassination of President James A. Garfield in 1881; and the appearance of ex-Confederates as pallbearers at Ulysses S. Grant's funeral in 1885.[19]

At the same time that Reconstruction was happily becoming a memory, the Lost Cause was becoming myth. As W. J. Cash cogently demonstrates, the 1880s marked a period of Southern flight from reality. The war took on a nostalgic glow, and the Cause seemed in danger of "slipping into the past." White Southerners therefore joined it there—at least in spirit—and the symbols of its expression began to abound. Plans for united Confederate action got under way, the erection of monuments became ever more frequent, the oratory of the Lost Cause flowered beyond its previous bloom, and Confederate museums—even a Battle Abbey—began to dot the landscape, taking on the aura of holy places.[20]

In 1883, friends of the late president of Washington College, Robert Edward Lee, gathered on the campus to inaugurate the mausoleum in the new Lee Chapel. Its central focus was the recumbent figure of Lee, stationed, like the altar of a great cathedral, so that all eyes would rest upon it. The work of Richmond sculptor Edward V. Valentine, it depicts Lee in sleep, with an expression of contentment, "irradiated by that nobility of soul that characterized the living man and endeared him to the Southern heart." As an awestruck visitor reported: "The light falls from above the ceiling of semitranslucent, compartmented glass which strikes the outstretched marble figure at an admirable angle, filling the chamber and illuminating the figure with a soft but powerful radiance." Perhaps the speaker at the inauguration, Sen. John W. Daniel, shared that reporter's feeling of wonder. Daniel described Lee as a Christ figure, as "the Priest of his people," who came to share their miseries. "He shared them, drinking every drop of Sorrow's cup." No wonder a later president of Washington and Lee University provoked a storm of protest when he suggested changes in the chapel. Wrote one editor, "Lay not hand upon it . . . for it is a holy place."[21] The Lost Cause had clearly erected a sacred shrine.

Further dramatizing the growth of Lost Cause sentiment, Jefferson Davis emerged from self-imposed exile. In 1886, Henry W. Grady, editor of the *Atlanta Constitution*, resurrected Davis from his beloved Beauvoir and invited him to appear at the dedication of an Atlanta monument to the late Confederate lawmaker Benjamin Harvey Hill. In reality an act in the political drama of Georgia (Grady sought Davis's presence on stage with John B. Gordon to boost the latter's gubernatorial campaign), Grady used the moment of Davis's appearance to intone a theme of the culture religion. "This moment," he began, "in this blessed Easter Week, witnessing the resurrection of these memories that for twenty years have been buried in our hearts, has given us the best Easter that we have seen since Christ was risen from the dead."[22] Grady's words appropriately punctuated the most important decade in the *Confederacy*'s rise from the dead.

Under the impetus of this resurgent spirit, Confederate veterans moved quickly to launch a national organization. On June 10, 1889, sixty Confederates representing ten organizations gathered in New Orleans, adopted a constitution, and elected Maj. Gen. John B. Gordon as the first commander in chief of the United Confederate Veterans. When the newly created organization held its first reunion on July 3, 1890, at Chattanooga, it was obvious that the UCV would contain all the trappings of a culture religion. A tableau on "the Wounding of Stonewall Jackson" featured a hundred-voice women's chorus singing "Nearer My God to Thee," and an enactment of the surrender at Appomattox was accompanied by the clearly religious words of Father Abram Joseph Ryan's "The Conquered Banner":

> Furl that Banner, softly, slowly!
> Treat it gently—it is holy—
>   For it droops above the dead.
> Touch it not—unfold it never,
> Let it droop there, furled forever,
>   For its people's hopes are dead![23]

Only nineteen camps sent delegations to that initial convocation, and the ceremonies attracted only four thousand visitors, but the UCV would grow enormously during the nineties—more than ten thousand old soldiers representing 850 camps attended the Richmond reunion in 1896. Its spirituality would grow as well. For well over a decade—the very years the Lost Cause myth thrived—the UCV was the primary institutional home for the Southern culture religion.[24]

Naturally, the women of the South, with their well-known fervor for the Lost Cause, echoed the sentiments of the veterans in gray. After their initial involvement in Memorial Day activities, they gave their attention to assisting the old soldiers in monumental and historical tasks. It was not until the 1890s, though, that Daughters of the Confederacy chapters began to spring up at local levels. The first came into being in St. Louis in 1890, and during the next few years similar societies formed in Savannah, Georgia, and Nashville, Tennessee. By 1894 the "Daughters" were ready to call for a national organization.[25] The United Daughters of the Confederacy began in the rooms of the Frank Cheatham Bivouac at Nashville in September of that year, and from its founding its members were faithful votaries at the shrine of the Lost Cause. Indeed, as C. Vann Woodward has written, the UDC gave the cult of the Confederacy "a religious character." According to the motto suggested by the Opelika, Alabama, chapter, the Daughters of the Confederacy were to be "the ark in which is laid up the political faith of their fathers."[26]

The organizational foundations now having been laid, worshipers at the shrine of the Lost Cause could carry on the process of sacralization by elevating the symbols of the Confederacy to sacred status.

Confederate emblems, of course, did not have to be described in religious metaphor in order to be powerful. They already manifested all the characteristics that equip symbols with potency. But postwar Southerners chose to give them sacred status, and therein lies their significance. They functioned not as mere emblems but as *religious* symbols, as collective representations of the Southern historical experience interpreted in the light of transcendence. It was no doubt to this singular aspect of Confederate symbols that Brig. Gen. Clement A. Evans, Methodist circuit rider and onetime commander of the UCV, pointed in a Memorial Day address in 1896. "We have a deep and honorable respect for some things which we call our mementoes," he said. "They are many, and all are sacred; but I will mention only three, each of which deserves our perpetual commemorations." Evans's choices read like a trinity of the culture religion: "Dixie," the battle flag, and the old soldier's gray jacket.[27]

Without question, the banners of the Lost Cause evoked the most reverent response. These, after all, were the totems under which the warriors in gray fought and fell. They were not mere fragments of cloth but representations of the homeland itself, of the reality for which the soldier struggled. Thus, Confederates believed they should be treated as if they *were* that reality, for they contained the essence and meaning—and often literally the blood—for which Southern heroes gave their lives. In the days just after Lee's surrender, Father Ryan, a former Catholic chaplain and noted poet, gave expression to this sentiment in "The Conquered Banner." A man whose life revolved around his two principal loves, God and the Southland, Ryan often united them in his verse and, on this occasion, his lyric description of the torn and tattered battle flag, drooping sadly on its broken staff as if weeping for the hands that had grasped it, touched the ardent feelings of his fellow Confederates, thus ushering in decades of sacralization of that flag. Ryan's verse became a leading anthem of the cultural faith and spurred other poets into singing the praises of Confederate banners. Employing biblical figures, for instance, Harry Lynden Flash, an aide-de-camp to Maj. Gen. Joseph Wheeler in wartime, depicted the Confederate flag leading the chosen Southern nation like Moses' "pillar of cloud by day,/ of fire by night." Symbol of "a people's hope," the Stars and Bars, like the soldiers who carried it into the fray, succumbed as a sacrifice for the cause:

> It fell—but stainless as it rose,
> Martyred, like Stephen, in the strife—
> Passing, like him, girdled with foes,
>   From Death to Life.[28]

At veterans' reunions and other patriotic convocations, old soldiers sanctified their flags in countless orations. At a Baltimore gathering of the Association of the Maryland Line in 1889, Maj. Gen. Thomas L. Rosser struck a chord intoned at myriad veterans' meetings, portraying the old battle flag's meaning in almost sacramental terms. "This is the cross which we bore with a courage, patience and fortitude which entitles every true, brave and tried Confederate soldier to a Patriot's immortal crown!" he bellowed. "This banner is consecrated by baptism in the blood of Stonewall Jackson, Turner Ashby, J. E. B. Stuart, and other Christian knights of the South whose proud names and glorious fame shall endure forever!"[29] Confederate banners were objects of devotion well into the twentieth century, but the focus of that adoration underwent significant change, for the wearers of the gray came to believe that, as sacred symbols, the flags prefigured the eventual resurrection of the Confederacy. In the poetic expression of Augustus J. Requier, the wartime State's Attorney for Alabama, the "shrouded ensign," like the Confederacy itself, would know resurrection: "A warrior's Banner takes its flight, / To greet the warrior's soul."[30]

Whether or not they would carry the battle flag on resurrection morn, there was little doubt in Southern minds that most Confederates would rise singing "Dixie." The battle hymn of the South served as a symbol of the land and the cause that no veteran wanted to forget. At every reunion of Southern soldiers its lively strains called them to look "away down South in Dixie"—to the land in which they had taken their stand "to lib an' die." Although written in 1859 by Ohioan Daniel Decatur Emmett of Bryant's Minstrels, and clearly lacking the language and sentiment of religious symbolism, it became an emblem of the cultural faith as a result of postwar controversies over its words. At the June 1904 reunion of the UCV, a resolution calling for the formation of a joint committee with the Sons of Confederate Veterans and the UDC "relative to the selection of suitable words for our immortal battle hymn" prompted a fierce reply by Brig. Gen. William L. Cabell. While he loved the Daughters and respected their opinion, he stated that it was nonetheless a "sacrilege to talk about changing dear old 'Dixie.'" Later that year, Cabell, who had a reputation as a vehement Lost Cause curmudgeon, wrote Mrs. W. M. Camper of Florence, Alabama:

> Then let old "Dixie" alone, and when I am lying in my grave, wrapped in my old gray jacket, pierced in a dozen places with Yankee bullets, and when the man of God is through, let the daughters of the South, the prettiest and the most glorious women on earth, sing "Dixie," so that my spirit may be taken to heaven, to join my comrades who have gone before.[31]

In his letter, Cabell mentioned still another of the South's potent symbols: the gray Confederate jacket. Along with many of his comrades, he expressed a desire to be buried in his old uniform coat, no matter its condition. This intent, while seemingly morbid and gloomy, was actually reflective of the role played by hope in the resurrection—both of the soldier and of his cause—which pervaded the culture religion. Fannie H. Marr, for example, portraying the role of an old warrior, had her protagonist utter the wish that he might be shrouded in his battle coat: "For I want to rest, till the Great Captain calls, / In my suit of Confederate gray." Another Daughter, Fannie Downing, offered a like plea:

> Old suit! Once more you will be worn,
>   When I am in my coffin laid,
> Upon the Resurrection morn
>   I wish to stand in you arrayed,
> When with hosannas loud and sweet,
>   Beatified with bliss intense,

Our Southern soldiery shall meet
    Confederate in the highest sense.[32]

Apparently, on the day of resurrection the "Dixie"-singing choir would
be clad in knightly garments of gray.

Of course, some sacred symbols could not be worn in coffins or transported to heaven: heroes, for example. And if there was anything at
which the South excelled in those years, it was the creation of heroes.
Therefore, along with "Dixie" and the Stars and Bars, Confederate
braves became sacred symbols—and chief among them were the South's
wartime leaders, most especially Robert E. Lee and Jefferson Davis.

Lee began his rise to sainthood during the war, but it was not until
after his death in 1870 that his deification would reach complete fruition
and he would be placed, as Charles Reagan Wilson put it, "at the apex
of the Lost Cause Pantheon." Almost with his last breath, he rose to
godlike stature in the mind of his countrymen. At Lexington, on the
very day of his death, the movement started that eventually would result
in the erection of the Lee Chapel. Within months of their former commander's passing, veterans of the Army of Northern Virginia laid the
foundations for a Lee cult and formulated the dogmas for the canonization of the South's leading Christian knight.[33]

Among these doctrines the most basic was a belief in Lee as the incarnation of the Lost Cause. Benjamin Morgan Palmer, the New Orleans
Presbyterian whose wartime services earned him the title "Orator-
Preacher of the Confederacy," spoke of Lee as "the representative of his
people" and "the true type of the American man, and the Southern
gentleman." In 1903, at the Confederate Home in Pikesville, Maryland,
Rev. William M. Dame told the old soldiers that "God's greatest gift to
a race and a time is some one man in whom that race shall see the embodiment of its highest ideals." Only a few ever reach such heights,
Dame noted, but among them were "Moses, David, George Washington, and Robert E. Lee."[34]

Most of the images that veterans projected of Lee—embodiment of
the South, a second Washington, the Christian knight—served as the
basis for the major culture religion view of Lee as a godlike figure, mani-
festing the traits of Christ. Even during the war, soldiers, reported ex-
Confederate officer Robert Stiles, had a habit of calling God "Old Marster," and it was not uncommon for them to request a clarification of the
term—whether the speaker referred to "the one up at headquarters or
the one up yonder." Like Christ, Lee appeared to Dixie's soldiers as
God's model of manhood. Randolph H. McKim, an officer on Brig.
Gen. George H. Steuart's staff and later a leading Episcopal priest,

wrote of Lee: "from the day when he publicly gave himself to the service of God in old Christ Church, Alexandria, he lived not to himself but to God and his fellow men." Lee was, McKim continued, infused "by the Christ-like spirit of self-sacrifice," and "the sign of the Cross was upon his life."[35]

On the occasion of the dedication of the recumbent figure in the Lee Chapel, John W. Daniel spoke of the general's agonizing decision to resign from the United States Army in order to offer his services to his native Virginia: "Since the Son of Man stood upon the Mount and saw 'all the kingdoms of the earth and the glory thereof' stretched before him, and turned away from them to the agony and bloody sweat of Gethsemane, and to the Cross of Calvary beyond, no follower of the meek and lowly Saviour can have undergone more trying ordeal, or met it with higher spirit of heroic sacrifice."[36]

Other veterans also compared this particular moment of the general's life with Christ's experiences, but they differed in their interpretations: To some it was Lee's "Gethsemane," whereas others called it his "crucifix moment." Daniel himself added another dimension by hinting that Gettysburg's Seminary Ridge was "the mount of [Lee's] transfiguration, where, sublimating all earthly instincts, the Divinity in his bosom shone translucent through the man, and his spirit rose up into the Godlike."[37]

Unlike Lee's apotheosis, Jefferson Davis's began long before his death. His countrymen bitterly attacked him when the Confederacy collapsed, but his arrest and lengthy imprisonment in Fort Monroe spurred Southerners to respond to his plight with sympathy and renewed devotion. By the time of his release in May 1867, the former chief executive had become a heroic martyr—the crucified Christ of the Southern people who had suffered on their behalf.[38] When in 1886 Henry Grady summoned the ex-president from his self-styled exile at Beauvoir to appear at the unveiling of the Hill memorial in Atlanta, Davis's journey became "a continuous ovation." A veteran described the scene in Atlanta in words reminiscent of another triumphal entry: "Along the streets and sidewalks . . . hobbled the veterans of the Confederate Army and thronged the carriage in which rode their defeated king and kissed its very wheels, while little children threw flowers before his horse's feet, and women . . . bowed their heads and wept. This was the triumph of the victim." To the special car that later bore Davis from Atlanta to Savannah was affixed the inscription, "He Was Manacled For Us."[39] Davis's role as a sacred symbol had been assured.

The strength of that role, as was the case with Lee, rested upon Davis's status as "the embodied history of the South." Even more than

Lee, Davis became the incarnation of the Confederacy's major principles, especially that of states' rights. According to Charles Colcock Jones, Davis "remained faithful even unto death" to his belief in state sovereignty, and a member of the Texas House of Representatives noted the former president's allegiance to that tenet while striking a central theme of Davis's deification. "The embodiment of a political ideal," the solon declared, "he became the very impersonation of faith and devotion; immersing himself in duty, he became a sacrifice to all the misfortunes following defeat, and, with a fortitude approaching stoicism, he offered himself a scapegoat to bear the so-called sins of his people."[40]

Here was Davis the Christ figure. Confederates firmly believed that, like the Christ crucified as the expiation for human iniquity, "Davis was the sacrifice selected—by the North or by Providence—as the price for Southern atonement." William Dame, rector of Baltimore's Memorial Protestant Church, theologized about the purpose of Davis's "passion." As the "chosen vicarious victim," Dame said, the former chieftain stood mute as Northerners "laid on him the falsely alleged iniquities of us all." And, as late as 1923, a second-generation Confederate bard would repeat the endless theme:

> Jefferson Davis! Still we honor thee!
> Our lamb victorious, who for us endur'd
> A cross of martyrdom, a crown of thorns,
> A soul's Gethsemane, a nation's hate,
> A dungeon's gloom! Another god in chains.[41]

If Lee and Davis reminded Southerners of Christ, another leader in gray—Thomas Jonathan "Stonewall" Jackson—made them think of Moses. Jackson was a natural candidate for Confederate sainthood since he combined in his character all the traits that Southerners admired. A devout Christian of the Calvinist variety, he also was a gallant warrior in the chivalric tradition and an ardent champion of Southern rights. Moreover, his death shortly after the battle of Chancellorsville made him a martyr, and the use of the newly adopted national flag as his burial shroud gave that martyrdom special meaning. In fact, his death was the primary reason Jackson entered the Confederate canon as a Moses figure. Presbyterian clergyman and scholar Robert Lewis Dabney wrote that Jackson "was to his fellow citizens the man of destiny, the anointed of God to bring in the deliverance for his oppressed Church and Country." Out in front of his men, "leading the van of victory," he commanded "such trust as the ancient Hebrews reposed in their kings and judges." Even his habit of praying in the midst of combat recalled Moses-like behavior. Reminiscent of that Old Testament deliverer "upon the mount of God," lifting his hands while Israel defeated Amalek, Jackson regularly appeared to pray in like manner during battles. Dabney observed him at Cross Keys, dropping the reins upon his horse's neck and raising "both his hands toward the heavens while the fire of battle in his face changed into a look of reverential awe. Even while he prayed, the God of battles heard; or ever he had withdrawn his uplifted hands the bridge was gained, and the enemy's gun was captured."[42]

But it was the fact that Jackson never lived to see Confederate victory that sealed his image. In 1899 a veteran wrote *The Lost Cause* magazine of his remembrances of being at the young general's funeral, and he posed a poignant question to God. "Why put out this lamp before the day of our independence had dawned?" he asked. "Why leave us in the midst of this great struggle without a Jackson, in the dark of doubt?" And poet Harry Lynden Flash wrote:

He entered not the nation's Promised Land
At the red belching of the cannon's mouth;
But broke the House of Bondage with his hand—
    The Moses of the South.[43]

The Confederacy's captains, however, were not the only heroes to suffer for the cause, and its devotees knew it. The most common human symbols were the thousands of nameless soldiers, living and dead, whose courage, they vowed, must never be forgotten. Around these anonymous figures a cult of the Confederate soldier developed, marked by a commitment never to let him die in vain. Determined that the private soldiers would "live in song and story," Southerners sought to preserve their memory in word and monument. One man of the ranks spoke for many of his comrades: "And with uncovered head and profoundest reverence I bow before those dauntless heroes, feeling that . . . they deserve to stand shoulder to shoulder with Lee and his lieutenants in the brotherhood of glory."[44] As with the leaders, rank-and-file Confederates bore the marks of the Christian knight; nineteenth-century Ivanhoes, they were men of principle and honor.

Since he bore those marks, the martyred Sam Davis—the South's Nathan Hale—served as the ultimate model of the common soldier. In the young Tennessean, hanged by Union soldiers as a spy in 1864, postwar Confederates found an emblem of valor, honor, and sacrifice which contained all their images of the Confederate fighting man. His last words, vowing his loyalty to his comrades and his refusal to inform on them, were compared to those of Jesus: "Greater love hath no man than this, that he lay down his life for his friends." Described as one of God's "own instruments" who, "touched by the hand divine, . . . rose from the gallows to the crown," Sam Davis became another Confederate Christ:

> On Calvary the Son of God died with cruel nails driven through his quivering flesh, the crown of thorns pressing down on his agonized brow, and since then the cross has been the Christian's sign in every land; and which of us has the right to say that He who created the earth and the sky and every living thing on sea and land, whose mysteries baffle, but whose providence is over all, could give the Son of Mary to teach men how to live could not also give this son of Tennessee to teach men how to die?[45]

In like manner to Sam Davis, all the Confederate martyrs were seen as spotless, blameless soldiers who ventured all for self-rule and died in a holy cause. References abound in Confederate speeches and poetry to the common soldier as a sacrificial lamb whose shed blood baptized and sanctified Dixie's soil.[46]

But not all Confederates received elevation to sainthood. Indeed, at least one officer in gray, James Longstreet, provided the culture religion with a personification of evil. Thanks largely to the writings of Jubal A. Early, J. William Jones, William Nelson Pendleton, and others in the so-called Virginia Coalition in the pages of the *Southern Historical Society Papers*, Longstreet became the Judas of Lost Cause religion. Lee devotees all, they joined Pendleton in accusing Lee's "Old War Horse" of "culpable disobedience" at Gettysburg, thus causing the failure of Pickett's assault on the third day. Longstreet, Pendleton charged, betrayed Lee, but the Christlike commanding general took the blame when he uttered his famous words, "It is all my fault." William Garrett Piston correctly observes: "As Christ assumed the burden of sin at Golgotha, so had Lee assumed the sins of Longstreet the Judas at Gettysburg."[47] Nor did Longstreet's later political activities as a Louisiana scalawag, and his service as leader of mostly African-American troops against former Confederates in the New Orleans White League fight of 1874, erase his image as the "absolute malefactor" of Gettysburg. By then he had become the culture religion's Antichrist. At his death in 1904, the Savannah UDC refused to send flowers, and a North Carolina UCV encampment withheld any expression of condolence. Not all the Confederate leaders were saints in the eyes of many Lost Cause devotees. There was a Judas Iscariot among them.[48]

To insure that the holy symbols of the Lost Cause would not be forgotten, Dixie's patriotic groups engaged in numerous ceremonial activities, the most important of which were Memorial Day and the UCV reunions.[49] Like all rituals, these Confederate experiences were carriers of meaning for Lost Cause devotees during which, in Charles Wilson's words, "a holy Confederate spirit descended and touched those present." Their purpose was to recall the past, to resurrect the days when the holy symbols were still living and viable. In short, Confederates sought through ritual to provide, for themselves and their posterity, a sense of attachment to their sacred history.[50]

Undoubtedly, the central ritual occasion for telling the story was Memorial Day, the Sabbath of the South. This solemn observance was more than simply a cult of the dead. It was a religious ritual for the living as well. As Paul Buck indicates, Memorial Day provided one of the few holidays for postbellum America, and this was especially true in the South. Consequently, "a visit to the graves of the dead was not merely a sad rite of remembrance but also a diversion." The excitement of marching veterans, the drama of children bearing floral offerings, the sounds of martial airs, and the sentiments of oratory made the day a highlight of the community's calendar.[51]

Wherever held, the day's activities followed a common pattern. The ceremonies on April 26, 1898, at Columbus, Georgia, were typical. Although Company G of the Albany Guards, accompanied by the Fourth Georgia Regimental Band, arrived in town at midmorning after their long trek to Columbus, the day's festivities did not begin until two o'clock in the afternoon. At that time, the procession of soldiers, Confederate veterans, marching bands, and dignitaries formed at the city armory. As the bands played martial music, all marched to the Confederate monument on Broad Street and then on to the Presbyterian Church, "where the Ladies Memorial Association and the Daughters of the Confederacy took their places in the line of march, which moved thence to the opera house, where the exercises took place." By now the military airs, the tramping feet of the old soldiers, and the glimpse of the monument had served to recall the past and its glorious emblems. The ritual activities at the opera house only needed to add word symbols to those already witnessed. With "hardly standing room in the building," the services opened with musical selections, followed by a prayer intoned by a local pastor. The orator of the day then proceeded to discuss the meaning of the solemn occasion. The ritual closed with a reading of the history of Memorial Day, a recitation on "Our Confederate Dead," and a solo rendition of Father Ryan's "The Conquered Banner." Proceeding to the cemetery, "where thousands of people were waiting," the throng decorated the graves with flowers, and the experience ended with the firing of salutes.[52]

It was at the cemetery that ex-Confederates transcended time in a symbolic meeting with the martyrs of the Lost Cause. Over their graves, the living comrades sounded the major themes of the Sabbath of the South. They spoke of sacrifice, death, and rebirth, and they embodied their words in ritual acts, chief among them the strewing of immortelles upon graves and monuments.

Occasionally, the ritual enactments of the day centered on the desire for reconciliation. At Little Rock, Arkansas, in 1875, the exercises were held at the spot where Union and Confederate dead lay in adjacent cemeteries. Since the speakers' platform had been constructed to overlap portions of the adjoining burial grounds, when the orations were completed the ex-Confederate speaker buried a hatchet in the Union earth, while the Yankee veteran did the same in the Southern plot. Seldom has a cliche been so dramatically enacted![53]

The annual reunions of the UCV likewise contained ritualistic expressions of the cultural faith; indeed, they were virtual revivals of the Lost Cause religion. The elaborate plans of Southern cities for each year's reunion, the intense exhilaration of the veterans and their frequent outbursts, the appeal of parades and balls, and the centrality of oratory and the mythmaking of UCV historical work, the intertwining of elements of Southern evangelicalism with the Confederate story—these were crucial ceremonial aspects of the Lost Cause movement.[54]

The veterans not only wanted their reunions to recall the past but *intended* for them to do so. They therefore ordered their activities during their annual meetings around the goal of reviving and "recounting sacred memories of the past." At times this recollection of the past, under the impact of the drama of ritual, could become graphically vivid. When Commander Clement A. Evans asked to hear the famed rebel yell from those gathered in Memphis in 1909, one veteran felt he was back in wartime again:

> And didn't they yell?
> You could hear Jackson's legions thundering down the slope and catch the dust of Forrest's brigade clattering by like a whirlwind in that yell. It came again and again, circled three times from the pit to the very peaks of the roof of that great building and died away in the hum of laughter and approval that bordered upon tears.

A poetic Southerner expressed it more succinctly:

> Backward, turn Backward, O Time, in your flight.
> Make me a Reb again just for tonight.[55]

Preparing for veterans to return to the past every year was a major undertaking for Southern cities. Plans had to be made for adequate transportation, for lodging the old soldiers, for feeding the anticipated

crowds, and for procuring and equipping a suitable hall. Huge throngs
overtaxed rail systems and made it difficult for reception committees to
provide accommodations. People came from everywhere to attend. In
1898 the *Atlanta Constitution* reported that veterans attended that city's
gathering from as far away as "Missouri, Indian Territory, and other
remote places." On the eve of the 1892 meeting in New Orleans, one
resident observed: "The old Confeds are arriving in force, and tomorrow and next day will own the town. . . . Everything is free for them,
drinks, shaves, cabs, theaters. The barbers, bar keeps, boot blacks are
ordered to serve them free, and call on the Comm. for reimbursement.
Just fancy 1500 Texans, well-primed with corn whiskey, turned loose
on the bully—and behind a half-dozen brass bands playing the Bonnie
Blue Flag!"[56]

The impact of the reunions on their host communities seemed tame,
however, compared to the emotional involvement of the veterans themselves. The erstwhile warriors, aroused by the excitement of seeing former leaders and comrades, and by the powerful remembrance of the Lost
Cause, were quick to unleash pent-up enthusiasm for everyone who es-
poused the sacred principles. No matter how loudly the band played
"Dixie" or "The Bonnie Blue Flag," no matter how attractive the decorations in the hall, nothing distracted the veterans when someone they
loved appeared on stage. Commander Gordon's arrival always prompted
instantaneous pandemonium—the waving of hats and handkerchiefs, the
screech of the rebel yell, the strains of a battle hymn. The appearance
of Winnie Davis, "The Daughter of the Confederacy," at the Houston
Assembly in 1895 provoked a wild melee: "People clambered onto the
stage from the front by the hundred, tearing away the plants and destroying the decorations, intent upon just one thing—touching the hand
of the daughter of their great chieftain of thirty-four years ago."[57]

Punctuated by such bursts of feeling, UCV reunions seldom displayed consistent ritual patterns. No single reunion, in other words, was
ever "typical." Perhaps it is best to say that Confederate gatherings consisted of a series of spontaneous, loosely connected ceremonial acts. For
example, within the business sessions themselves the elevation of sacred
symbols took place in unscheduled ways, interspersed throughout the
proceedings in orations, recitations, impulsive cheers for "Dixie" or the
Confederate flag, or wedged between resolutions. Likewise, in the more
public events—the parades, balls, and banquets—spontaneous occur-
rences would spark expressions of love and loyalty to the Lost Cause.
Instantaneous singing of "Dixie" or "The Bonnie Blue Flag" might
capture the veterans' fancy, or occasionally a church hymn would be
sung, and frequently the old soldiers chose to join in "We Are Old-Time

Confederates," a tuneful recollection of the past sung to the catchy revival song, "That Old-Time Religion":

> We are a band of brothers,
> We are a band of brothers,
> band of Southern brothers,
> Who fought for Liberty.
> We're old-time Confederates,
> We're old-time Confederates,
> We're old-time Confederates,
> They're good enough for me.[58]

That interesting song, which normally ended with a rebel yell, illustrates a major dimension of Lost Cause ritual: the yoking of evangelicalism with the Confederate spirit. Prayers combining the symbols of the culture religion with the God of the Bible, Christian hymns interspersed with Confederate battle anthems, "altar calls" to join Davis and Lee at the throne of grace—all marked the revivalistic nature of UCV reunions. Chaplain John William Jones consistently opened the meetings with a prayer that melded Christianity and Confederacy:

> Oh! God our help in ages past, our hope for years to come, God of Israel, God of Abraham, Isaac, and Jacob—God of the centuries—God of our Fathers—God of Stonewall Jackson and Robert Lee and Jefferson Davis—Lord of Hosts—God of the whole of our common country—God of our Southland—our God!

Moreover, Commander Gordon regularly asked the gray-clad veterans to stand and sing the doxology or another favorite hymn. In 1902 the doxology was followed by "Dixie" and "the crowd went wild." At the 1914 reunion, a memorial song reminiscent of the sawdust trail that was sung to the tune of "When the Roll Is Called Up Yonder" lifted the spirits:

> On that mistless, lovely morning, when the saved of Christ shall rise,
> In the Father's many-mansioned home to share;
> When our Lee and Jackson call us to their home beyond the skies,
> When the reveille is sounded, let's be there.[59]

However, the clearest expression of the union of evangelicalism with the Lost Cause appeared in the chaplains' sermons. In 1900, Jones asked the veterans if, "when the roll is called up yonder," they would be prepared to "'Cross over the river and rest under the shade of the trees' with Davis and Lee and Jackson and other Christian comrades who wait and watch for your coming?" As late as 1926, chaplain and novelist

Henry L. Wharton shouted: "Brother, if Jesus Christ walks at your side
—you and I are proud to say that we followed General Lee, . . . but
prouder shall we be when we stand beside our Commander General Lee
and look into the face of our Greater Commander, Jesus Christ." A voice
replied, "Amen!" Then, insisting that "the religion and faith that could
stand by Jefferson Davis in all his tremendous suffering is good enough
for you and it is good enough for me," Wharton closed by saying:

> sometime up in Heaven there will be a Grand Reunion of our men,
> women, daughters, sons, because we have followed our Great Cap-
> tain of Salvation. . . . I think we will get David to come and sit
> upon the platform with his harp and he will say, "What hymn shall
> we sing?" I think I would say, "Give us 'All Hail the Power of
> Jesus' Name' first and foremost, and wind up with 'The Bonnie
> Blue Flag.'"[60]

Here is a cogent reminder of Charles Reagan Wilson's conclusion that
"Each Lost Cause ritual and organization was tangible evidence that
Southerners had made a religion out of their history."[61] Even more tangible were the ways in which they interpreted that history—ways which
constituted the mythic elements of the culture religion.

Benjamin Harvey Hill, the former Confederate States senator from
Georgia, knew that there was but one way postwar Southerners could
justify their region's course during the "late unpleasantness": Though
defeated on the fields of bloodshed, they must emerge victorious on the
pages of history. Hill articulated this belief at an Atlanta gathering of
the Southern Historical Society in 1874. He declared: "we have but one
resource left us for defense or vindication. The resource is history—impartial and unpassioned, un-office-seeking history!" For the sake of the
Confederate dead, and as a gift to their children, Southerners "should
be active in the work of preserving the truth, and repelling the falsehoods," so that they may receive "just judgment from the only tribunal
before which we can be fully and fairly heard"—the bar of history.[62]
Seen in the context of the culture religion, this plea stood at the very
heart of that faith's mythic structure. Postwar Southerners, viewing
their Confederate experience as a redemptive event, transmuted it into
myth. For them, history *became* myth or, to be more precise, history
assumed the function of myth. Looking back on the Golden Age when
they wore the gray, they embodied its truths and lessons in a sacred
story, a history-oriented, history-shaping force of much cultural potency.[63]

To begin with, as Howard Dorgan has written, Confederates "spoke
of the South as a land and a culture apart." The Old South which they

had taken up arms to defend, they believed, had lived by the noblest of motives and its way of life had been, in the words of Edwin Mims, "the most glorious in the history of the world." Dabney H. Maury, for instance, told a veterans reunion in 1883: "no higher civilization has ever existed on earth than was here; and you can have no nobler work than the preservation of the memories of our struggle to maintain that civilization, and of the people who bravely made it."[64]

A second doctrine followed logically from this image of a noble South, namely, that the Cavalier South was forced to take up arms against money-seeking Puritan invaders. The South was torn asunder precisely because of its honor and nobility, its purity and grace. For, put very simply, while Cavaliers of aristocratic manners and polite sentiments shaped existence in the South, in the other section there ruled an opposite extreme—"the cold Covenanter types of the Puritan and the Knickerbocker." Lucian Lamar Knight, reminding his listeners in Danville, Kentucky, in 1902 that slavery was universal and that the North's role in its propagation was as crucial as the South's, asserted that "New England's conscience never hurt her in regard to slavery until her profit in the institution began to diminish." But Robert Catlett Cave, a St. Louis pastor speaking in Richmond in 1894, probably explained this element of the myth best:

> On one side of the conflict was the South, led by the descendants of the Cavaliers, who with all their faults, had inherited from a long line of ancestors a manly contempt for moral littleness, a high sense of honor, a lofty regard for plighted faith, a strong tendency to conservatism, a profound respect for law and order, and an unfaltering loyalty to constitutional government. Against the South was arrayed the power of the North, dominated by the spirit of Puritanism, which, with all its virtues, has ever been characterized by the pharisaism which worships itself, and is unable to perceive any goodness apart from itself, which has ever arrogantly held its ideas, its interests, and its will higher than fundamental law and covenanted obligations, which has always "lived and moved and had its being" in rebellion against constituted authority.[65]

The chivalrous Southerners, according to a third doctrine of the culture religion, also fought only for the noblest motives and on the most honorable bases. Building upon this theme, veterans laid the blame for the hostilities squarely on the shoulders of the North. Brigadier General Bradley T. Johnson characterized the conflict in these words: "Repeat and reiterate that the war waged upon the South was an unjust and causeless war of invasion and rapine, of plunder and murder, not for patriotism or high motives, but to gratify ambition and lust for power in the promoters of it." He went on: "the war of the South was a war of self-defence justified by all laws sacred and divine, of nature or of man."[66]

For precisely this reason, Confederates rejected the notion that they had gone to war for the purpose of maintaining or extending the institution of slavery. This refutation was a cardinal element in the myth of the culture religion, and about none were they so vociferous. To accuse Southerners of warring for the sake of holding others in bondage, they retorted, was a cruel affront. Randolph McKim, rector of the Episcopal Church of the Epiphany in Washington, D.C., speaking to his fellow veterans at the UCV reunion in 1904, responded to that charge in typical fashion. "Think of it, soldiers of Lee!" he shouted. "You were fighting, they say, for the privilege of holding your fellow man in bondage! Will you for one moment acknowledge the truth of that indictment? Oh, no! That banner of the Southern Cross was studded with the stars of God's heaven, . . . You could not have followed a banner that was not a banner of liberty!"[67]

If Southerners did not fight to preserve slavery, neither did they wage a rebellion against the United States. According to the mythmakers in gray, the Confederacy, not the government in Washington, represented the sacred constitutional principles of the American system. Nearly every book or speech that originated in the mind of an ex-Confederate included a detailed examination—or at least an impassioned proclamation—of the South's right to secede from the Union. Most rested, in the final analysis, upon the dogma that the Constitution of 1787 had been a compact among equally sovereign states. As Benjamin Morgan Palmer told veterans in 1900: "Whatever may have been the occasion of the war, its *cardo causae,* the hinge on which it turned, was the old question of state sovereignty as against national supremacy."[68] Secession, then, was the constitutional right of free and independent states.

In that case, the struggle for Southern independence was no "War of the Rebellion," as the federal government persisted in calling it, and adherents of the myth squelched the use of that term at every available instance. If the war was not a rebellion, then obviously the warriors in gray were neither rebels nor traitors. At the UCV's Houston meeting in 1895, Chaplain J. William Jones admitted—no doubt with unveiled pride—that he was known as "an unreconstructed rebel," but he sharply denied that any who had worn the gray were ever rebels. "George Washington and his compatriots were 'rebels' because they fought against properly constituted authority," he averred, "but we were not 'rebels' because we fought to uphold the constitution of our fathers."[69] Quite the contrary, the soldiers of Dixie, in the rhetoric of their comrades, were patriots who fought to maintain the noble principle of self-government, a cause sacred to the American tradition.

A final element in the mythic pattern of the cultural faith was the Confederates' belief that the Lost Cause was never genuinely lost. In affirming this belief, Southerners formed analogies between their own and other seemingly lost causes—especially that of Christ—and noted that truth, once overcome, generally rises again. Wade Hampton asked veterans in Savannah some pointed questions in 1892: "Did the river which swept the ashes of Huss to the sea bury in its waves forever the truth he had proclaimed? When our Divine Master perished on the cross, did the doctrines for which he died die with him?" And, in 1879, former private James N. Dunlop made it clear to his "fellow comrades" of the Army of Northern Virginia that the cause of the Confederacy, similar to Christ's mission, was not lost at Appomattox. "Truth, subjected to mock trial and condemnation, scourged and spitted on, betrayed by secret foes, staggering under its Cross, and sealed to-day in its sepulchres," he proclaimed, "bursts tomorrow the gates of death, rises with the crown, triumphant reigns throughout the world."[70] The myth of the culture religion thus wrested the promise of victory from the despair of defeat.

Lawyer Gavin Stevens, a William Faulkner character, would understand those sentiments. In *Intruder in the Dust*, he explains to his young nephew, Chick Mallison:

It's all *now* you see. Yesterday wont be over until tomorrow and tomorrow began ten thousand years ago. For every Southern boy fourteen years old, not once but whenever he wants it, there is the instant when it's still not yet two oclock on that July afternoon in 1863, the brigades are in position behind the rail fence, the guns are laid and ready in the woods and the furled flags are already loosened to break out and Pickett himself with his oiled ringlets and his hat in one hand probably and his sword in the other looking up the hill waiting for Longstreet to give the word and it's all in the balance, it hasn't happened yet, it hasn't even begun yet, it not only hasn't begun yet but there is time for it not to begin against that position and those circumstances which made more men than Garnett and Kemper and Armstead [*sic*] and Wilcox look grave yet it's going to begin, we all know that, we have come too far with too much at stake and that moment doesn't even need a fourteen-year-old boy to think *This time. Maybe this time* with all this much to lose and all this much to gain: Pennsylvania, Maryland, the world, the golden dome of Washington itself to crown with desperate and unbelievable victory the desperate gamble, the cast made two years ago; or to anyone who ever sailed a skiff under a quilt sail, the moment in 1492 when somebody thought *This is it:* the absolute edge of no return, to turn back now and make home or sail irrevocably on and either find land or plunge over the world's roaring rim.[71]

Returning to the time when their sacred symbols roamed the land, Lost Cause worshipers and their descendants stood at the center of their collective experience, realizing that in it history had happened to them and that its meaning could be captured only in that sacred moment and its countless extensions. Because they remembered it, they did not "plunge over the world's roaring rim" but found land—a Sacred South, an Immortal Confederacy.

Notes

This essay is dedicated to the memory of Robert M. Taylor Jr., good friend, colleague, and co-laborer in the vineyard of good history.

1. *Official Proceedings of the Tenth Annual Reunion and Convention of the Missouri Division, United Confederate Veterans* (Jefferson City, Mo.: UCV, 1906), 42. Hereafter cited as *Minutes UCV* (Mo.), followed by the reunion number in parentheses.

2. Robert Penn Warren, *The Legacy of the Civil War: Meditations on the Centennial* (New York: Random House, 1961), 15, 56.

3. That the Lost Cause myth served as an agent of Dixie's religious self-image has been acknowledged by historians for over two decades. As early as 1973, Rollin G. Osterweis, building on Ernst Cassirer's insight that "myth is from its very beginning potential religion," observed that the Lost Cause became "the dominant faith of a region." See Osterweis, *The Myth of the Lost Cause, 1865–1900* (Hampden, Conn.: Archon Books, 1973), 29. See also Ernst Cassirer, *An Essay on Man* (Garden City, N.Y.: Doubleday, 1954), 116. It was not until the publication of Charles Reagan Wilson's pioneering *Baptized in Blood: The Religion of the Lost Cause, 1865–1920* (Athens: University of Georgia Press, 1980), however, that the central role of religion in Lost Cause ideology and practice came forcefully to the attention of historians of the South. In his provocative "study of the afterlife of a Redeemer Nation that died," Wilson described the Lost Cause myth as "a Southern civil religion" which focused on "the religious implications of a nation"—in this case, a dead nation. From his perspective, the Lost Cause served as the tie that bound together Christian communities and Southern culture. In this interpretation, Wilson contends that ministers, many of them former Confederate chaplains, "were the prime celebrants of the religion of the Lost Cause," although the Southern civic faith, he

warned, should not be equated with Southern Protestantism. See Wilson, *Baptized in Blood*, 1, 5–7, 11–14; and "The Religion of the Lost Cause: Ritual and Organization of the Southern Civil Religion, 1865–1920," *Journal of Southern History* 46 (May 1980): 219–38. A second major examination of the Lost Cause is Gaines M. Foster, *Ghosts of the Confederacy: Defeat, the Lost Cause, and the Emergence of the New South, 1865 to 1913* (New York: Oxford University Press, 1987). Foster eschews the terms *myth* and *civil religion* in describing the Lost Cause phenomenon, viewing it not as a religious experience, but as "primarily a cultural movement" which helped Southerners cope with defeat and social change by providing conservative values and ideas for the creation of a New South. See Foster, *Ghosts of the Confederacy*, 4–8, 195–97.

The current study, while benefiting greatly from those of Wilson and Foster, breaks with them in distinctive ways. For one thing, Wilson's use of the term *civil religion* seems inadequate to capture the full dimensions of the cultural impact of the Lost Cause religion. As such students of American civic faith as Robert Nisbet, Gail Gehrig, and John A. Coleman have cogently demonstrated, civil religion by definition requires the existence of a definable, organized state—an entity clearly lacking in the postbellum South. See Robert Nisbet, "Civil Religion," in *The Encyclopedia of Religion*, 16 vols., ed. Mircea Eliade et al. (New York: Macmillan, 1987), 3:524–26; Gail Gehrig, "The American Civil Religion Debate: A Source for Theory Construction," *Journal for the Scientific Study of Religion* 20 (March 1981): 51–63; John A. Coleman, "Civil Religion," *Sociological Analysis* 31 (Summer 1990): 75–76. More recently, William C. Davis underscored this point. With the exception of the fact that the Confederacy did launch "a working, if rickety, civil government," Davis rightly contends that it lacked all other elements of nationhood and therefore "cannot be regarded as anything more than a very organized insurrection or separatist movement." See Davis, *The Cause Lost: Myths and Realities of the Confederacy* (Lawrence: University Press of Kansas, 1996), 179.

Secondly, the Lost Cause centered not on the present state of the nation, but rather on past images and ideals of the *region*, on the particular *culture* postwar Confederates sought to remember and, in a sense, rebuild. I therefore choose to describe the Lost Cause as a "culture religion," a term borrowed from German historian Fritz Stern. In *The Politics of Cultural Despair*, Stern chronicles the growth of a Germanic faith—what he calls *Kulturreligion*—among German nationalist leaders during the late nineteenth and early twentieth centuries. This new religion, its followers believed, would recapture Germany's "cultural uniqueness and her imperial destiny." See Stern, *Politics of Cultural Despair* (Berkeley: University of California Press, 1963), xv–xxviii, 48. As a fusion of several strains of the Southern spirit, and as an attempt to adjust to the culture shock of the days after the war, the Lost Cause functioned as precisely such a cultural religious longing.

Finally, the present study differs from those of Wilson and Foster in two additional ways. Unlike Wilson, who contends that Southern clergy were the primary figures in the propagation of the Lost Cause religion, I locate the organizational and institutional bases for the cultural faith in Confederate patriotic groups, especially the UCV and the UDC. This is to say that, rather than being essentially ecclesiastical in its focus, the Lost Cause religion institutionally encompassed a far broader spectrum of Southern culture. Furthermore—and here I agree with Wilson—the Lost Cause faith has been much more tenacious than Foster contends. Far from being of "temporary cultural importance," as Foster states (8), the South lives with the remnants of the Lost Cause religion to this very day—as flag controversies in South Carolina and Georgia, conflicts over "Dixie" at Ole Miss, and the confrontations over the death of a battle flag–displaying youth in Kentucky testify. On these legacies, see Charles Reagan Wilson, *Judgment and Grace in Dixie: Southern Faiths from Faulkner to Elvis* (Athens: University of Georgia Press, 1995), chap. 2; Thomas L. Connelly and Barbara Bellows, *God and General Longstreet* (Baton Rouge: Louisiana State University Press, 1982); Tony Horwitz, *Confederates in the Attic: Dispatches from the Unfinished Civil War* (New York: Pantheon Books, 1998); John M. Coski, "The Confederate Battle Flag in American History and Culture," and Kevin Thornton, "The Confederate Flag and the Meaning of Southern History," *Southern Cultures* 2 (Winter 1996): 195–245.

4. James McBride Dabbs, *Who Speaks for the South?* (New York: Funk and Wagnalls, 1964), 254, 256, 259.

5. Howard Becker, "Sacred and Secular Societies," *Social Forces* 28 (May 1950): 363, 373; John B. Boles, *The Great Revival, 1778–1805* (Lexington: University Press of Kentucky, 1972), 196, 198–99. See also Samuel S. Hill Jr., *Southern Churches in Crisis* (New York: Holt, Rinehart, and Winston, 1967), 68–69.

6. Richard W. Comstock, *The Study of Religion and Primitive Religions* (New York: Harper and Row, 1972), 44–45, 47–48. See also Clifford Geertz, "Religion as a Cultural System," in *Anthropological Approaches to the Study of Religion,* ed. Michael Banton (London: Tavistock, 1966), 19, 23–24.

7. An understanding of sacralization may be derived from the following definition of sanctification by Thomas Ford Hoult: "that culture pattern(s) which, in any given society, is concerned with the sanctification of behaviors and beliefs associated with the most permanent survival, materially or spiritually conceived." See Hoult, "A Functional Theory of Religion," *Sociology and Social Research* 42 (March–April 1957), 277–80.

8. Susanne K. Langer, *Philosophy in a New Key: A Study of the Symbolism of Reason, Rite, and Art* (Cambridge, Mass.: Harvard University Press, 1963), 41.

9. Emile Durkheim, *The Elementary Forms of the Religious Life* (New York: Free Press, 1965), 251–52, 260. Emphasis in original.

10. Raymond Firth, *Symbols: Public and Private* (Ithaca, N.Y.: Cornell Univer-

sity Press, 1973), 328, 332–35, 338–42, 365. For a fuller treatment of the representational role of symbols as applied to the Lost Cause religion, see Lloyd A. Hunter, "The Sacred South: Postwar Confederates and the Sacralization of Southern Culture" (Ph.D. diss., St. Louis University, 1978), 18–25.

11. Clyde Kluckhohn, "Myths and Rituals: A General Theory," in *Reader in Comparative Religion: An Anthropological Approach*, ed. William H. Lessa and Evan S. Vogt (Evanston, Ill.: Row, Peterson, 1958), 141.

12. Paul Gaston, *The New South Creed: A Study of Southern Mythmaking* (New York: Alfred A. Knopf, 1970), 9; Robert N. Bellah, *The Broken Covenant: American Civil Religion in Time of Trial* (New York: Seabury Press, 1975), 3; Thomas J. J. Altizer et al., eds., *Truth, Myth, and Symbol* (Englewood Cliffs, N.J.: Prentice-Hall, 1962), 107. See also Hunter, "Sacred South," 25–30.

13. Ernst Cassirer, *The Myth of the State* (New Haven, Conn.: Yale University Press, 1946), 278–80. For a direct application of this concept to the myths of the Confederacy, see Davis, *Cause Lost,* 175–76.

14. On ritual and its role in religious life, see Hunter, "Sacred South," 30–34; Comstock, *Study of Religion,* 31, 35; Orrin E. Klapp, *Ritual and Cult: A Sociological Interpretation* (Washington, D.C.: Public Affairs Press, 1956).

15. Confederated Southern Memorial Association, *History of the Confederated Memorial Associations of the South* (New Orleans: CSMA, 1904), 29–30; Anne Bachman Hyde, *An Historical Account of the United Daughters of the Confederacy* (Little Rock: Memorial Chapter No. 48, n.d.), 3–4; Charles Colcock Jones Jr., *Georgians During the War Between the States* (Augusta: Chronicle, 1889), 32, in Pamphlet Files, Ray D. Smith Collection, Knox College, Galesburg, Illinois (hereafter cited as Smith Collection). An excellent discussion of the memorial associations appears in George C. Rable, *Civil Wars: Women and the Crisis of Southern Nationalism* (Urbana: University of Illinois Press, 1989), 236–39.

16. Anna Caroline Benning, "Preface," in *A History of the Origins of Memorial Day,* United Daughters of the Confederacy, Georgia Division, Lizzie Rutherford Chapter (Columbus: Thomas Gilbert, 1898), 6.

17. Ibid., 5–7, 17–18, 24–25; CSMA, *Confederate Memorial Associations,* 30–34, 39–40. On one state's memorial experience, see Martha E. Kinney, "'If Vanquished I Am Still Victorious': Religious and Cultural Symbolism in Virginia's Confederate Memorial Day Celebrations, 1866–1930," *Virginia Magazine of History and Biography* 106 (Summer 1998): 237–66.

18. William W. White, *The Confederate Veteran,* Confederate Centennial Studies, no. 22 (Tuscaloosa, Ala.: Confederate, 1962), 7–16. See also Hunter, "Sacred South," 77–87.

19. Paul H. Buck, *The Road to Reunion, 1865–1900* (Boston: Little, Brown, 1938), 101–103, 134–42, 249.

20. W. J. Cash, *The Mind of the South* (New York: Random House, 1941), 157–

59; Richard M. Weaver, *The Southern Tradition at Bay: A History of Post-bellum Thought* (New Rochelle, N.Y.: Arlington House, 1968), 348–49; Osterweis, *Myth of the Lost Cause*, 10.

21. Unidentified newspaper clipping, n.d., in United Confederate Veterans Scrapbooks, 11 vols., Louisiana State University Archives, Baton Rouge, vol. 1; *Ceremonies Connected with the Inauguration of the Mausoleum and the Unveiling of the Recumbent Figure of General Robert Edward Lee at Washington and Lee University, Lexington, Virginia, June 28, 1883* (Lynchburg: J. P. Bell, 1883), 5–7, 69, 80 (hereafter cited as *Lee Memorial Ceremonies*); Thomas L. Connelly, *The Marble Man: Robert E. Lee and His Image in American Society* (New York: Alfred A. Knopf, 1977), 128.

22. Quoted in Raymond B. Nixon, *Henry W. Grady: Spokesman of the New South* (New York: Russell and Russell, 1969), 229, see also 225–34; Ralph Lowell Eckert, *John Brown Gordon: Soldier, Southerner, American* (Baton Rouge: Louisiana State University Press, 1989), 260–73; Michael B. Ballard, "Cheers for Jefferson Davis," *American History Illustrated* 16 (May 1981): 8–11, 14–15.

23. White, *Confederate Veteran*, 27–30; Herman Hattaway, "The United Confederate Veterans in Louisiana," *Louisiana History* 16 (Winter 1975): 8–12; United Confederate Veterans, Arkansas Division, *Confederate Women of Arkansas in the Civil War, 1861–'65: Memorial Reminiscences* (Little Rock: UCV, 1907); Howard Dorgan, "Southern Apologetic Themes as Expressed in Selected Ceremonial Speaking of Confederate Veterans, 1889–1900" (Ph.D. diss., Louisiana State University, 1971), 24; Dixon Wecter, *When Johnny Comes Marching Home* (Cambridge, Mass.: Riverside Press, 1944), 253; Abram J. Ryan, *Poems, Patriotic, Religious, Miscellaneous* (New York: P. J. Kenedy and Sons, 1896), 168.

24. Dorgan, "Southern Apologetic Themes," 26; Herman Hattaway, "Clio's Southern Soldiers: The United Confederate Veterans and History," *Louisiana History* 12 (Summer 1971): 214–15; White, *Confederate Veteran*, 34–35.

25. Unidentified newspaper clipping (February 1902) and handwritten notes of Mrs. A. C. Cassidy, in Patriotic Clubs Papers, United Daughters of the Confederacy, Missouri Historical Society, St. Louis (hereafter cited as MHS); Constitution of the Daughters of the Confederacy of Missouri, in John S. Bowen Papers, MHS; Mary B. Poppenheim et al., *The History of the United Daughters of the Confederacy* (Richmond: Garrett and Massie, 1938), 2–6; Susan S. Durant, "The Gently Furled Banner: The Development of the Myth of the Lost Cause, 1865–1900" (Ph.D. diss., University of North Carolina, 1972), 162–65. On the early years of the Nashville organization and its challenge to St. Louis's claim to having the first UDC chapter, see Patricia Faye Climer, "Protectors of the Past: The United Daughters of the Confederacy, Tennessee Division, and the Lost Cause" (Master's thesis, Vanderbilt University, 1973), 10–11, 14.

26. C. Vann Woodward, *Origins of the New South, 1877–1913* (Baton Rouge:

Louisiana State University Press, 1951), 156; Hyde, *United Daughters of the Confederacy*, 4–5; Poppenheim, *History of the United Daughters*, 8–11; *Minutes of the Eighth Annual Meeting of the United Daughters of the Confederacy* (Nashville: Foster and Webb, 1902), 153 (hereafter cited as *Minutes, UDC*, reunion number). See also John M. Coski and Amy R. Feely, "A Monument to Southern Womanhood: The Founding Generation of the Confederate Museum," in *A Woman's War: Southern Women, Civil War, and the Confederate Legacy*, ed. Edward D. C. Campbell Jr. and Kym S. Rice (Richmond and Charlottesville: The Museum of the Confederacy and the University Press of Virginia, 1996), 137–38; Angie Parrott, "'Love Makes Memory Eternal': The United Daughters of the Confederacy in Richmond, Virginia, 1897–1920," in *The Edge of the South: Life in Nineteenth Century Virginia*, ed. Edward L. Ayers and John C. Willis (Charlottesville: University Press of Virginia, 1991), 219–38.

27. *The Confederate Veteran* 4 (July 1896): 228.

28. Harry Lynden Flash, *Poems* (New York: Neale, 1906), 158. On the influence of Father Ryan, see Wilson, *Baptized in Blood*, 58–61; Gardiner H. Shattuck, *A Shield and Hiding Place: The Religious Life of the Civil War Armies* (Macon, Ga.: Mercer University Press, 1987), 114–15; Durant, "Gently Furled Banner," 25–27.

29. T. L. Rosser, "The Cavalry, A. N. V.," Address at the Seventh Annual Reunion of the Maryland Line, Baltimore, February 22, 1889, 12, in Other Veterans' Organizations Papers, 1872–1924, Louisiana Historical Association Papers, Tulane University, New Orleans, La.

30. Edwin A. Alderman et al., *Library of Southern Literature*, 17 vols. (Atlanta: Martin and Holt, 1907–32), 10:4395–97. See also Hunter, "Sacred South," 133–40.

31. *Minutes of the Fourteenth Annual Meeting and Reunion of the United Confederate Veterans*, reissued as *Minutes U.C.V.*, 6 vols. (New Orleans: UCV, 1907–13), 3 (14th), 58. (Hereafter cited as *Minutes UCV* followed by the volume number and then the reunion number in parentheses.) The Cabell letter appears in the *New Orleans Daily Picayune*, November 6, 1904 (clipping) in United Confederate Veterans Scrapbooks, 11 vols., vol. 4. See also John A. Simpson, "Shall We Change the Words of 'Dixie'?" *Southern Folklore Quarterly* 45 (1981): 19–40.

32. *The Confederate Veteran* 10 (June 1902): 260; *The Land We Love* 2 (November 1866): 37. On other objects of veneration, see Hunter, "Sacred South," 143–51.

33. Wilson, *Baptized in Blood*, 48–49; Connelly, *Marble Man*, 43. As Lee's elevation to sacred status evolved, an intense rivalry developed between the Lexington group and its Richmond counterpart, the Lee Memorial Association, led by Jubal Early. For details on this internal war among Lost Cause followers, see Connelly, *Marble Man;* Connelly and Bellows, *God*

and General Longstreet, chap. 3; Charles C. Osborne, *Jubal: The Life and Times of General Jubal A. Early, C. S. A.* (Chapel Hill, N.C.: Algonquin Books, 1992), chap. 27; Foster, *Ghosts of the Confederacy,* chap. 4.

34. Thomas Cary Johnson, *The Life and Letters of Benjamin Morgan Palmer* (Richmond: Presbyterian Committee on Publication, 1906), 349–51; *Baltimore Sun,* June 4, 1903, in United Confederate Veteran Scrapbooks, vol. 4.

35. Robert Stiles, *Four Years Under Marse Robert* (New York: Neale, 1903), 21; Randolph H. McKim, *The Soul of Lee* (New York: Longmans, Green, 1918), 200, 202, 210.

36. *Lee Memorial Ceremonies,* 32.

37. Homer Richey, ed., *Memorial History of the John Bowie Strange Camp, United Confederate Veterans* (Charlottesville, Va.: Michie, 1920), 218; *Stone Mountain Magazine,* April 1924, 11; J. William Jones, *Army of Northern Virginia Memorial Volume* (Richmond: Randolph and English, 1880), 122. Recent historians have sought forthrightly to deal with the apotheosizing of Lee in their treatments of his life and accomplishments. See Connelly, *Marble Man;* Alan T. Nolan, *Lee Considered: General Robert E. Lee and Civil War History* (Chapel Hill: University of North Carolina Press, 1991); Emory M. Thomas, *Robert E. Lee: A Biography* (New York: W. W. Norton, 1995), 13, 20, 408–409, 416–17; William Garrett Piston, *Lee's Tarnished Lieutenant: James Longstreet and His Place in Southern History* (Athens: University of Georgia Press, 1987), 175–77.

38. Thomas J. Pressly, *Americans Interpret Their Civil War* (New York: Free Press, 1965), 109–10; Jonathan T. Dorris, *Pardon and Amnesty Under Lincoln and Johnson: The Restoration of the Confederates to Their Rights and Privileges, 1861–1898* (Chapel Hill: University of North Carolina Press, 1953), 284–86; Charles M. Blackford, *The Trials and Trial of Jefferson Davis* (Richmond: John T. West, 1900), 45–46, in Davis Folder, Smith Collection.

39. Woodward, *Origins of the New South,* 155; John A. Simpson, "The Cult of the 'Lost Cause,'" *Tennessee Historical Quarterly* 34 (Winter 1975): 353 n 10; Hudson Strode, *Jefferson Davis, Tragic Hero: The Last Twenty-five Years, 1864–1889* (New York: Harcourt, Brace, and World, 1964), 482–85.

40. C. C. Jones Jr., "Funeral Oration," in *Life and Reminiscences of Jefferson Davis* (Baltimore: R. H. Woodward, 1890), 331, 338; Texas House of Representatives, *In Memoriam: Jefferson Davis,* in Memorial Association Papers, Louisiana Historical Association Collection, Tulane University.

41. William C. P. Breckenridge, Address at Army of Northern Virginia Reunion, 1892, quoted in Dorgan, "Southern Apologetic Themes," 187; *Baltimore Sun,* June 4, 1903, in United Confederate Veteran Scrapbooks, vol. 4; Lucian Lamar Knight, *Stone Mountain, or the Lay of the Gray Minstrel* (Atlanta: Johnson-Dollar, 1923). See also Michael Ballard, *A Long Shadow:*

Jefferson Davis and the Final Days of the Confederacy (Jackson: University Press of Mississippi, 1988), 171–73.

42. Robert Lewis Dabney, *Life and Campaigns of Lieut. Gen. Thomas J. Jackson* (New York: Blelock, 1866), 110, 142–43, 413, 727.

43. L. Dix Warren, "Recollections of a Confederate Veteran," *The Lost Cause* 2 (June 1899): 82, in John M. Richardson Papers, 1854–1901, Southern Historical Collection, University of North Carolina, Chapel Hill; Flash, *Poems*, 150. For an excellent study of Jackson's image in Southern myth and history, see Davis, *The Cause Lost*, chap. 10.

44. *Minutes UCV* (Mo.) (5th), 16; Robert Catlett Cave, *The Men in Gray* (Nashville: Confederate Veteran, 1911), 37.

45. *The Confederate Veteran* 4 (June 1896): 176, 190 and 8 (March 1900): 99; Bettie A. C. Emerson, *Historic Southern Monuments* (New York: Neale, 1911), 329. See also Edythe J. R. Whitley, *Sam Davis: Confederate Hero* (Smyrna, Tenn.: Sam Davis Memorial Association, 1947). The finest recent study of the transformation of Sam Davis into a sacred icon is in John A. Simpson, *S. A. Cunningham and the Confederate Heritage* (Athens: University of Georgia Press, 1994), chap. 21.

46. On the common soldiers as "sacred martyrs," see Rod Andrew Jr., "Martial Spirit, Christian Virtue, and the Lost Cause: Military Education at North Georgia College, 1871–1915," *Georgia Historical Quarterly* 80 (Fall 1996): 486–87, 496–97; Rod Andrew Jr., "Soldiers, Christians, and Patriots: The Lost Cause and Southern Military Schools, 1865–1915," *Journal of Southern History* 64 (November 1998): 695, 704–706; Kinney, "'If Vanquished I Am Still Victorious,'" 256–57; Hunter, "Sacred South," 164–68. Southern women also were objects of veneration, although more as "ministering angels" who exhibited patriotic self-denial during the war and who, afterward, were "last at the cross and first at the sepulchre." See Hunter, "Sacred South," 168–71; Francis W. Dawson, *Our Women in the War: An Address Delivered February 22, 1887, at the Fifth Annual Reunion of the Association of the Maryland Line* (Charleston, S.C.: Walker, Evans, and Cogwell, 1887); *Southern Historical Society Papers* 5 (1878): 303.

47. Piston, *Lee's Tarnished Lieutenant*, 122. On the effort of the Virginia Coalition to blame Longstreet for Gettysburg, see ibid., chaps. 6–8; Jeffry D. Wert, *General James Longstreet: The Confederacy's Most Controversial Soldier—A Biography* (New York: Simon and Schuster, 1993), chap. 20; Connelly, *Marble Man*, 27, 64, 83–90; Connelly and Bellows, *God and General Longstreet*, chap. 1; Osborne, *Jubal*, chaps. 27–28.

48. Connelly and Bellows, *God and General Longstreet*, 38; Wert, *Longstreet*, 413–16; Piston, *Lee's Tarnished Lieutenant*, 111–28.

49. Monument dedications were likewise major ritual events for the ex-Confederates, but their ritualistic patterns and oratory replicated those of Memorial Day and reunions. For more on these occasions, see Foster, *Ghosts of the Confederacy*, 41–42, 128–31; Stephen Davis, "Empty Eyes,

Marble Hand: The Confederate Monument and the South," *Journal of Popular Culture* 16 (Winter 1982): 2–21; W. Stuart Towns, "Honoring the Confederacy in Northwest Florida: The Confederate Monument Ritual," *Florida Historical Quarterly* 57 (October 1978): 205–12; Lawrence J. Nelson, "Memorializing the Lost Cause in Florence, Alabama, 1966–1903," *Alabama Review* 41 (July 1988): 179–92.

50. Wilson, *Baptized in Blood*, 22.

51. Buck, *Road to Reunion*, 118.

52. UDC, Georgia Division, *Origin of Memorial Day*, 13–16.

53. Buck, *Road to Reunion*, 120–21. For scholarly accounts of other Memorial Day rituals, see Kinney, "'If Vanquished I Am Still Victorious,'" 677–78, 704–706; Andrew, "Martial Spirit, Christian Virtue," 497–503.

54. For more detailed descriptions of the UCV reunions, see Foster, *Ghosts of the Confederacy*, 131–42; Wilson, *Baptized in Blood*, 30–32.

55. Durkheim, *Elementary Forms*, 240; *Minutes UCV,* 1 (8th), 24; poem quoted in H. C. Nixon, "Paths to the Past: The Presidential Addresses of the Southern Historical Association," *Journal of Southern History* 16 (February 1950): 39.

56. White, *Confederate Veteran*, 36–37; *Minutes UCV,* 1 (8th), 11; Foster, *Ghosts of the Confederacy*, 133. On preparations for these big affairs, see Dolly Blount Lamar, *When All Is Said and Done* (Athens: University of Georgia Press, 1952), 144–48; Ray Hanley, "The Gray Reunion," *Civil War Times Illustrated*, January–February 1992, 42–63.

57. Quoted in Dorgan, "Southern Apologetic Themes," 56; Wallace Evan Davies, *Patriotism on Parade: The Story of Veterans' and Hereditary Organizations in America, 1783–1900* (Cambridge, Mass.: Harvard University Press, 1955), 132–33; Eckert, *John Brown Gordon*, 326–29.

58. *The Confederate Veteran* 4 (October 1896): 333; Alderman et al., *Library of Southern Literature*, 14:6127–28.

59. *Minutes UCV,* 1 (6th), 7; 2 (12th), 32; 6 (24th), 95.

60. Ibid., 2 (10th), 108; Stenographic report of the 36th Reunion, UCV, 6, 100, 102, in UCV Records, Louisiana State University Archives.

61. Wilson, *Baptized in Blood*, 36. The UDC meetings, while not as revivalistic as those of the veterans, contained a brief ritual replete with sacred imagery that resembled a church devotional moment. Simple, brief, and more liturgical than UCV rituals, it contained an opening litany, the singing of "How Firm a Foundation," and a prayer written by Bishop Ellison Capers of South Carolina. See UDC, *Minutes of the Twelfth Annual Meeting, UDC* (Nashville: Foster, Webb, and Parkers, 1906), 265–66.

62. Benjamin H. Hill Jr., *Senator Benjamin H. Hill of Georgia: His Life, Speeches, and Writings* (Atlanta: T. H. P. Bloodworth, 1893), 405–406.

63. This is to say that Confederate mythmaking emerged from their foremost goals of providing their posterity with the truths of the War Between the

States through writing and preserving their version of its history. Their goal was to justify and vindicate their actions during the war. In addition to the indefatigable work of the Southern Historical Society, the UCV and UDC each had Historical Committees that saw their work as *the* central component in the telling of the Confederate story, i.e., their myth. Unquestionably, the foremost champion of proper history was Mildred Lewis Rutherford, long-time Historian General of the UDC. See her Scrapbooks in sixty-one volumes in the Eleanor S. Brockenbrough Library, The Museum of the Confederacy, Richmond, Virginia. See also Fred Arthur Bailey, "Mildred Lewis Rutherford and the Patrician Cult of the Old South," *Georgia Historical Quarterly* 3 (Fall 1994): 509–35. For detailed portraits of UCV and UDC historical work, see Hunter, "Sacred South," 204–45; Hattaway, "Clio's Southern Soldiers": 213–42; and the following insightful articles by Fred Arthur Bailey: "Free Speech and the Lost Cause in the Old Dominion," *Virginia Magazine of History and Biography* 103 (April 1995): 237–66; "Free Speech and the 'Lost Cause' in Texas: A Study of Social Control in the New South," *Southwestern Historical Quarterly* 97 (January 1994): 453–77; "Free Speech and the 'Lost Cause' in Arkansas," *Arkansas Historical Quarterly* 55 (Summer 1996):143–66; and "The Textbooks of the 'Lost Cause': Censorship and the Creation of Southern State Histories," *Georgia Historical Quarterly* 75 (Fall 1991): 507–33.

64. Dorgan, "Southern Apologetic Themes," 210; Edwin Mims, *The Advancing South* (Garden City, N.Y.: Doubleday, Page, 1927), 2; *Southern Historical Society Papers* 11 (1883): 544.

65. Thomas C. DeLeon, *Belles, Beaux, and Brains of the 60's* (New York: Dillingham, 1909), 17; Lucian Lamar Knight, *Memorials of Dixie-Land* (Atlanta: Byrd, 1919), 189–90; Cave, *The Men in Gray*, 20–21.

66. Confederate Memorial Literary Society, *In Memoriam Sempiternam* (Richmond: Waddey, 1896), 49–50.

67. *Minutes UCV,* 3 (14th), Appendix, 27. See also Durant, "Gently Furled Banner," 109–18; Hunter, "Sacred South," 252–57.

68. Johnson, *Benjamin Morgan Palmer,* 566. The classic statement of the compact theory in defense of secession and the war is Jefferson Davis, *The Rise and Fall of the Confederate Government,* 2 vols. (Richmond: Garrett and Massie, 1939), Memorial Edition.

69. *Minutes UCV,* 1 (5th), 33. See similar sentiments by Jubal Early in Osborne, *Jubal,* 436. See also Durant, "Gently Furled Banner," 184–86; Foster, *Ghosts of the Confederacy,* 117–18.

70. UCV, Georgia Division, *Addresses Delivered Before the Confederate Veteran Association of Savannah* (Savannah: Confederate Veterans Association, 1893–98), 104; *Southern Historical Society Papers* 8 (January 1880): 15–16.

71. William Faulkner, *Intruder in the Dust* (New York: Random House, 1948; Vintage Books, 1972), 194–95.

Contributors

Keith S. Bohannon earned an M.A. in history from the University of Georgia and received his doctoral training in American history at Penn State University. He is the author of *The Giles, Alleghany, and Jackson Artillery* and the coeditor of *Campaigning with "Old Stonewall": Confederate Captain Ujanirtus Allen's Letters to His Wife*, and has contributed essays and articles to various scholarly publications.

Peter S. Carmichael is a member of the Department of History at the University of North Carolina at Greensboro. The author of *Lee's Young Artillerist: William R. J. Pegram*, as well as several essays and articles in scholarly and popular journals, he is completing a study of Virginia's slaveholders' sons and the formation of Southern identity in the antebellum years.

Gary W. Gallagher is the John L. Nau III Professor of History at the University of Virginia. His books include *The Confederate War* and *Lee and His Generals in War and Memory*.

Lesley J. Gordon is a member of the Department of History at the University of Akron (Ohio). She is the author of *General George E. Pickett in Life and Legend* (1998), coeditor and coauthor of *Intimate Strategies: Marriages of the Civil War* (forthcoming), and a contributor to various journals and volumes of essays. She is currently working on a study of the Sixteenth Regiment Connecticut Volunteers.

Charles J. Holden is a member of the Department of History at St. Mary's College of Maryland. A specialist on late-nineteenth- and early-twentieth-century Southern history, he is the author of a forthcoming book on South Carolina conservatives and their adjustment to the post-bellum world.

Lloyd A. Hunter, a professor of history and religion and director of American Studies, occupies the Roger D. Branigin Chair in History at Franklin College, Franklin, Indiana. He has written a number of articles for popular and scholarly journals and contributed to volumes of essays in the fields of American studies and American religious history.

Alan T. Nolan is a lawyer in Indianapolis. A member of the Indianapolis Civil War Round Table, he has written *The Iron Brigade: A Military History* and *Lee Considered: Robert E. Lee and Civil War History;* with Sharon Vipond he edited *Giants in Their Tall Black Hats: Essays on the Iron Brigade.*

Brooks D. Simpson is a professor of history and humanities at Arizona State University. He has written or edited several books, the most recent of which are *Ulysses S. Grant: Triumph over Adversity, 1822–1865* (2000) and *Sherman's Civil War: Selected Correspondence of William T. Sherman, 1860–1865* (1999; with Jean V. Berlin).

Jeffry D. Wert, a high school history teacher, is the author of several books, including *General James Longstreet: The Confederacy's Most Controversial Soldier—A Biography* (1993); *Custer: The Controversial Life of George Armstrong Custer* (1996); and *A Brotherhood of Valor: The Common Soldiers of the Stonewall Brigade, C.S.A., and the Iron Brigade, U.S.A.* (1999).

Index

221